LONG-WAVE RHYTHMS IN ECONOMIC DEVELOPMENT AND POLITICAL BEHAVIOR

D0905472

Brian J. L. Berry

THE JOHNS HOPKINS UNIVERSITY PRESS
Baltimore and London

The Johns Hopkins University Press
701 West 40th Street
Baltimore, Maryland 21211
The Johns Hopkins Press Ltd., London

Cartoons by Bill Fountain
Graphics by Debbie Partain and Christopher Müller-Wille
at the Cartographics Laboratory, Texas A&M University

The paper used in this book meets the minimum
requirements of American National Standard for
Information Sciences—Permanence of Paper for Printed
Library Materials, ANSI Z39.48-1984.

Library of Congress Cataloging-in-Publication Data

Berry, Brian Joe Lobley, 1934–
Long-wave rhythms in economic development and political
behavior / Brian J. L. Berry.
p.   cm.
Includes bibliographical references and index.
ISBN 0-8018-4035-X (hardcover). —
ISBN 0-8018-4036-8 (pbk.).
1. Long waves (Economics).   2. Business cycles—Political
aspects.   3. Economic development.
4. Leadership.   I. Title.
HB3729.B47   1990
338.9—dc20   90-4586   CIP

CONTENTS

FIGURES AND TABLES

Figures

Tables

ACKNOWLEDGMENTS

Reviews of a 1987 proposal to the National Science Foundation in which I sought funding to investigate long swings of urban growth provoked me to prepare this book. Some of the reviewers' comments were paradigmatic: "No one takes long waves seriously any more." Others were more personal: "Berry knows nothing of the current research on the topic"; he "has been tarnished [by] his years in administration."

Nemo me impune lacessit. As Winston Churchill said, "Remember the turtle; he only makes progress when his neck is out." While I did receive a small grant to support my research on urban growth, I decided to pursue the long-wave question free of foundation sponsorship, helped by my research assistant Lyssa Jenkens (who worked on the data analysis) and eight University of Texas at Dallas graduate students (Ibrahim Akoum, Nicholas Alozie, James Ibe, Eun Sup Kim, Phillip Rotman, Gregg Selby, Brahma Sinha, and Sunday Uzuh), who spent a semester with me delving into the byways that other investigators have taken.

A year later, when I had a manuscript in first-draft form, my colleagues in the School of Social Sciences at the University of Texas at Dallas took the time to attend seminars devoted to critical assessments of my work and made a broad range of constructive recommendations. My thanks go in particular to Edward Harpham and Royce Hanson, as well as to Tony Champagne, Jeff Dumas, Paula England, Don Hicks, Irv Hoch, Doug Kiel, Richard Scotch, Vibhooti Shukla, Marianne Stewart, and Greg Thielemann, for their tough questions and thoughtful critiques.

A variety of other friends and professional colleagues were good enough to read the first draft, at that time titled *The Clocks That Time Development*, responding with yet more excellent suggestions. Robert McCormick Adams, John R. Borchert, E. C. Conkling, Andre Gunder Frank, Peter Gould, Hans Mark, William H. McNeill, and Anders Richter each made comments that I heeded in recasting the initial draft into the present form.

Readings of the revised draft by Charles Dale, Paul Ove Pederson, Vibhooti Shukla, Edward Harpham and his students, Doug Kiel, C. D. Cantrell, Jack Meltzer, and Walt W. Rostow helped in the fine tuning.

Cynthia Keheley converted my initial papyrus rolls into an attractive first draft, and Giselle Nunez took the similarly butchered revised version and converted it into the manuscript that was finally delivered to the publisher. Without their technical expertise in desktop publishing, I would not have been able to bring the project to fruition with as much dispatch.

Bill Fountain prepared the cartoons, and Christopher Müller-Wille and Debbie Partain drafted many of the graphs.

Last, but never least, I should acknowledge the immense help by my wife, Janet, who recognizes the faraway look when the ideas finally come together, and who protects the cloister, giving me the uninterrupted time that is so important when it is time to set pen to paper.

This has been a journey into a contentious land. I came away excited by my discoveries, yet painfully aware of the exploration that remains to be done. It is a difficult land, populated by tribes with different cultures and languages, separated by their world-views and by the boundaries they defend. I doubt that I will convert many of the true believers, but perhaps, in the spirit of the geographers who have preceded me, I can provide a more accurate map, a better understanding of the people and places, and a set of questions to be researched by other, more innovative investigators.

Time present and time past
And both perhaps present in time future
And time future contained in time past.

T. S. ELIOT

INTRODUCTION

I had not intended to work on long waves. Like many of you, I was taught to view the topic with suspicion. Too many "long wavers" have insufficient regard for the soundness of evidence. At the fringe are crackpots and mystics, charlatans who play on peoples' fears by writing popular books proclaiming an imminent economic Armageddon—not particularly savory company to be associated with, even peripherally. In truth, if I had not been provoked by some of the critics, I would not have begun the research that led to this book, for I, too, was taught to believe that Kondratiev waves and Kuznets cycles are both examples of the Emperor's new clothes. Once provoked, however, my research led me to resolve a number of important questions about the rhythmic upswings and downturns of prices and economic growth and the clocklike timing of turning-point crises in American development—questions that cut across economy, society, and politics. I discovered that there *is* something to the long-wave idea, even though it takes a form that may be unfamiliar to many of its advocates. Suitably reconstructed, this idea provides important insights about where we have been and where we might be heading. In this book I will try to (1) persuade you that I am not one of the crackpots, (2) point you to the important historical regularities, (3) lay out the essentials of an explanation, and (4) chart the margins of knowledge beyond which myths and mysticism still prevail.

We should begin at the beginning. I had been happily exploring the relation-

1

ship between urbanward migration and economic growth in another, quite different study. Using data on the gross national product of the United States for each decade from 1790 to the present, I charted the average annual growth rates of both nominal and real GNP for the first two centuries of the nation's history (Figure 1). There appeared to be an approximately half-century-long pattern of accelerations and decelerations in the rate of U.S. economic growth. I also calculated the average annual growth rates of U.S. urban areas due to migration. A similar pattern of accelerations and decelerations seemed to emerge (Figure 2). Evidently, each quickening of economic growth was followed by a burst of

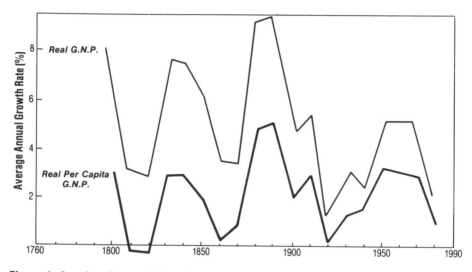

Figure 1. Accelerations and Decelerations in the Average Annual Growth Rates of Real GNP in the United States, 1790–1980

This illustration is merely suggestive. The base data are for each decennial year: 1790, 1800, 1810, etc. Decadal growth rates were calculated (e.g., for the period 1790–1800) and annualized by dividing by ten. These average annual growth rates were then plotted at the end-point years (i.e., in 1800 for 1790–1800, etc.) and the points linked by straight-line segments. Computed this way, the growth rates are sensitive to the specific values of GNP in each decennial year, and variations within each decade are smoothed out. You will want to compare this graph with Figure 34, appearing in Chapter 3, which plots the actual annual growth rates, as well as Figures 35–39 and the graphs in Appendix B. The additional graphs smooth the annual growth rates using moving averages of different lengths to identify the long swings. The more finely grained information reveals within-decade slowdowns in the 1840s and 1890s, the Great Depression, and the 1950s and 1970s, and in fact I conclude in Chapter 3 that beyond the 7-to-11-year business cycle, economic growth pulsates with the 25-to-30-year rhythm of the Kuznets cycle. Plots of decennial data such as the one presented here pick up the very long rhythms revealed by moving averages of eighteen or twenty years. As we shall see later, these rhythms involve accelerating growth rates in the quarter-century between stagflation crises and deflationary depressions, and decelerating growth rates in the quarter-century from depressions to stagflation crises.

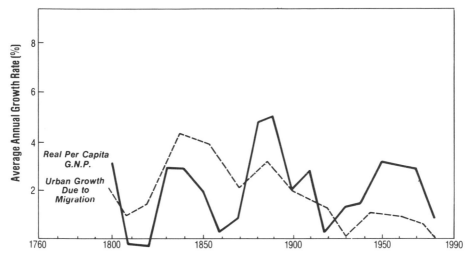

Figure 2. Fluctuations in the Average Annual Rates of Growth of Urban Areas due to Migration, Compared with Accelerations and Decelerations in the Growth of Real Per Capita GNP, 1790–1980

Urban growth has two sources: natural increase (excess of births over deaths) and net migration (excess of immigration over emigration). What is plotted here is the part of the urban growth rate attributable to net migration, computed and plotted in the same manner as the data in Figure 1. The same problems with the use of decennial data outlined in the discussion of Figure 1 apply, but, subject to these caveats, the rates of economic and urbanward migration appear to be synchronized. Reinforcing this observation, I show in Chapter 4 that immigration into the United States actually oscillated every 25–30 years, helping to drive the nation's city-building with Kuznets-cycle rhythms.

urbanward migration. Each slowdown in the growth rate was accompanied by a slackening of urban growth.

The half-century-long waves were no surprise, even though all my training cautioned me to view them with suspicion. Nikolai Kondratiev's idea that capitalist economies follow an approximately 50-year cycle of crisis, recovery, prosperity, and stagnation was familiar to me, but I had not explored it in any depth.[1] I must admit, however, that I was taken aback when I read Alfred Ma-

---

1. Nikolai Dmitryevich Kondratyiev (often transliterated as Kondratieff, but I prefer Kondratiev) was not the first to suggest the idea. In an article in the *British Railway Journal* in 1847, Dr. Hyde Clark published a paper describing a 54-year long wave from 1793 to 1847 that included five apparent cycles, each 10–11 years in length (cited in Nathan H. Mager, *The Kondratieff Waves* [1987], p. 21). The idea was restated in a 1901 pamphlet written by "Parvus" [Alexander I. Helphand] and soon thereafter by two Dutch socialists, J. van Gelderen and S. De Wolff. Van Gelderen, writing in 1913 under the pseudonym "J. Fedder," talked of a cycle including a quarter-century of slow growth, followed by a "new springtide," a surge of new growth. De Wolff focused on the causes of depressions, attributing their regularity to the effective depreciation rate of "long-living fixed capital" (capitalist infrastructure). Kondratiev's contribution is discussed at length in Chapter 2 of this volume.

labre Jr.'s 1987 book, *Beyond Our Means,* which is typical of the genre. Echoing Paul Samuelson's alleged dictum that "long waves are science fiction," Malabre asserts that they "appear to be figments of the imagination of their various sponsors . . . the best known of these dubious cycles [being] the so-called Kondratieff Wave." "Using modern techniques," he continues, "there is no evidence of the long wave."[2] This was certainly not what Figures 1 and 2 of my own study seemed to be suggesting. Were my graphs deluding me?

Perhaps, but the negative assessments could just as easily have arisen because statistical techniques requiring dozens of repetitions to prove the existence of mathematically correct cycles having fixed periodicities were the wrong tools to apply. After all, in 200 years of American history there have been only four long waves of varying shapes and timing. The critics may have been deluded by the demanding technical wizardry of cyclical testing methods ill-suited to the data at hand! I had obtained other evidence that appeared to belie their negative views. The familiar graph of variations in the U.S. wholesale price index also showed a long-wave pattern in its sequence of inflationary peaks and intervening troughs (Figure 3). The same long-wave fluctuations were seen in the growth of the nation's money supply and in its annual inflation rate (Figure 4). Even more interesting was my finding that the price cycles and growth waves seemed to have inverse rhythms (Figure 5). Peaks on one coincided with troughs on the other. The possibility that long-wave rhythms had been at work looked increasingly real to me.

I suddenly had many questions and no answers. Would this rhythmic behavior stand up to more detailed investigation? If so, what mechanisms could produce such contrapuntal rhythms over periods of a half-century and more? And why the visceral negativism of those who deny the reality of the long wave in economic history?

This question was also asked by Joshua S. Goldstein in his 1988 book, *Long Cycles: Prosperity and War in the Modern Age.* "Why," he wrote, "has there been such a hostile reception to long cycles among the established academic disciplines, especially economics? I think that the answer has to do with a paradigm shift required to take long cycles seriously. Long cycles require thinking on a new time scale, looking at history differently, thinking about the connections of economics and politics in new ways" (p. xii). I agree with Goldstein.

2. Alfred L. Malabre, Jr., *Beyond Our Means: How Reckless Borrowing Now Threatens to Overwhelm Us* (1987). Malabre, news editor for the *Wall Street Journal,* tried to have it both ways. Following a group of University of Montreal statisticians, he was critical of the idea of cyclical rhythmicity ("man bound to a large, slow-turning wheel, unable to avoid having his head dunked in the mire at regular intervals") but hedged his bets by suggesting that "longer repetitive patterns, transcending the familiar business cycle, may well be at work" (p. 101). However, "not all proponents of the long-wave idea agree that the wave runs for about fifty years. Among other waves named for their particular sponsors . . . is the so-called Kuznets cycle. . . . It was conceived by Simon Kuznets, a Nobel-laureate economist. . . . Barely half as long as the Kondratieff cycle, the Kuznets cycle hinges on periodic swings in construction activity. . . . The prudent course may be to recognize that long-term as well as short-term patterns play a crucial role in how the economy behaves."

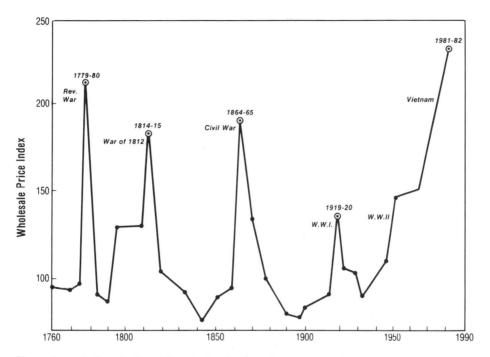

Figure 3. Variations in the U.S. Wholesale Price Index, 1760–1982

The data most commonly used to document Kondratiev waves come from the U.S. Bureau of the Census, *Historical Statistics of the United States*. For the years 1760–1890, what is plotted is the Warren-Pearson wholesale price index for all commodities. See George F. Warren and Frank A. Pearson, *Wholesale Prices in the United States for One Hundred Thirty-five Years, 1797 to 1932* (1932). For 1890–1932, the Bureau of Labor Statistics' wholesale price index for all commodities is used. To prepare the graph, I inspected the annual series and identified the peaks and troughs. Then, decennial values of the index were plotted in between the peaks and troughs, and the points linked by straight-line segments to reveal the 50-year rhythms of upswings and downswings in wholesale prices. In contrast with Figures 1 and 2, what are shown here are *levels* of the index, not rates of change. However, in Chapter 1 I switch and examine the annual rates of change. The essential long-wave pattern does not change.

Long waves extend across generations, far beyond the time horizons of any results-oriented profession committed to instrumental rationality. Perhaps this explains why our political leaders and economic managers appear, like the rest of us, to be capable only of reacting to the longer rhythms, and not of changing them.

As I worried about these questions, I was drawn more deeply into an often uninviting literature in which I found a morass of conflicting opinion but precious little reliable data analysis. In this literature, truth-by-assertion often passes for evidence, speculation masquerades as theory, and fantasy has a strong

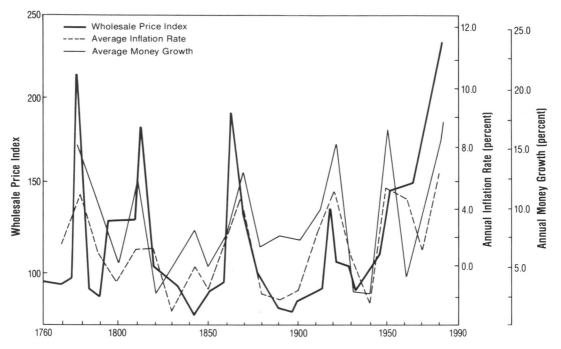

Figure 4. Covariations of Money Growth, Inflation, and the Wholesale Price Index in the United States, 1760–1982

This illustration, like the others in this Introduction, is meant to be no more than suggestive of Kondratiev waves of money growth, inflation, and wholesale prices. I used the same sources of data on money growth and the inflation rate as Ravi Batra used in his strange book *The Great Depression of 1990: Why It's Got to Happen. How to protect yourself* (1987, p. 187), namely: Milton Friedman and Anna Schwartz, *A Monetary History of the United States* (1983), and John G. Gurley and Edward S. Shaw, "The Growth of Debt and Money in the United States, 1800–1950: A Suggested Interpretation" (1957). The difference in peaking of the wholesale price index and the other two series is an artifact. In Figure 3 and here, I plotted actual peaks of the wholesale price index, but the two new variables were computed as decennial averages, in the manner described for Figures 1 and 2, smoothing through the actual peaks. Elizabeth B. Schumpeter gives the conventional explanation of the relationships revealed by this graph in a paper that deals with another country at an earlier time, "English Prices and Public Finance, 1660–1882" (1938): "Rising prices . . . occurred simultaneously with a relatively large volume of government expenditure for war purposes, met to an appreciable degree by borrowing. This borrowing resulted in credit inflation. . . . At intervals financing of the unfunded debt put a real strain on the Bank of England and its resources, and extensive increases in the unfunded debt always had a direct and immediate effect on the volume of credit" (p. 31). Friedman and Schwartz argue that "from 1867 to 1960 there have been two major price inflations . . . the periods during and after each of the two world wars. In both wars, there was also a more than doubling in the money stock. So large a rise in the money stock did not occur in any other period" (pp. 676–677). There is, however, a considerable (and hotly debated) literature on long-wave cycles of war, and as prescient as Elizabeth Schumpeter was about the relationship of inflation and war, more measured increases in money growth and inflation occurred far in advance of the final, war-induced spirals.

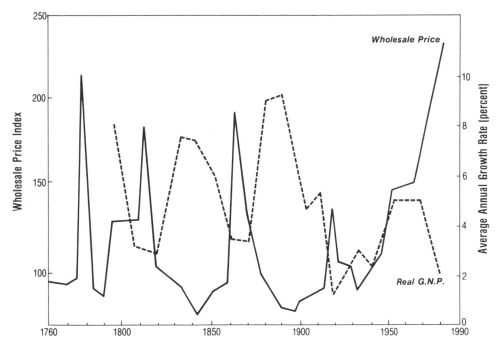

Figure 5. The Inverse Rhythms of Growth Rates and Price Levels, 1760–1982

The accelerations and decelerations of real GNP are taken from Figure 1, while the wholesale price index comes from Figure 3, revealing inverse 50-year rhythms. Following an inflation peak (coinciding with a growth-rate trough in a stagflation crisis), there is a period of deflationary growth acceleration. Following a growth-rate peak (coinciding with a price-index trough), there is a period of reflationary, then inflationary, growth deceleration. The idea that there may have been such repetitive phases or trend periods in economic history has been an issue of much interest and debate, and was used by Walt W. Rostow to structure his text *The World Economy*. Chapter 6 of the present volume is devoted to a more detailed analysis of such trend periods. Whereas my analysis deals only with American data, many authors, including Rostow, argue that the story of long waves makes sense only within the overall history of the world economy; however, in that story, the recurrence of patterns may only be suggestive given the cumulative and irreversible dynamics of history and the high noise ratio in history. I am sympathetic to this view, but feel that the United States is as good a place as any to reevaluate the long-wave idea, providing thereby a basis for other investigators to make the global extensions. Where others have provided evidence on other countries, I cite that evidence in the data that follows.

foothold. Tension has been added by clashing ideologies. Nikolai Kondratiev was a star witness at the Menshevik trial in March 1931. According to Alexander Solzhenitsyn, Kondratiev died in one of Stalin's gulags, where he had been sent because his ideas were at odds with party orthodoxy.

The work that culminated in the present book began as an attempt to find a way out of the morass. The key problem, I decided, was evidentiary: Have there, in fact, been long waves of rising and falling prices and of accelerating and decelerating economic growth, interlinked in harmonious rhythms? Without a sound evidentiary footing, all so-called long-wave "theory" is specious. I therefore chose to examine the evidence first, and to join the theoretical debate only after each piece of the puzzle had been put in place. Methodological purists would say I am naive to work this way, putting things the wrong way around; what I should be doing, in their view, is testing explicit hypotheses derived from a theory. But the long-wave theories are diverse, having been derived from widely different propositional schemes, and much of the previous long-wave research has been poorly executed. In my view, *sound data analysis is a necessary first step* in finding our way out of the morass. I am willing to be charged with brute-force empiricism if, ultimately, the facts can be made to speak for themselves, for facts can be stubborn things.

In their comprehensive work *Measuring Business Cycles* (1946), Arthur F. Burns and Wesley C. Mitchell of the National Bureau of Economic Research suggested that long cycles should "appear usually as accelerations and retardations in the original data" (p. 427). But they felt that their own data, extending only to the 1930s, offered too brief a span to determine whether Kondratiev's waves were a continuing feature of modern economies, or whether building cycles (the 25-to-30-year growth cycles documented by Simon Kuznets) were synchronized with them. Burns and Mitchell's worries were echoed by Gary S. Becker in his presidential address, "Family Economics and Macro Behavior," delivered to the American Economic Association in December 1987. "If long cycles of the Kondratieff or Kuznets type exist," Becker argued, "we will need another 200 years of data to determine whether they do exist or are just a statistical figment of an overactive imagination" (p. 7). I took up the Burns and Mitchell challenge by focusing on rates of change rather than levels of prices and other economic indicators. I had at my disposal 50 years of data beyond those that Burns and Mitchell had used. Looking back, I believe that I was able to answer their questions without waiting Becker's 200 years!

Because my method is largely graphical, it will, I hope, make the argument reasonably accessible to the less-numerate as well as the more mathematically inclined reader. Because they deal with change rather than levels of prices or economic activity, these graphs require care in interpretation, however. In order to fully understand the material in the chapters that follow, the reader needs to assure him- or herself of the necessary level of "graphicacy" by first studying Figure 6 and the discussion that accompanies it. What will be immediately clear upon looking at this graph is that I am dealing with nonlinear *dynamics*, not statics: with *changes in the rate of change* and with the *critical turning points* that mark shifts in direction. With the facts of long-term price and growth dynamics clarified, the fantasies in the long-wave literature will become transparent, and the task of sorting out sound theory from speculative hypotheses will become much easier.

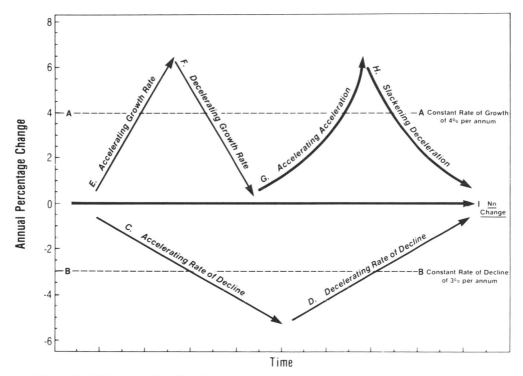

Figure 6. Guide to Reading the Graphs

In each of the graphs in the chapters that follow, the ordinate (*vertical axis*) plots annual growth rates in percentages. Above zero, the annual growth rate is positive; the base data are increasing. Below zero, the rate is negative; the base data are decreasing. The abscissa (*horizontal axis*) shows time; in the succeeding graphs time is measured in years. Now study the various cases shown. Horizontal (dashed) line *AA* depicts a constant growth rate of 4 percent per annum. Horizontal (dashed) line *BB* shows a constant rate of decline of 3 percent per annum. Horizontal (solid) line *I* shows no change over time (growth rate zero). Line *C* shows the rate of decline accelerating from 1 to 5 percent annually, and Line *D* shows the converse, the rate of decline decelerating from 5 to 1 percent annually. Line *E* shows an accelerating rate of growth, and line *F* depicts a growth rate that is decelerating. Line *G* illustrates the acceleration of an accelerating growth rate, and Line *H* shows the deceleration of a decelerating growth rate. The transition from *E* to *F* is a peak turning point at which growth acceleration tops out and shifts to deceleration; that from *C* to *D* is a trough turning point at which the rate of decline reaches a maximum and then begins to slacken. *To reiterate: the graphs you will see in the next chapters will show change, not levels:*

• Horizontal lines will show constant rates of growth or decline.

• Non-horizontal lines will reveal accelerations or decelerations of the rate of growth or decline.

• If the non-horizontal lines are curved, they will show accelerating acceleration or decelerating deceleration.

• Peaks and troughs will capture turning points where there are changes in the direction of change.

Having said that, I realize that my graphics may, individually, fail to meet the econometrician's most exacting standards of proof of mathematically regular cycles, but such proof may be beside the point if there have been waves of varying amplitude and period. I have tried to address each methodological objection that has been published, and in the interest of looking at the data in as many ways as possible, I have added the powerful insights provided by the recently developed perspective of chaos theory. "Chaos" exists if the data are apparently random but are in fact the outcome of an underlying deterministic process. According to William A. Barnett et al., "Stochastic-appearing outcomes from non-stochastic economies . . . define the concept of deterministic chaos" (*Economic Complexity: Chaos, Sunspots, Bubbles, and Nonlinearity* [1989], p. vii). It is from the *repetitions of the patterns and sequences* that emerge from multiple views of the data that one can build an understanding of this underlying process. And by adding to this empirical foundation insights into the internal mechanisms that produce it, one can make a persuasive case for the long wave as a complex, driven oscillator.

I conclude that, within the inherently high noise levels of history, prices and economic growth move in synchronized rhythms in which alternating stagflation crises and deflationary depressions separate cycles of deflationary and inflationary growth. Historically, major stagflation crises have spawned innovation in the ensuing periods of deflationary growth, thereby precipitating waves of technological change. Deflationary depressions have pruned old industries and regions; the industries, regions, and nations in the process of reaching economic maturity remain and lead the next wave of growth. The substance of each phase differs because of the irreversible and cumulative dynamics of history, but the defining qualities of successive sequences of phases repeat themselves: they are the signals within the noise.

What drives the oscillator is an endogenous historical process: each phase is a consequence of the sequence that precedes it, and the phases are synchronized in approximately 55-year waves within which 25-to-30-year cycles are embedded. These rhythms are longer than the two-, four-, and six-year electoral time horizons of politicians, the payback periods of profit-maximizing investors, and even the period of career development that each of us shares with members of our cohort. As a result, we do not plan and act with long-wave periodicity in mind, and the longer rhythms become context—the environment within which we shape our lives. In seeking short-term gains, we unconsciously adjust our behavior to the long-term trends, thereby reinforcing the directions of change. Viewed individually, each decision appears to make sense, but taken together, the resulting "collective unconscious" becomes a recipe for periodic disaster. Bandwagon effects produce overshoot and collapse: overinvestment in new technologies, overfunding of industries, and unsustainable levels of valuation in property and stock markets at one extreme; excessive pruning and panic sales at the other. By reacting in concert when crises are upon us, we guarantee that reversals of direction will recur and will once again be reinforced as the turning point passes.

Like it or not, our lives appear to be embedded in a higher order of complexity: collectively, we are a societal organism that displays self-regulating fluctuations around a path of growth, a dynamic equilibrium. Long waves should be numbered among these fluctuations, the processes by which innovative change is introduced, diffuses, saturates, overshoots, and ultimately is succeeded. Our failure to think of this higher order of complexity guarantees that the oscillations will continue and that the succession of historical phases will be repeated. Yet, if we take full advantage of the fruits of the information age, it is possible to think of stabler alternatives. History need not be destiny if we solve the problems of imperfect information and lagged reactions that are at the heart of the rhythmic repetition of overshoot and collapse.

CHAPTER 1

THE KONDRATIEV QUESTION: HAVE THERE BEEN LONG WAVES OF PRICES?

That skepticism about long waves is well founded, despite the graphs presented in the Introduction, is illustrated no more clearly than by Figure 7, which charts oscillations of the annual growth rate of the U.S. wholesale price index for the last two centuries. The growth rates have fluctuated in a manner that would pass most standard tests of randomness, clear evidence of the trial-and-error process by which markets manage growth. The question is whether, clouded by this year-to-year seesawing, there have been half-century-long accelerations and decelerations of the underlying growth rates of prices around which the annual movements have oscillated. This is the Kondratiev question.

One way to answer the question, perhaps the most typical, has been to smooth out the year-to-year oscillations by computing moving averages. This was Walt Whitman Rostow's procedure in *The World Economy*. Yet many economists would reject such a procedure, citing for authority the 1937 *Econometrica* article "The Summation of Random Causes as the Source of Cyclic Processes," in which E. Slutsky argued that a moving average applied to random numbers can create cyclical fluctuations where none existed before.

Slutsky showed that the length of the resulting cycle is L where $\cos(2\pi/L) = r(1)$, and $r(1)$ is the first-order correlation of the terms of the sinusoid. The formula holds when the second differences of the series in question are inversely

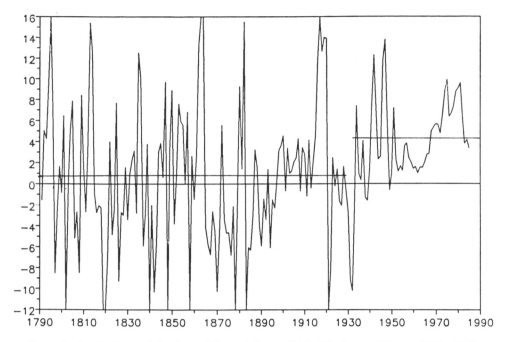

Figure 7. Oscillations of the Annual Growth Rate of U.S. Wholesale Prices, 1790–1988

The sources for the base data are the same as those for Figure 3, but what are plotted are the annual rates of growth in the wholesale price index, not the levels of the index itself. The growth rates have oscillated widely, with both accelerating and decelerating increases and decreases. The average growth rate around which these oscillations occurred was 0.65 percent annually from 1790 to 1930. In the aftermath of the Great Depression, prices rose rapidly, the result of a devaluation following departure from the gold standard which had a differential impact on the wholesale price level, a number of explicit measures to raise prices with government assistance and encouragement (among them the Agricultural Support Act, the Guffey Coal Act, and the National Labor Relations Act), and the advent of Keynesian economic management financed in part by large government deficits followed by its speedy transition into "military Keynesianism" (Keynesian deficits allied with massive shares of the budget flowing to the military-industrial complex). Since 1930, the annual growth rate of the wholesale price index has averaged 4.36 percent. Before the Great Depression, fluctuating growth rates produced an alternating pattern of inflation and deflation. Since the 1930s, we have lived in an era of permanent inflation, and the fluctuations have carried the economy from inflation to disinflation and back again. The oscillations continue, but around a higher setting.

proportional to the ordinate at that point—that is, it is a sinusoid in the limit. Slutsky's thesis was supported in a 1985 article by Roger C. Bird, Meghad J. Desai, Jared J. Enzler, and Paul J. Taubman, "Kuznets Cycles in Growth Rates." These authors showed that if the original data have only a short cycle, a long cycle, and a trend, the use of overlapping (i.e., moving) averages will diminish the amplitude of the short cycle more than that of the long cycle. By selecting points at the same stage in the short cycle, the long cycle will be revealed. How-ever, if there are random errors in the data, Slutsky's caveat may hold: moving averages may introduce cycles into the data where none existed before. There-fore, Bird et al. concluded, "if long cycles have been found in economic data after using (*a moving average*) transformation, it can mean that long cycles actually exist, or that they were created by the transformation" (p. 239).

This concern that long cycles may simply be artifacts, consequences of the transformation of the data, is a serious one and *must* be addressed. Accordingly, the first step I take in this chapter is to lay to rest the Slutsky criticism. Then, by examining the underlying data from alternative perspectives, I show that consis-tencies of pattern and rhythm emerge regardless of method. One alternative to the use of moving averages is suggested by the recent interest in the phenomenon known as *chaos,* a circumstance under which the *dynamic mechanism* may be simple and deterministic but the resulting time path is so complicated that it passes the standard tests for randomness. An important difference between the two is that in a random series behavior is independent of prior conditions, but in a chaotic system there is dependence upon initial states. If a system can be shown to be chaotic, there is evidence that endogenous mechanisms are at work. Why is this important? The real issue is that of prediction. If the system is com-pletely deterministic, perfect prediction is possible. If the fluctuations are ran-dom, prediction is impossible, and all forecasts are equally likely. If, however, the fluctuations are chaotic, prediction is possible within a limited interval of time that depends upon the specific characteristics of the chaotic system. In this sense, a chaotic system lies somewhere between one that is perfectly periodic and one that is a random walk. After setting aside the Slutsky criticism, I provide evidence that the movements of prices may have been chaotic: there have been systematic rhythms, but there has also been lots of noise.

A good discussion of the economic applications of chaos theory appears in the 1989 article by William J. Baumol and Jess Benhabib, "Chaos: Significance, Mechanism, and Economic Applications."[1] According to these authors, "Chaos

1. In a 1989 paper entitled "Searching for Chaos in Economic Systems," read to the Sixth Gen-eral Assembly of the World Future Society, Charles Dale identifies Richard H. Day's 1982 publica-tion, "Irregular Growth Cycles," as the first description of the possibility of chaotic movements of prices, GNP, and industrial production to appear in the economics literature, antedating Dale's 1984 "A Search for Business Cycles with Spectral Analysis." Other attempts to use chaos formulations are those of Brock and Sayers (1987) on business cycles, Sayers (1988) on strikes, and Scheinkman and Le Baron (1987) on stock market prices. None of these attempts survived what Dale calls the "NYU Meat Grinder"—Ramsey et al.'s demanding statistical tests (1988)—or the evaluation pro-cedures (the BDS test) developed by Brock and his associates at the University of Wisconsin. Dale concludes that "a successful finding of a chaotic system would have such a tremendous impact on the economic profession that the huge potential rewards outweigh what currently appear to be a relatively small probability of success." As Henderson argued in her 1985 paper, "Post-economic Policies for Post-industrial Societies," however, perhaps the reason for lack of success has been the attachment of economists to the wrong kind of mathematics, an attachment that appears to be waning as some now turn to nonlinear dynamics. Techniques to test for chaos are most developed in the field of physics. Important recent papers are Peter Grassberger's "Estimation of the Kolmo-

theory shows that a simple relationship that is deterministic but nonlinear, such as a first order nonlinear difference equation, can yield an extremely complex time path. Intertemporal behavior can acquire an appearance of disturbance by random shocks and can undergo violent, abrupt qualitative changes, either with the passage of time or with small changes in the values of the parameters" (p. 79). "It warns us that apparently random behavior may not be random at all" (p. 80). Baumol and Benhabib go on to suggest a straightforward graphical approach to testing for the presence of chaos. I use the approach they recommend.

What I thus present in this chapter is an examination of the data graphed in Figure 7 using both moving-average techniques and the relatively simple methods for identifying chaos suggested by Baumol and Benhabib. In using moving averages, I have been careful to control for the possibility that cycles are propagated by the smoothing technique—the heart of the Slutsky criticism. In testing for chaos, I show that the behavior of prices is inherently noisy and that the problem is to separate the long-wave signals from the noise. But with such separation, clear evidence of the "boom and bustiness" of certain kinds of chaotic systems appears.

The analysis is graphical and the graphical evidence is cumulative. For that reason, the rest of this chapter consists of a series of graphs accompanied by discursive text. To follow my argument, begin with Figure 8 and examine each graph in sequence, reading the accompanying text and getting a feel for the rhythms in the data. *For the reader who wishes to skip the intervening details, the "bottom line" of the analysis appears in Figure 21, an illustration that reveals the remarkable consistencies of price behavior in each of the four long waves that have unfolded in the last two centuries. There have indeed been long waves of prices!*

With this consistent long-wave behavior of prices firmly established, I turn in Chapter 2 to the various theories that have been advanced to account for it. In Chapters 3 and 4, I repeat the procedure for economic growth: Chapter 3 consists of graphs that build the evidentiary base; Chapter 4 discusses the alternative theories that account for the behavior depicted. Chapters 5 and 6 put the patterns of price behavior and economic growth together, exploring the synchronization of Kondratiev waves and Kuznets cycles, and the types of crises and phases of growth in American economic history that have resulted from the

---

gorov Entropy from a Chaotic Signal" (1983) and Grassberger and Procaccia's "Characterization of Strange Attractors" (1983). It is the value of the Kolmogorov entropy that tells the researcher whether the system is multiperiodic/deterministic, chaotic, or random. The most recent, and by far the most positive, work by economists dealing with various types of nonlinear dynamics, including chaos, is William A. Barnett, John Gewecke, and Karl Shell, eds., *Economic Complexity: Chaos, Sunspots, Bubbles, and Nonlinearity* (1989). I cite the conclusions that appear to be consistent with mine in what follows. Of particular significance in this book is one application of the BDS tests to data on real per capita GNP in the United States, 1870–1986, which concludes that once account is taken of the Great Depression, the hypothesis of deterministic chaos cannot be rejected.

synchronous rhythms. What is suggested is that there is an underlying long-wave clock.

From the firmer ground of the evidentiary base laid out in Chapters 1, 3, 5, and 6, I then embark on a more perilous journey across the shifting sands of Elliott waves in the stock market, cycles and critical elections in American politics, the periodic incidence of global wars and the rise and decline of world powers, and more. The task is to separate mirage and myth from that for which there is a reasonable evidentiary footing. The literature is immense, and I choose not to deal with many of the ghosties and ghoulies, looking instead to those arenas in which groups of academics are engaged in active research. But even then I traverse pathways that end in a blue haze.

Finally, in Chapters 11 and 12, I ask: What time is it now on the long-wave clock? Where are we headed? I conclude that, in phase, a decade after the stagflation crisis of 1980–1981, an epoch of disinflationary growth has seen the emergence of new technologies and the decline of old industrial regions, but the growth acceleration is ending. Signaling the turning point, a booming stock market has peaked and crashed. Falling prices and collapsed asset values have precipitated a major crisis in the savings and loan industry, and have given a further downward nudge to depressed agricultural regions. We have seen this conjunction before—in the 1760s, the 1820s, the 1870s, and the 1930s. But the current policy environment is different. Price oscillations that formerly moved from inflation to deflation and back again now cycle between inflation and disinflation, and growth now fluctuates within a narrower range.

What, then, lies ahead? Are we condemned to repeat the experiences of those past phases of growth? Or do we now have the freedom to construct alternatives? To understand my answers, join me in my journey of exploration and discovery, beginning with Figure 8.

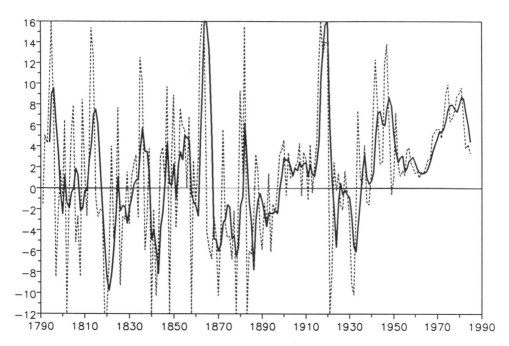

Figure 8. Four-Year Moving Averages (Computed Annually) Superimposed on the Annual Growth Rates of U.S. Wholesale Prices, 1790–1988

The first important step is to show the way in which the annual seesawing of growth rates of prices shown in Figure 7 is smoothed by taking moving averages. In this example, a four-year moving average is selected. Each average is calculated for the four-year period, including the end-point year at which the resultant is plotted (i.e., 1801-1802-1803-1804 plotted in 1804; 1802-1803-1804-1805 plotted in 1805). Why four years when I could have taken two or three or six or seven years as the smoothing interval? I simply selected one for illustrative purposes. The entire series of moving averages (for two-, four-, six- through twenty-year intervals) was calculated and plotted and appears in Appendix A for inspection by those who are worried about the effects of the smoothing interval on the analysis. What I conclude from the present figure is that the four-year moving average, while reducing the annual noise, still tracks the growth rates of prices well, peaking where it should in the inflation crises of 1815, 1865, and 1920, and revealing alternating periods of inflation and deflation through 1930 and an inflation-disinflation cycle thereafter.

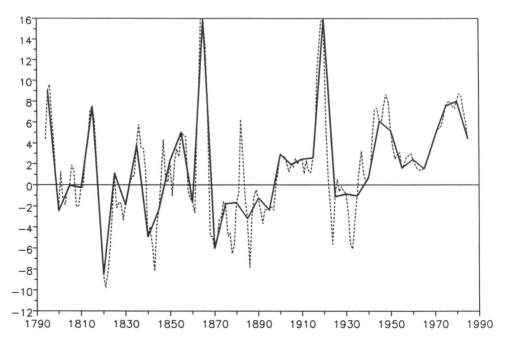

Figure 9. Four-Year Averages Computed Every Fifth Year (*solid lines*) Superimposed on the Four-Year Moving-Average Growth Rates of U.S. Wholesale Prices

The next step is to check the Slutsky argument that long waves in moving averages are artifacts of the smoothing technique, the result of propagation of deviations when the underlying data are random. To do this I computed the four-year averages at five-year intervals and overlaid them on the four-year moving averages that were plotted in Figure 8. Four-year average growth rates computed every fifth year have a one-year gap that precludes propagation, because the individual averages are decoupled. The graph shows quite clearly that the decoupled averages track very closely the four-year moving averages that were introduced in Figure 8. I therefore conclude that *nothing is being propagated by the smoothing technique;* the rhythms are a quality of the data, not of how the data have been handled. The moving average simply tracks the underlying movements of the growth rates, helping separate signals from the noise of the year-to-year seesaw. Further confirmation of this conclusion is provided in Appendix A, which presents moving averages of the growth rates of prices smoothed by successively longer averaging periods.

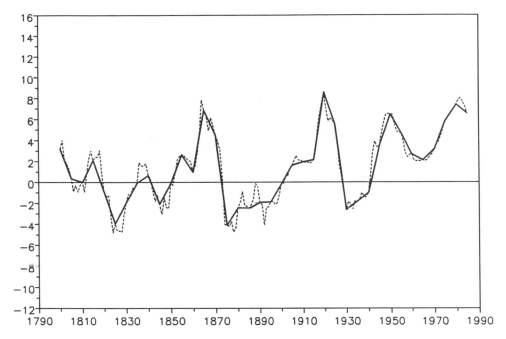

Figure 10. Ten-Year Moving Averages of the Growth Rates of U.S. Wholesale Prices Computed Annually (*dotted lines*) and Once Every Fifth Year (*solid lines*)

A higher level of generalization is achieved if ten-year moving averages are used, in the manner of Walt W. Rostow in *The World Economy,* rather than four-year averages. Depicted in this graph are ten-year averages computed annually, plotted at the end-point years (i.e., 1791–1800 in 1800) and joined by dotted lines. Superimposed on them are ten-year averages computed and plotted every fifth year, joined by solid lines. Symmetries of pattern begin to appear—for example, the acceleration of the growth rate of prices from the 1840s to the inflationary spiral of 1865, and again from the 1890s to the spiral of 1920, as well as the plunges from these two spirals into the deflationary vortexes of the early 1870s and the 1930s. These symmetrical patterns are Kondratiev's long-wave rhythms.

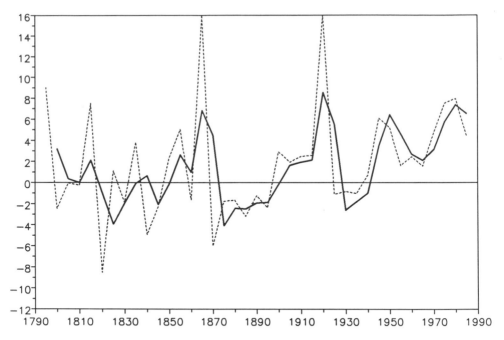

Figure 11. Ten-Year Moving Averages of the Growth Rates of U.S. Wholesale Prices Computed Every Fifth Year (*solid lines*) Superimposed on the Four-Year Averages Computed Every Fifth Year (*dotted lines*)

Do different averaging periods produce different cycles, or do the ten-year moving averages track the rhythms of the more detailed four-year averages reasonably well? From this diagram, which is an overlay of the ten-year moving averages of Figure 10 on the decoupled four-year averages of Figure 9, I conclude that the story is essentially the same: Different averaging periods do not produce different cycles, as Bird et al. (1985) suggested they would. Nor is there any propagation of cycles where none existed before. The only differences between the two lines in the graph are that the ten-year averages fluctuate within a narrower range (because of the longer smoothing period) and are pulled to the right (because the inflationary spirals remain within the averaging period for a longer number of years when a ten-year smoothing is used). Once the noisy annual seesaw of growth rates is smoothed away, not only does an underlying rhythm begin to emerge but it remains consistent across smoothing intervals.

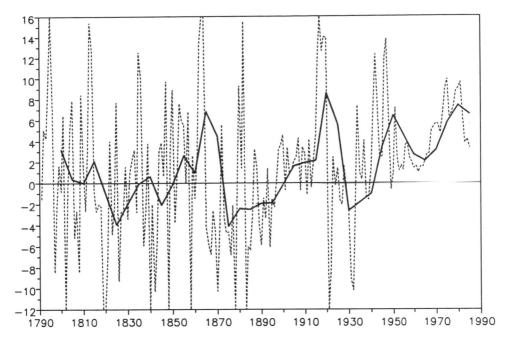

Figure 12. Ten-Year Moving Averages of the Growth Rates of U.S. Wholesale Prices (Computed Every Fifth Year) Superimposed on the Original Annual Growth Rates

This underlying rhythm within the very noisy pattern of oscillations of the annual growth rates of wholesale prices is suggested by superimposing the ten-year moving averages (*solid lines*) on the annual data of Figure 7. Over long periods of time, the annual seesaw ratchets the growth rate of prices upward, ending in a major inflationary spiral, followed by a rapid collapse into a deflationary vortex. The ratcheting seesaw then resumes. Deflation initially decelerates, but gradually prices are pushed upward into modest and then successively higher rates of increase, ending in yet another inflationary spiral and collapse.

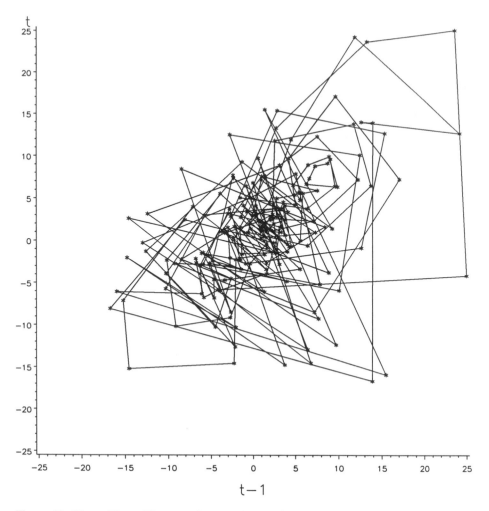

Figure 13. Chaos Phase Diagram: Average Annual Growth Rates of U.S. Wholesale Prices in Year _t_ Plotted as a Function of Growth Rates in Year _t − 1_ for the Years 1790–1987, with Successive Pairs of Years Joined by Straight-Line Segments

Will a different look at the data bring out the same rhythms suggested in Figure 12? Are the oscillations of the growth rates chaotic—i.e., apparently random, but in fact the result of an underlying deterministic process? To test this, the growth rates are plotted in a $t/t-1$ "phase space," as suggested by Baumol and Benhabib (1989). The growth rate at time t is shown on the vertical axis, the growth rate at time $t − 1$ on the horizontal axis. When plotted, a point thus shows the relationship between the previous year's and the current year's growth rate. If subject to random influences, the points plotted in the phase space will scatter in a wide, two-dimensional region. If chaotic, the paths taken by successive points should converge on a "strange attractor," a particular path in the space. "An _attractor_ is . . . the equilibrium or limit time path of a stable dynamic system, whether or not that system is chaotic" (Baumol and Benhabib 1989, p. 91). "A _strange attractor_ [is] a set of points (in the phase diagram) toward which complicated paths starting in its neighborhood are attracted" (ibid., p. 92). See also Robert Pool, "Where Strange Attractors Lurk"

(1989). There clearly is a wide scatter in the graph, but the oscillations are reminiscent of the behavior of finite difference equation functions of the quadratic form $y_t = \lambda y_{t-1}(1 - y_{t-1})$ for higher degrees of nonlinearity (i.e., when λ is large, resulting in what Robert May calls "boom and bustiness"). See James Gleick, *Chaos* (1987), pp. 176–178; and Leon Glass and Michael C. Mackey, *From Clocks to Chaos* (1988), pp. 26ff. Remember, however, that the difference equations suggested here relate to *rates of growth*, not *levels* of prices.

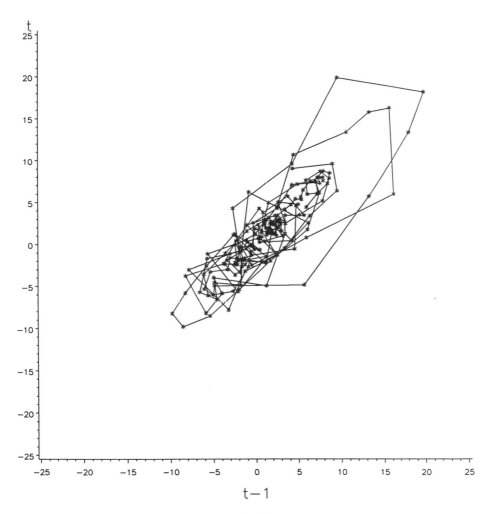

Figure 14. Convergence on the "Strange Attractor": Four-Year Moving Averages of the Growth Rates of Prices in Year *t* Plotted as a Function of the Growth Rates in Year *t* − *1*

Perhaps the smoothed data will help separate the long-wave signals from the noise, revealing more about the strange attractor that lurks within the oscillations formed by accelerating and decelerating growth rates of prices. The four-year moving averages do indeed appear to be "attracted" to an acceleration-deceleration path within the phase space, cycling from higher to lower rates of change and back again. What the smoothing has removed is much of the shorter-term oscillatory behavior that was evident in Figure 13, exposing within the oscillations a set of self-reinforcing processes, evidence of endogenous mechanisms at work. These processes destabilize the tendency to oscillate around a stable growth rate. On the one hand, as National Bureau of Economic Research investigators Joseph Haubrich and Andrew Lo say in their study *The Sources and Nature of Long-Term Memory in the Business Cycle* (1989), the economy moves toward its average level of moderate growth. On the other hand, as is evident in this illustration, there is pressure to accelerate. The result is that oscillations are forced to rotate around successively higher rates of inflation until the acceleration reaches a critical upper limit, "bursts," and is followed by a collapse down to rapid rates of deflation. The resulting pattern is one of extreme "boom and bustiness" played out over decades. One recent examination of chaos in the context of such self-reinforcing economic mechanisms is W. Brian Arthur's paper, "Self-reinforcing Methods in Economics," in P. W. Anderson and K. J. Arrow's *The Economy as an Evolving Complex System* (1988). In his 1989 paper ("Endogenous Financial-Production Cycles in a Macroeconomic Model"), Duncan K. Foley says it is possible to think "of a self-contained explanation of cyclical motion [which] assumes that the steady-state growth path is unstable, so the economy can never be observed on it. . . . [But] real capitalist economies never make unbounded excursions from [this] growth path . . . [so] a local instability of the steady-state growth path can be contained by nonlinear effects to prevent the economy from exploding" (p. 89).

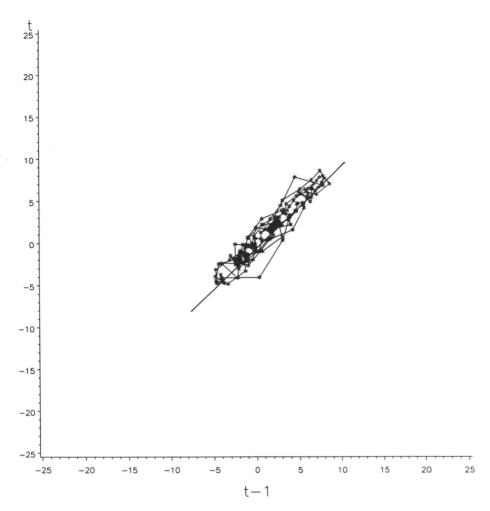

Figure 15. The Long-Wave Acceleration-Deceleration Path: Ten-Year Moving Averages of the Growth Rates of Prices in the Chaos Phase Space

When the ten-year moving averages are plotted in the phase space, the nature of the strange attractor is revealed even more starkly. The oscillations are continually drawn back to a stable, long-run growth rate in which $y_t = y_{t-1}$. A stable growth rate is the "preferred" moving equilibrium. Yet the tendency toward stable growth is continually deflected by an accompanying pressure to accelerate, with the result that actual growth rates surge and sag along the self-reinforcing path of boom until an upper limit to the inflation rate is reached and a major bust returns the system to a trough marked by rapid rates of deflation. There is much seesawing, but inside the fluctuations there is evidence of chaos, a simple and deterministic endogenous process at work. There is also evidence of "self-organized criticality": a ratcheting of growth up to an unsupportable rate of acceleration that precipitates a crash.

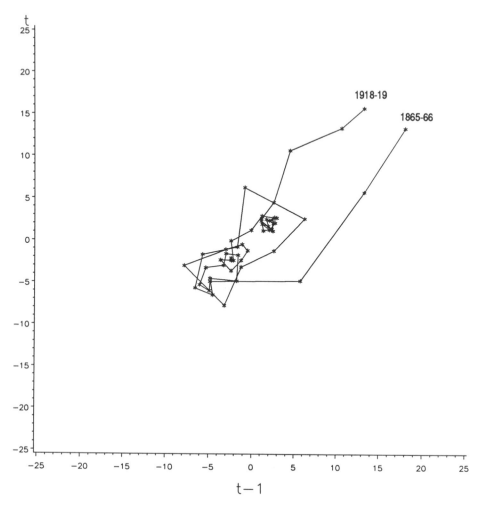

Figure 16. Time Path of the Four-Year Moving Averages between the 1865 and 1920 Inflation Peaks, Plotted in Phase Space

More can be learned about this process by breaking the 200-year series into segments, in this case the period between the 1865 and 1920 inflationary spirals. Growth rates are at the peak of an inflationary spiral in 1865–1866, but plummet down thereafter into a deflationary vortex. There is then a long period of oscillatory movement in which growth rates are ratcheted up to successively higher levels of increase, at each level trying to stabilize around a constant growth rate, but from that rate being pushed upward to the next until another upward spiral occurs and prices skyrocket into the next inflationary peak, that of 1919–1920.

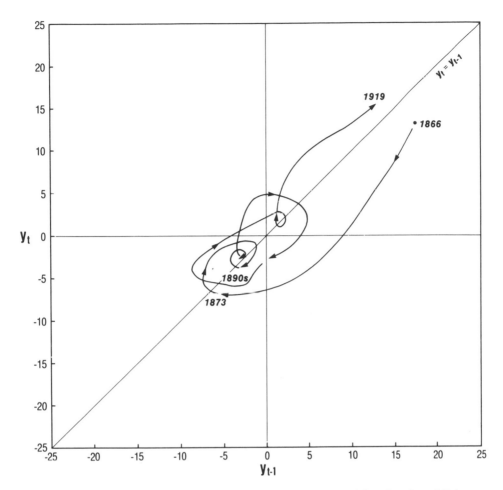

Figure 17. Interpretation of Figure 16: Chaotic Deceleration and Acceleration of Price Changes between Two Inflation Peaks

The pattern in Figure 16 includes the plunge from the 1865 inflationary spiral to a primary deflationary vortex in 1873, thereby indicating convergence on the strange attractor but at a rapid rate of deflation. There is then a ratcheting upward to an initial constant growth rate followed by an upward surge and a loop downward into the depression of the 1890s, a ratcheting up to another loop, and then acceleration to the spiral of 1919–1920.

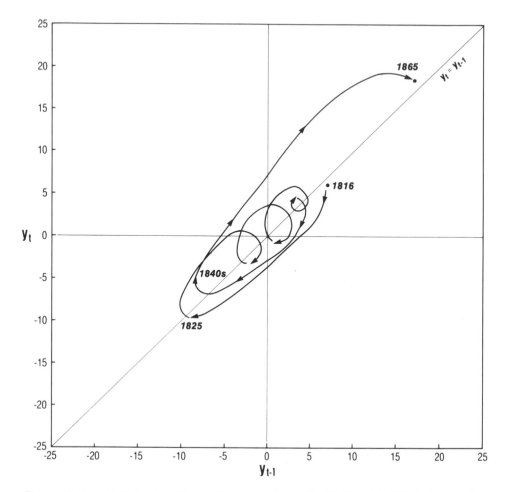

Figure 18. Chaotic Behavior of Price Changes between the 1815 and 1865 Inflation Peaks

The pattern between the 1815 and 1865 inflation peaks was the same as that between 1865 and 1920. There was a rapid plunge of growth rates from the 1815 inflationary spiral to the primary vortex of 1825, followed by upward looping around the strange attractor to the brief inflationary peak of 1837, a collapse into the deflationary depression of the 1840s, and an upward surge to the inflationary spiral of 1865.

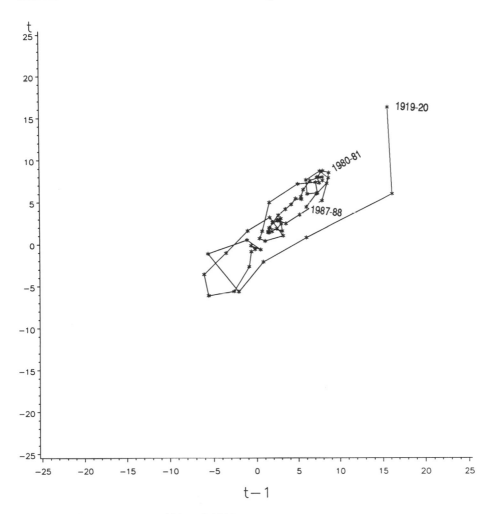

Figure 19. Chaos between 1920 and 1988

The chaotic repetitions continued after 1920. First came the rapid plunge of prices into a primary vortex, the Great Depression, followed by a process of ratcheting and looping upward which culminated in the inflationary spiral of 1981. In the years since 1981, there has been a downward, disinflationary move. Thus, in each long wave the essential pattern is repeated, providing clear evidence of chaos rather than randomness. Growth rates plunge rapidly from the peak acceleration rates of inflationary spirals to the trough deceleration rates of the primary vortex. They then ratchet upward in long loops and tight oscillations from vortex to spiral, moving upward along a strange attractor—at each point a constant growth rate. On the one hand, the attraction is to stable growth, but as price changes oscillate around this attractor, the pressure to accelerate ratchets the regime upward until a final surge into an inflationary spiral takes place and growth rates reach their upper limit. This is followed by a collapse to the opposite extreme, the deflationary depression, after which the process begins anew. Each long-term boom-and-bust cycle takes half a century or more to complete.

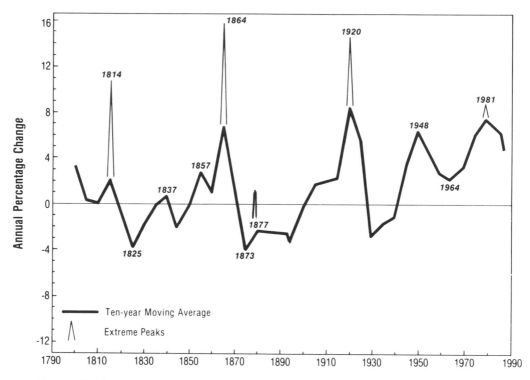

Figure 20. The Long-Wave Trend, Summarized from Figure 11

The long-term price movements may now be summarized. In previous research, the inflationary spirals of 1814-1815, 1864-1865, 1919-1920, and 1980-1981 have been characterized as *Kondratiev peaks,* fifty-five years apart on the average, while the mid-1840s and the mid-1890s have been characterized as *Kondratiev troughs,* similarly spaced. In addition, there have been *inflationary turning points* in 1837, 1857, 1877, and 1948, and *primary deflationary vortexes* in 1825, 1873, and 1929. Have the successive Kondratiev cycles been similar? Within the inherent noisiness of economic history, have there been repetitive regularities? This question can be answered by slicing the long-term trend into trough-to-trough segments, then overlaying the segments by centering them on a common vertical axis corresponding to their inflationary peaks. The resulting graph, shown in Figure 21, reveals the essential form of the long wave.

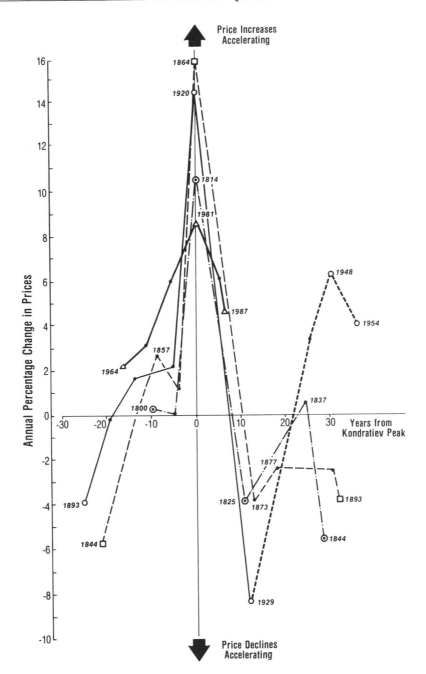

Figure 21. The Long Waves Superimposed

There is remarkable consistency in this graph, which is the proper form of the accelerations and decelerations of the growth rates of prices suggested by the (unlabeled) "idealized long-wave model" presented in Robert Beckman's book *Into the Upwave* (1988, p. 34). *Long waves* of price acceleration and deceleration extend over half a century or more, and the rhythms are repetitive. The chaos formulation suggests that a simple deterministic mechanism may be at work. *A common, four-phase pattern stands out:*

- In each wave there is first a progressive acceleration of the rate of price increase over a period of some twenty years, ending in the brief paroxysm of an *inflationary spiral* that rushes upward to a peak (1814–1815, 1864–1865, 1919–1920, 1980–1981).
- This is followed by a rapid collapse of prices into a *primary vortex* (1825, 1873, 1929).
- Then there is a *secondary recovery* in which prices move upward to another turning point, at a lesser peak (1837, 1877, 1948).
- Finally, from this secondary peak, prices decelerate into the *Kondratiev trough* (1844, 1893, 1954).

The timing suggested by Kondratiev is confirmed for the long waves 1789-1815-1844 and 1844-1864-1893. The patterns indicate that the third Kondratiev long wave should be defined as 1893-1920-1954, the fourth as 1954-1981-(?). Within this chronology, the Great Depression is properly identified as one of the free-fall "primary vortexes" along with those of 1825 and 1873, although it was much deeper than either of them, and the New Deal is grouped with the secondary recoveries of 1825–1837 and 1873–1877, even though its policy-driven price recovery was much sharper. In several seminars I have been criticized for this classification of the Great Depression and the New Deal, for it runs counter to many of the chronologies of the long wave that define the third Kondratiev wave as ending in the 1930s and show the fourth peaking in 1973 and entering a downwave phase thereafter (see, e.g., Robert Beckman, *Into the Upwave* [1988], p. 31). Walt W. Rostow and Jay W. Forrester have debated the resulting question of whether we are now in an "upwave" or a "downwave." Some minds are made up. In a letter, Andre Gunder Frank writes: "You will shock people not to define the 30s as the (Kondratiev trough) . . . derived from trying to fit the facts into your procrustean bed." My answer is twofold. First, simply examine Figure 21: *the facts can be stubborn things;* I think they speak for themselves. I believe they resolve the Rostow-Forrester debate. Second, read two perceptive essays written by Joseph A. Schumpeter. In the first, entitled "Depressions—Can We Learn from Past Experiences?" (1934), Schumpeter argued that 1929 was initially simply a first free-fall of prices after the 1920 inflation peak, just as 1825 had followed 1815 and 1873 had followed 1865. But then, "supernormal sensitivity of the economic system to adverse occurrences and to the weaknesses in the institutional set up of the country" took over ("The American Economy in the Interwar Period" [1946]). In the 1930s, Schumpeter noted, the Coolidge-prosperity investment and building boom came to an end as prices continued to fall and profits began to sag. The stock market boomed and crashed. All of which had happened in previous historical experiences of the same kind. There was the *normal depressive tendency* of the turning point. But *supernormal sensitivity* meant that certain sectors of the economy—the most defenseless of all being agriculture—developed severe difficulties or breakdowns from which a downward vicious spiral, attended by widespread unemployment, began. According to Schumpeter, there were three sources of supernormal sensitivity:

- The speculative stock market mania of 1927–1929, with its "wild excesses and the attendant financial practices [that] were clearly abnormal; they can be explained only by a specifically American mass psychology." When the market crashed, it annihilated that part of the consumers' demand that had been financed by largely unrealized capital gains.

- The weakness of the U.S. banking system (a "nebula of inefficient pygmies"), which enabled successive banking crises to break the morale of the public and spread paralysis throughout business.
- The mortgage situation, characterized by reckless borrowing and lending, which affected both urban and rural areas, but particularly farmers as commodity prices sagged and the drought of the 1930s affected productivity.

Confirming Schumpeter's assessment, John Kenneth Galbraith wrote in *The Great Crash* (1929): "No inevitable rhythm required the collapse and stagnation of 1930–40" (p. 177). Instead, he defined the causes of this anomalously large disruption as follows:

- A highly unequal distribution of income, which made high-bracket spending and investment especially susceptible to the crash of October 1929.
- Bad corporate structure: "American enterprise in the twenties had opened its hospitable arms to an exceptional number of promoters, grafters, swindlers, imposters, and frauds. This, in the long history of such activities, was a kind of flood tide of corporate larceny" (p. 183).
- Bad banking structure: "The bankers yielded to the blithe, optimistic, and immoral mood of the times. . . . one failure led to other failures, and these spread with a domino effect" (p. 184).
- Dubious foreign balance: The United States was a major creditor nation, and countries had to pay their debts to it in gold or in increased exports. But a sharp increase in the tariff eliminated the latter possibility. International debts went into default, and there was a precipitate fall in American exports.
- Poor state of economic intelligence: "In the months and years following the stock market crash, the burden of reputable economic advice was invariably on the side of the measures that would make things worse. . . . The Democratic platform in 1932 called for an immediate and drastic reduction of governmental expenditures . . . [but] instead of inflation the country was experiencing the most violent deflation in the nation's history. Yet every sober advisor saw . . . the danger of run-away price increases" (pp. 187–190).

Charles P. Kindleberger adds (in *The World in Depression, 1929–1931* [1973]) that the shocks to the system from overproduction of primary products, or from the stock market crash of 1929, were not so great; similar shocks had been experienced before without such dire consequences. The problem was that no one assumed any leadership position, and all of the reactions were inappropriate:

- The Smoot-Hawley Tariff Act of 1930 was a reaction to agricultural overproduction. It helped precipitate an international crisis as debtor nations found it more difficult to export to the United States in a contracting spiral of world trade.
- Britain withdrew from a world leadership role, folding itself into protected Commonwealth markets.
- The gold standard collapsed in 1931 during the interregnum when monetary leadership in the United States was shifting from New York to Washington. Severe contractions in the money supply helped propel deflation.

The combination of banking failures, personal and corporate bankruptcies, and lack of credit drove the primary trough into the Great Depression. What would normally have been the secondary recovery phase was delayed, and when it occurred it was boosted by the wholesale price inflation accompanying the departure from gold, by the New Deal's national-recovery and price-stabilization policies, and by the deficit spending that became the hallmark of strong central governments committed to Keynesian economic policy. World War II, followed by Korea, distorted the third-wave trough as war production and mobilization churned the U.S. economy into a period of war prosperity some years before the third wave should have bottomed out. There was then only a minor sag after the Korean war ended before the main thrust of post-depression growth began in the late 1950s. It was therefore only from the 1950s that a fourth long wave unfolded, reaching its inflationary spiral in 1981 and moving downward since, heading toward yet another primary vortex. Interestingly, there is no reference to Schumpeter's articles in Kathryn M. Dominguez, Ray C. Fair, and Matthew D. Shapiro's 1988 paper, "Forecasting the Depression: Harvard versus Yale," in which these authors conclude that the Depression was largely unforecastable due to mistakes made by the Federal Reserve which compounded the financial panic and the collapse of commodity prices.

CHAPTER 2

LONG-WAVE EXPLANATIONS:
KONDRATIEV AND HIS SUCCESSORS

WHAT KONDRATIEV SAID

Having established quite clearly, at least for the United States, that prices have accelerated and decelerated in a succession of long waves, it behooves us to take a closer look at what Nikolai Kondratiev (for whom the long waves are named) said, and how subsequent scholars have tried to explain the 50-year long wave.[1]

1. Two good treatments of Kondratiev can be found in Nathan H. Mager, *The Kondratieff Waves* (1987), and a four-part series by Ralph D. Cato that was published in *Futures: The Magazine of Commodities*, March–June 1986. Kondratiev wrote six pieces on long waves between 1920 and 1928; all except the first and fourth were initially published in the *Economic Bulletin of the Conjuncture Institute*, which he edited. His book *The World Economy and Its Condition during and after the War* was published in 1922. "Some Controversial Questions Concerning the World Economy and the Crisis" (1923) and "On the Notion of Economic Statics, Dynamics, and Fluctuations" (1924) appeared in the *Economic Bulletin*. "Long Business Cycles" was published in *Problems of Economic Fluctuations* (1925); "Major Economic Cycles" (1926a; published in 1928 with an extensive critique by D. I. Oparin) and "Dynamics of Industrial and Agricultural Prices" (1928a) were published in *Economic Bulletin*. Kondratiev's work is largely known via his 1925 article, published in abridged form as "Die langen Wellen der Konjunktur," *Archiv für Sozialwissenschaft und Sozialpolitik* 56 (1926b), and his 1928 article, published as "Die Preisdynamik der industriellen und landwirtschaftlichen Waren," *Archiv für Sozialwissenschaft und Sozialpolitik* 60 (1928b). An abridged version of the 1926 article was translated into English by W. F. Stolper and published as

Kondratiev was born in 1892. He was sufficiently precocious that after join-
ing the Chayanov Institute in 1916 he became vice-minister for food in Alexander Kerensky's provisional 1917 government. His mentor was Mikhail I.
Tugan-Baranovskij, Russia's greatest prerevolutionary economist, and when he
died in 1919, Kondratiev prepared the eulogy (part of the reason for his later
downfall).

Surviving the November Revolution, he became active in the left-wing
agrarian Socialist Revolutionary Party, and in 1920 he was appointed founding
director of the Conjuncture Institute, a post he held until 1928. The prime purpose of the institute was to study capitalist crises and to predict the crisis that
would lead to the collapse of capitalism.

During this time, Kondratiev was also a professor at the Timiryazez Agricultural Academy and an associate of the U.S.S.R. Popular Commissariats of Finance and Agriculture. He devised the "peasant indices"—price indexes for
products bought and sold by farmers—and in 1923–1924 he was in charge of
drafting the First Five-Year Plan for Soviet agriculture. He was more conservative than many of his colleagues, and he believed that Soviet agriculture could
be collectivized without eliminating the wealthier peasant class, the kulaks. He
was at the British Exhibition in 1924 and in the United States for economic talks
in 1925.

But Kondratiev's hypothesis that long waves were an organic part of the capitalist system—that there was complete interdependency in capitalism between
political and social development, war, economics, and finance (particularly his
view that capitalist crises were self-correcting and that successive cycles were
therefore repetitive)—brought vigorous criticism. In a 1926 paper he wrote:
"*Each consecutive phase [of the long wave] is a result of a cumulative process
during the preceding phase, and, as long as the principles of the capitalistic
economy are conserved, each new cycle follows its predecessor with the same
regularity with which the different phases succeed each other*" (italics added).
Clearly, he was a heretic; capitalism was not supposed to be able to renew itself.

Kondratiev also deviated by supporting the Socialist Revolutionary Party's
populist agrarian position that expropriated land be redistributed to the peasants who cultivated it.

He was removed as director of the Conjuncture Institute in 1928 and the
institute was dissolved. In 1928, the *Soviet Russian Encyclopedia* said of his
long-wave idea, "This theory is wrong and reactionary." He was arrested in
1930 and charged with heading an illegal "Working Peasants' Party." In March

---

"The Long Waves in Economic Life," *Review of Economic Statistics* 17 (1935); and a critique by
Estonian émigré and research director of the Federal Reserve Bank in New York, George Garvy,
"Kondratieff's Theory of Long Cycles," appeared in the *Review of Economic Statistics* in 1943.
There is also *Nikolai Kondratieff's "The Long Wave Cycle"* [1928], translated by Guy Daniels, with
an Introduction by Julian M. Snyder (1984).

1931 he was a witness at the Menshevik trial, and both his long-wave hypotheses and his views on agriculture were denounced. In the *Gulag Archipelago*, Alexander Solzhenitsyn says that Kondratiev was put into solitary confinement and became mentally ill before his death.

Subsequently, the *Great Soviet Encyclopedia* called the "Theory of Long Cycles" a "vulgar bourgeois theory of crises and economic cycles." "The concept of the long cycle in theory is directed against the basic Marxist thesis concerning the inevitability of economic crises under capitalism, and it conceals the unsolvable contradiction of capitalist society." However, the October 9, 1987, issue of *Science* contained the following news item (p. 149):

Kondratiev Rehabilitated

The Soviet Union has rehabilitated the economist Nikolai Kondratiev. He is best known for his theory of economic cycles, which has recently seen a resurgence of interest among Western economists as an explanation of the link between technological innovation and economic growth. Kondratiev was one of a number of academic economists who were arrested during the purges of the early 1930s because of their opposition to the economic policies of Josef Stalin. He subsequently disappeared after a show trial. Another of those whose works can now be openly studied in the U.S.S.R. is Alexander Chayanov, a staunch opponent of the mass collectivization of agriculture who supported the gradual transformation and modernization of peasant smallholdings through cooperative farming. Chayanov was shot in 1939.

Kondratiev's rehabilitation, as the Soviet Union strives to restructure, is not inconsistent with the favorable assessment accorded his work by Western economists until the advent of the Keynesian paradigm thrust his ideas aside: "It was N. D. Kondratieff who brought the phenomenon fully before the scientific community and who systematically analyzed all the material available to him on the assumption of the presence of a Long Wave, characteristic of the capitalist process" (Joseph A. Schumpeter, *Business Cycles* [1939], 1:164).

Working first with wholesale price levels in England, France, and the United States, Kondratiev found long-term cycles that he said ran from trough to peak to trough as follows: 1789-1814-1849; 1849-1865(U.S.)/1873(Europe)-1896; 1896-1920-(?). He called them "waves of an average length of about 50 years." Writing in 1925, he predicted an inevitable plunge in commodity prices ahead. He then examined interest rates and found, as expected, an inverse relationship between the prices quoted for interest-bearing state bonds (French *rentes*, British *consoles*) and wholesale-price cycles. Examining other series, he noted that some supported and others were inconsistent with his central idea. He believed that the relationships were not accidental. Cyclical turning points coincided in many series, and coincident long-wave behavior occurred in many countries.

On this point—that long waves have been a global rather than specifically U.S. phenomenon—the majority of investigators concur. Writing from the later

vantage point of the 1940s, Burns and Mitchell offered a supportive comparison
of peak and trough dates (*Measuring Business Cycles,* p. 432):

Nature of turn	Turns in Kondratiev's long waves	Turns in long waves of wholesale prices			
		United States	Great Britain	Germany	France
Trough	ca. 1790	1789	1789	1793	—
Peak	1810–1817	1814	1813	1808	1820
Trough	1844–1851	1843	1849	1849	1851
Peak	1870–1875	1864	1873	1873	1872–1873
Trough	1890–1896	1896–1897	1896	1895	1896
Peak	1914–1920	1920	1920	1923	1926
Trough	—	1932	1933	1933	1935

More recently, reflecting the contemporary resurgence of interest in the phenomenon, Joshua Goldstein concludes in his book *Long Cycles* (1988) that
"there is remarkable consensus on dating among thirty-three scholars from
all theoretical schools of the long wave debate" (p. 74). "Empirical analysis
strongly corroborates long waves in price data—both before and after the onset
of industrialization in the late eighteenth century. Price waves go back as early
as the sixteenth century. . . . Since the late eighteenth century, price waves appear in, and are synchronous among, various European countries, reflecting the
expansion of the core of the world system and its increasing integration in the
industrial era" (p. 209).

To better interpret his long-wave idea, Kondratiev studied descriptive data on
capitalist nations. He discerned *three empirical patterns* that he suggested may
aid in understanding long waves:

1. Before and during the beginning of the rising wave of a long cycle, the
society's economic life undergoes considerable changes. These changes are usually seen in production and exchange techniques preceded by significant technical discoveries and inventions, gold-production and monetary-circulation conditions, and/or involvement of new countries in worldwide economic relations.

> The first upwave (1780s–1815) began at the height of the Industrial Revolution
> and at a time when the United States was emerging into the world's economic
> markets. The second upwave (1844–1875) was preceded by many technical inven-
> tions, including the turbine, harvesting machine, telegraph, steamboat, and sewing
> machine. The wave's rise was accompanied by expansion of the U.S. role in the
> world market and a considerable increase in gold production due to discoveries in
> the United States and Australia. The third upwave (1896–1920) also preceded by
> important technical inventions, including the vacuum pump, gas motor and engine,
> telephone, electric locomotive, railroad and streetcar, and transformer; these in-
> ventions triggered a second Industrial Revolution, particularly in the chemical and
> electrical industries. The wave's rise was accompanied by an increase in gold pro-
> duction, establishment of the gold standard in many countries, and the emergence
> into the world economy of Australia, Argentina, Chile, Canada, and others.

2. The period of the rising wave of a long cycle is characterized by a far greater number of social upheavals and radical changes to society than the period of the downward wave.

The first upwave (1780s–1815) covers the period when the United States gained independence, the French Revolution occurred, there were wars between Napoleonic France and other nations, Russia and Turkey fought, and Poland was partitioned. The second upwave (1844–1875) was marked by revolutionary movements in Italy, Germany, Austria, France, and Hungary, by the Crimean War, the founding of Rumania, the U.S. Civil War, the Franco-Prussian War, and the founding of the German Empire. The third upwave (1896–1920) spanned conflict or wars between Japan and China, Turkey and Greece, and Italy and Turkey, the Spanish-American War, the Anglo-Boer War, the Russo-Japanese War, the first and second Balkan Wars, World War I, and revolutions in Russia, Turkey, China, Germany, and Austro-Hungary.

3. The periods of downward waves of the long cycles are characterized by prolonged and serious depressions in agriculture.

During the first downwave (1815–1844), while the prices of both industrial and agricultural commodities dropped, those in agriculture exhibited relatively greater declines. Starting in 1818, land rents declined until 1840. In England, commissions were established by Parliament in 1820, 1821, 1822, 1833, and 1836 to study the causes and depth of the depression in agriculture. During the second downwave (1875–1896) a great depression in agriculture affected almost all major European nations and the United States. In several instances the price level of agricultural commodities declined absolutely and land rents dropped considerably. Again, commissions were established to study the causes and possible solutions to the depression in agriculture. Kondratiev noted that there were signs of an agricultural depression as the world entered the third long-cycle downwave; the signs were most pronounced in the United States, where commissions on the agricultural depression were formed in 1921 and 1924.

Kondratiev concluded that "the historical material relating to the development of economic and social life as a whole conforms to the hypothesis of long waves." Therefore:

• Prosperity and depression, with all their profound social implications, are tied to the upswings and downswings of the long waves.

• During long-wave downswings, "agriculture suffers an especially pronounced long depression."

• Also during long-wave downswings, "an especially large number of important discoveries and inventions in the technique of production and communication" occur, but these must wait for the next wave's upswing to be implemented on a large scale.

- Worldwide gold production increases on the wave's upswing, and the global market for commodities and manufactured goods is enlarged by the assimilation of new national territories and colonies.
- "It is during the period of the rise of long waves (during the period of high tension in the expansion of economic forces) that, as a rule, the most disastrous and extensive wars and revolutions occur." "The rising wave of a long cycle [also] is associated with the replacement and expansion of basic capital goods, and with the radical regrouping of, and changes in, society's productive forces."

Kondratiev's Soviet critics focused on the issue of causation, arguing that the long waves have been created by external circumstances such as inventions, wars and revolutions, international migrations, the assimilation of new countries into the world economy, and fluctuations in world gold production. Capitalism, they said, has internal contradictions that prevent self-renewal. Kondratiev's response was clear: "*These considerations . . . are not valid. Their weakness lies in the fact that they reverse the causal connections and take the consequence to be the cause, or see an accident where we really have to deal with a law governing the events*" (italics added). To Kondratiev, the alleged causes were neither exogenous nor random—they were part of the rhythms of the long wave, obedient to and symptomatic of it. The long wave is driven, he believed, by a set of self-correcting processes that are inherent to capitalism. For this belief, he died.

LONG-WAVE THEORIES AFTER KONDRATIEV

Kondratiev's long-wave formulation attracted many adherents, each of whom formulated his or her own explanation for the rhythms. Historian Walt Whitman Rostow used the long-wave idea to structure his interpretation of world economic history, centering his explanation of price waves on the problems of overshoot and lag that drive world commodity prices. Craig S. Volland introduced materials-substituting technology into the equation. John R. Borchert described successive technology transitions as leading to epochs of growth. And others, such as J. J. van Duijn, worked on the S shape of infrastructure life cycles. Other formulations include capital-lifespan theories, Joseph A. Schumpeter's innovation-wave concepts, Gerhard Mensch's neo-Schumpeterian metamorphosis model, and neo-Marxist profit-cycle notions.

Despite their differences, what emerges cumulatively from these contributions is the idea that the long-wave rhythms have something to do with the innovation and diffusion of major new transportation and energy technologies, with infrastructure development, and with collective behavior marked by lag and overshoot. But exactly what the relationship is—what the pattern of causation is—will remain unclear until we have dealt with issues of growth (the cycles of which have a 25-to-30-year periodicity) in Chapters 3 and 4, and have been able to draw together the synchronized rhythms of growth and prices in Chapter 5.

Rostow on Commodity-Price Movements

Rostow pointed to the fact that the evidence for 50-year long waves was in commodity prices. It was logical, then, to seek an explanation in commodity prices. Long-wave fluctuations, he said, could be understood only by relating forces set in motion by a leading sector in growth stemming from the introduction and progressive diffusion of a new technology; forces set in motion by changes in the profitability of producing foodstuffs and raw materials, whether from the side of prices or that of technology, including their effects on investment in new territories and mines, or capital movements, interest rates, terms of trade, and domestic international income distribution; and forces set in motion (notably in housing and infrastructure) by long waves of international or domestic migration, or other forces changing the rate of family formation, the demand for housing, and the size of the work force. All are aspects, he said, of the process of adjustment toward a never-attained dynamic equilibrium.

There were, he concluded, two principal kinds of trend periods (*The World Economy,* pp. 109–110):

1. Periods when prices in general, agricultural and raw-material prices in particular, and interest rates are rising or are high relative to previous and subsequent periods; when agriculture is expanding rapidly; and when income distribution tends to shift in favor of agriculture and profits, while urban real wages are under pressure (1790–1815, 1848–1873, and 1896–1920):

1790–1815: The expansion of the major leading sector, cotton textiles, was dampened by war and the necessity to expand agriculture to feed Britain's growing population. The war expanded the iron industry in Britain and led to its takeoff in New England in the United States.

1848–1873: The population-food imbalance operated in full force. Prices for grain shot up in the 1850s. The price of cotton also rose, and urban wages came under severe pressure. The British railroads expanded, but overall growth was affected by the American Civil War. Prices, interest rates, terms of trade, income distribution, and flows of capital were distorted in this period by a series of minor wars and, for the first time, by the attractions of gold mining.

1896–1920: Small wars led to relative shortages of foodstuffs and raw materials, the expansion of military outlays, and finally a great war. Industrial real wages came under pressure. By the late 1890s, the railroads were no longer a leading economic sector. Steel and its subsectors were decelerating. Electricity, new forms of chemicals, and the automobile sectoral complex were moving forward very rapidly. The Boer War was expensive, but in the United States, the prices of agricultural products fell.

2. Periods when the previous trends are reversed (1815–1848, 1873–1896, and 1920–1936):

1815–1848: The price of foodstuffs fell in this postwar period. The speedy expansion of the cotton industry in the 1830s led to a sharp increase in prices in the period 1833–1835. Although the period was not affected by wars, population pressure and the potato crisis of 1845–1847 in Ireland dislodged the food-population balance.

1873–1896: The railroads peaked out as a leading sector, but steel took root, and machine tools and steam engines for ships were born. At this time electricity and new forms of chemicals began to move from the stages of invention to an early phase of innovation. In the late 1800s, new economies (Sweden, Japan, Russia, and Italy) took off.

1920–1936: Although the prices of agricultural products were still low, this did not encourage a sufficiently accelerated diffusion of the new leading economic sectors in advanced economies.

The answer to long waves, Rostow concluded, lies in the fact that the opening up of new sources of food and raw materials requires substantial periods of time. "The lags involved in responding to a relative rise in food or raw material prices, and the fact that the response often required the development of whole new regions, led to an overshooting of world requirements and a period of relative surplus. A relative fall in the prices of food and raw materials then followed . . . until expanding world requirements caught up with the excess capacity" (*Getting from Here to There* [1979], p. 22). Commodity prices then shifted upward again, stimulating the opening up of new sources of food and raw materials.

Volland on Materials-substituting Technology

Taking Rostow one step further, Craig S. Volland argued in his article "A Comprehensive Theory of Long Wave Cycles" (1987):

• Long waves are caused by the growth of dominant technologies that strain the supply of natural resources upon which they are dependent.

• The mechanism that induces the wave is rising commodity prices. In the intermediate term (10–20 years), rising real prices initiate the search for new sources; capital requirements are huge and lead times are very long. In the long term (40–60 years), an exponential increase in demand causes resource-based technologies to become vulnerable to substitution by new technologies because the search for new sources leads to lower-grade ores, heavier hydrocarbons, smaller fields, and frontier areas where the cost of recovery is great.

• The depressionary leg of the cycle ends as new technologies gain acceptance and relieve the strain. These innovations may allow more-efficient use of existing materials, may be dependent on different materials in plentiful supply that can be more easily utilized, may be only mildly resource intensive, or may be based on renewable resources.

"At first blush," Volland says, "this would appear to be a rehash of Rostow's excellent work. This is not the case. Rostow assumed the rise of commodity prices was due to transient shortages that eventually were relieved by additional investment in the production of those same commodities. He did not take into account the clear historical record of price and technology-induced substitution between key commodities, particularly primary energy sources" (ibid., p. 130).

Borchert on Technology Transitions and Epochs of Growth

This notion of technology-induced substitutions was implicit in Minnesota geographer John R. Borchert's epochal study "American Metropolitan Evolution" (1961). Focusing on transportation technologies and energy sources in their initial phase of deployment, he argued:

• Before 1830 the location and spread of American cities was primarily influenced by wagon and sail technology. Eastern seaports dominated, and centers rising in importance were located on the nation's inland waterways.

• From 1830 to 1870, canals, iron rails, and the steamboat were the dominant innovations. Ports with large rail territories grew to dominance.

• Between 1870 and 1920 the major influences were the steel rail and the ocean-going vessel, combined with the major thrust of industrialization. The Northeastern Industrial Belt lay at the heart of a national rail network, with processing centers at rail nodes.

• After 1920, cities were reshaped by the automobile, while air travel and long-distance communications began to recast regional relationships.

It is new technology, Borchert said, that shapes the pattern of urban and regional development, serving as the leading growth sector. Recasting his supportive materials, we can see in Figure 22 how the inland waterways and the use of captive industrial water power reached their peak-development zenith in the inflationary spiral of 1864–1865 and declined thereafter. Railroad development and the coal industry peaked in the inflationary spiral of 1919–1920 and subsequently declined (Figure 23). Motor vehicles, surfaced-road development, and oil production were all still heading upward in the 1950s (Figure 24), but a more recent rendering of patterns of U.S. energy consumption shows that petroleum consumption peaked in the most recent inflation crisis (that of 1981), just as wood and coal use peaked in the inflation crises of the 1860s and around 1920, respectively (Figure 25).

What these graphics reveal is that the *life cycles* of energy use and dominant transportation technology have common features (Figure 26). The initial inno-

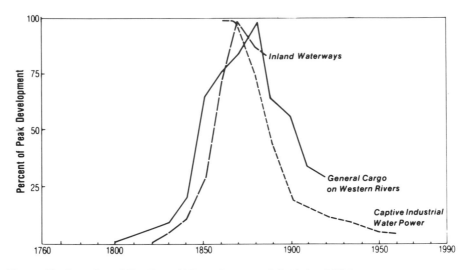

Figure 22. Growth and Decline of Water Power and the Inland Waterways

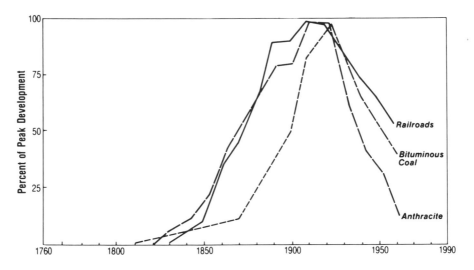

Figure 23. Growth and Decline of Railroads and the Coal Industry

vation (i.e., the first commercial application) may occur long before widespread acceptance. With such acceptance, there then is a period of accelerating deployment, a turning point, and a period of decelerating deployment until peak development is achieved during an inflationary crisis. Retrenchment follows as substitute technologies take over. The time period between initial acceleration

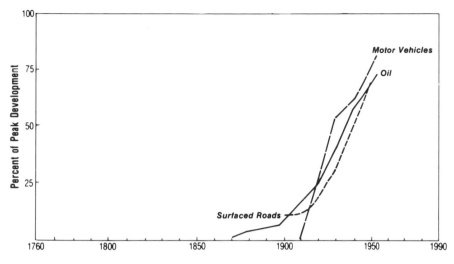

Figure 24. Growth of Surfaced Roads, Automobile Use, and the Oil Industry

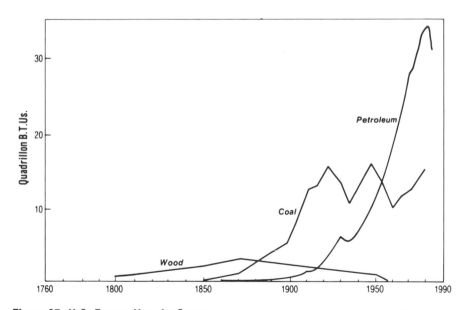

Figure 25. U.S. Energy Use, by Source

after one inflation crisis and peak deployment in the next is that of a single long wave. As Volland suggests, inflationary pressures on an old technology spark the growth of an alternative that diffuses until it, too, pressures resources and reaches the inflationary limits of its growth.

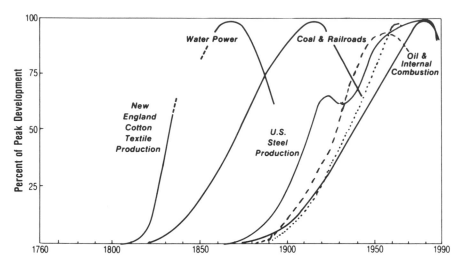

Figure 26. Technology Transitions: Transportation Infrastructure and Dominant Energy Sources

The unlabeled dashed line charts the percentage of electrically driven U.S. factories, and the unlabeled dotted line tracks the percentage of U.S. households wired for electricity. That such epochal arrangements may be the consequence of phase structures and regimes that are the outcome of the non-linear dynamics of deterministic chaos is explored by Richard Day and Jean-Luc Walter in their 1989 paper, "Economic Growth in the Very Long Run." "Evolution," they say, "is driven by an unstable, deterministic (intrinsic) process, not by a random shock (extrinsic) process" (p. 285). They thus add support to Walt W. Rostow's belief that "a satisfactory dynamic theory of production and prices must render substantially endogenous the sequence of major inventions and innovations—the leading-sector complexes—as well as the incremental improvements in productivity embraced under the case of increasing returns" (*Why the Poor Get Richer and the Rich Slow Down* [1980], p. 42).

The Infrastructure Life Cycle

What J. J. van Duijn suggests in his 1983 book, *The Long Wave in Economic Life* (echoing Simon Kuznets's 1930 *Secular Movements in Production and Prices*), is that "growth is an S-shaped phenomenon": basic innovations give rise to new industrial sectors that develop in an S-shaped life-cycle pattern. New sectors require their own infrastructure. But excess accumulation of physical stock will occur. The leveling off of demand in the innovation-incorporating sectors will accentuate the overexpansion of the capital sector. The combined effect of those two forces is a long-wave downturn. The pattern is that of a five-phase product life-cycle in which the phases are *introduction* (innovation), *growth, maturity, saturation,* and *decline* (Figure 27). Overlapping transportation and energy life cycles produced the *technological successions* that we saw in Figure 26. Such successions have been central to Eric Jantsch's work on technological forecasting.

In a 1989 paper entitled "The Third Kondratieff Wave," Christopher Freeman offers the following characterization of technological successions, which he equates with Kondratiev-phased modes of global economic development:

1. Early Mechanization Kondratiev, 1770s–1840s
   Key industries: cotton, pig iron

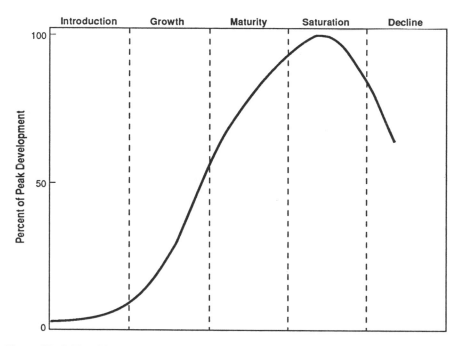

Figure 27. A Five-Phase Product Life Cycle

These S-shaped life cycles can be studied by fitting logistic curves to the data. Such curves yield both the saturation points and what some call "time constants" (the time required to go from 10 to 90 percent of the saturation level). Consistent with the long wave, 54-year time constants have been calculated for U.S. railroad development, construction of the Western Union telegraph system, and the building of the U.S. surfaced-road network and crude oil, petroleum, and natural gas pipeline systems. For discussions of methodology, see Cesare Marchetti's "Society as a Learning System: Discovery, Invention, and Innovation Cycles Revisited," *Technological Forecasting and Social Change* 18 (1980); *On a Fifty Year Pulsation in Human Affairs: Analysis of Some Physical Indicators* (1983); and "Infrastructures for Movement: Past and Future" (1988). See also Nebojsa Nakicenovic, "Dynamics and Replacement of U.S. Transport Infrastructures" (1988). Nakicenovic's 1984 Ph.D. dissertation at the University of Vienna was entitled "Growth to Limits, Long Waves, and the Dynamics of Technology."

Leading sectors and infrastructures: textiles, textile chemicals, textile machinery, iron-working and iron castings, water power, potteries, trunk canals, turnpike roads
Technological leaders: Britain, France, Belgium
Other industrializing countries: German states, the Netherlands

2. Steam Power and Railway Kondratiev, 1840s–1890s
   Key industries: coal, transport, heavy engineering
   Leading sectors and infrastructures: steam engines, steamships, machine tools, iron, railway equipment, railways, world shipping
   Technological leaders: Britain, France, Belgium, Germany, the United States
   Other industrializing countries: Italy, the Netherlands, Switzerland, Austria-Hungary

3. Electrical and Heavy Engineering Kondratiev, 1890s–1940s
   Key industries: steel, automobiles, aircraft, telecommunications, radio, aluminum, consumer durables, oil, plastics
   Leading sectors and infrastructures: electrical engineering, electrical machinery, cable and wire, heavy engineering, heavy armaments, steel ships, heavy chemicals, synthetic dyestuffs, electricity supply and distribution
   Technological leaders: Germany, the United States, Britain, France, Belgium, Switzerland, the Netherlands
   Other industrializing countries: Italy, Austria-Hungary, Canada, Sweden, Denmark, Japan, Russia

4. "Fordist" Mass-Production Kondratiev, 1940s–1990s
   Key industries: energy, computers, radar, machine tools, drugs, nuclear weapons and power, missiles, microelectronics software
   Leading sectors and infrastructures: automobiles, trucks, tractors, tanks, armaments for motorized warfare, aircraft, consumer durables, processing plants, synthetic materials, petrochemicals, highways, airports, airlines
   Technological leaders: the United States, Germany, other EEC, Japan, Sweden, Switzerland, the Soviet Union, other EFTA, Canada, Australia
   Other industrializing countries: other Eastern European, Korea, Brazil, Mexico, Venezuela, Argentina, China, India, Taiwan

5. Information and Communications Kondratiev, 1990s–?
   Key industries: "chips" (microelectronics), third-generation biotechnology products and processes, space activities, fine chemicals, SDI
   Leading sectors and infrastructures: computers, electronic capital goods, software, telecommunications equipment, optical fibers, robotics, flexible manufacturing systems, ceramics, data banks, information services, digital telecommunications networks, satellites
   Technological leaders: Japan, the United States, Germany, Sweden, other EEC, EFTA, the Soviet Union and other Eastern European, Taiwan, Korea, Canada, Australia

Other industrializing countries: Brazil, Mexico, Argentina, Venezuela, China, India, Indonesia, Turkey, Egypt, Pakistan, Nigeria, Algeria, Tunisia, other Latin American

"Transmaterialization"

Related successions take place in the mineral industries: *transmaterialization,* according to Lorna M. Waddell and Walter C. Labys, is "a characteristic behavior of materials markets through time" in which minerals demand changes as materials linked to mature industries undergo periodic replacement by higher quality or technologically more appropriate materials linked to new industries. The energy-source transitions that we have already seen are part of a much broader pattern of materials-demand successions that also follow five-phase life cycles. The notion is certainly clear enough in Figures 28, 29, and 30, as demand has shifted from the industries of the early twentieth century to those of the postwar boom, and now to those of the modern "high tech" complex.

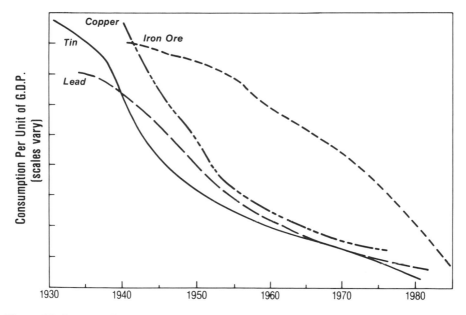

Figure 28. Consumption of Copper, Iron Ore, Tin, and Lead per Unit of GDP (adapted from L. M. Waddell and W. C. Labys, *Transmaterialization: Technology and Materials Demand Cycles* [1987])

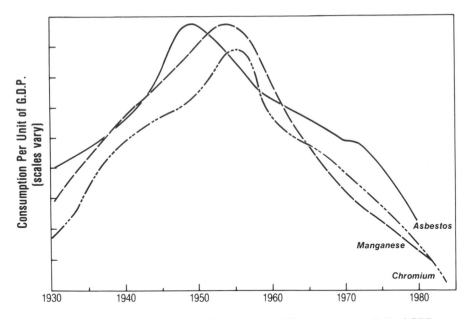

Figure 29. Consumption of Asbestos, Chromium, and Manganese per Unit of GDP

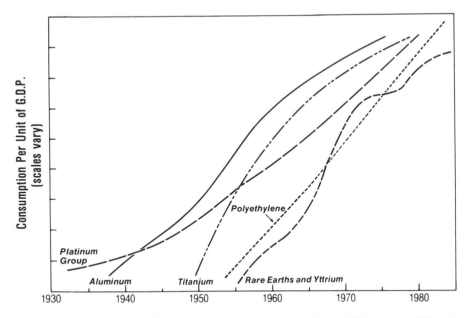

Figure 30. Consumption of Aluminum, Platinum, Rare Earths and Yttrium, and Titanium per Unit of GDP

Capital-Lifespan Theories

Kondratiev believed that "the material basis of the long cycles is the wear and tear, the replacement and increase of the fund of basic capital goods, the production of which requires tremendous investment and its long process." He echoed a number of earlier economists. His mentor Mikhail Tugan-Baranovskij had argued as early as 1894 that the main cause of cycles was the fluctuating rate of growth of fixed capital. In 1896, Knut Wiksell had written about discrepancies in the rate of return on investment caused by technological or other changes in opportunity. Albert Aftalion spoke in 1913 of the long period required to bring capital into being, the long life of capital goods, and the capacity of relatively minor changes in consumption to generate large changes in net additions to fixed capital required by business.

The view is not one on which Marxists look with disfavor. Marx had argued that the obsolescence of capital goods was the chief cause of depressions, with the efficiency life of machines determining the length of expansion periods. In 1920, Samuel De Wolff estimated that the depreciation rate for long-lived fixed capital ("capitalist infrastructure" such as railroads, bridges, and manufacturing plants) was 2.615 percent per year, leading to a 38-year lifespan.

After Kondratiev, the idea has continued to be developed. In 1939, Michal Kalecki asked what causes periodic crises. His answer was that investment is not only produced; it produces. Investment is a source of prosperity. Increasing investment improves business and stimulates a further rise in investment. But at the same time, investment is an addition to capital equipment. Right from birth it competes with an older generation of this equipment. Inevitably, more new investment creates a crisis for old investment.

Two ideas thus seem to be embedded in capital-lifespan concepts: (1) the idea of the lifespan itself; (2) the notion of substitution of newer capital for old. These ideas were developed by Jay W. Forrester and his associates at the Massachusetts Institute of Technology in the 1970s. They built an elaborate fifteen-sector System Dynamics National Model of the U.S. economy in which 50-year long waves were generated consisting of three decades of investment, one decade of market saturation, and one decade of depression. John D. Sterman (1985) emphasizes that this model produces results consistent with the idea of bounded rationality. Forrester (1977) concludes that sufficient causes for long waves are the long lifespan needed to change the production capacity of the capital sectors, the way capital sectors provide their own input capital as a factor of production, the need to develop excess capacity to catch up on deferred demands, and psychological and speculative forces that can cause overexpansion in the capital sector. The sequence is:

1. Decay of the capital plant below the level required for replacement needs
2. Development of shortages that promote demands for capital-intensive production

3. Self-ordering of capital by the capital sector of the economy in order to produce the capital needed by consumer-goods industries

4. Overexpansion of the capital sector to a capacity greater than needed for
   replacement to catch up with deferred needs

5. Excess accumulation of capital in the housing, consumer durables, and durable manufacturing sectors

6. Failure of capital users to absorb the output of the overexpanded capital
   sectors

7. Sudden appearance of unemployment and rapid collapse of the capital sector

8. Decline of excess capital through physical depreciation

See Figure 31.

Forrester writes that each major expansion grows around a highly integrated
and mutually supporting combination of technologies (particularly transport
and energy) which during good times tends to reject incompatible innovations.
The process culminates in excess debt and an overbuilding of the capital sectors,
followed by depression. During the depression the excess capital is worn out
and fully depreciated. Defaults and bankruptcies clean out the excess debt load.
The long wave involves an overbuilding of the capital sectors. Their growth
exceeds the capital-output rate needed for long-term equilibrium to a point beyond that justified by the marginal productivity of capital. Finally, the overexpansion is ended by a great depression during which excess physical capital is

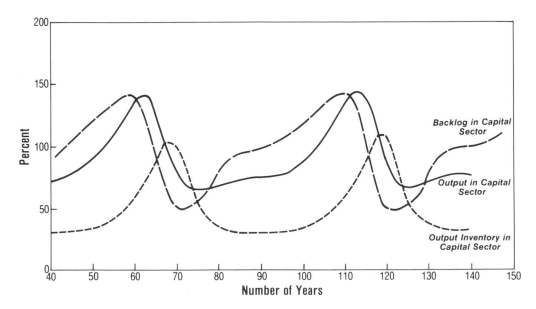

Figure 31. Forrester's Long Cycle in the Capital-Goods Sector

physically worn out and is financially depreciated on the account books until the economic stage has been set for a new era of rebuilding.

Graham and Senge (1980) also argue that the switchover to new technologies comes in the Kondratiev downwave. Near the peak of the wave, major industries suffer decreasing returns to capital. The resources required by a particular type of investment become more costly to acquire. As the economy slides toward depression, opportunities arise for inventions that have been waiting in the wings to be implemented. Thus, Ehrensaft (1980) could point to the clustering of agricultural innovations in the downswing as farmers adopted new technologies to increase production in the face of declining prices. These inventions become the basis of the next wave of growth; the next Kondratiev trough is the point of technology transition at which deployment of the new technology exceeds the old. George Ray (1980, 1983) argues that new energy sources are the central elements in the innovations that are adopted. A. Van der Zwan (1980) maintains that technologically advanced sectors shape the recovery from depression. All of which points to the critical role played by innovation.

Schumpeter on Innovation Waves

Kondratiev believed that during the long-wave recession "an especially large number of important discoveries and inventions in the technique of production and communication" occur, but that they must wait for the next wave's upswing to be implemented on a large scale. This was the point of departure for Joseph A. Schumpeter, who tried to build an innovation-wave theory of long cycles.

Schumpeter, once Austria's Minister of Finance and later a professor at Harvard University, undertook as his life's work a detailed account of the economic histories of England, Germany, and the United States after 1787, and provided strong empirical support for the idea of long waves.[2]

He concluded that any fully comprehensive economic history necessarily had to take account of multiple cycles, and in *Business Cycles* (1968) he was the first to name three of them after their discoverers: *Kitchins* (inventory cycles now acknowledged to run 3–4 years), *Juglars* (investment cycles running 7–11 years), and *Kondratievs* (long waves of 45–60 years).[3]

2. Works by Joseph A. Schumpeter: *The Theory of Economic Development* (1934), a translation of the first German edition of 1912; *Business Cycles: A Theoretical, Historical, and Statistical Analysis of the Capitalist Process* (1939); *Capitalism, Socialism, and Democracy* ([1942] 1976). See also Michael I. Stevenson, *Joseph Alois Schumpeter: A Bibliography, 1905–1984* (1985). John Maynard Keynes wrote, in his *Treatise on Money* (1930): "In the area of fixed capital it is easy to understand why fluctuations should occur in the rate of investment. Entrepreneurs are induced to embark on the production of fixed capital, or are deterred from doing so by their expectations of the profits to be made. Apart from the many minor reasons why these should fluctuate in a changing world, Professor Schumpeter's explanation of major movements may unreservedly be accepted" (p. 85).

3. Joseph Kitchin had proposed a 3.3-year farm commodity cycle in 1923, although his analysis of economic fluctuations did distinguish between these "minor cycles" and what he called "major cycles" (Juglars) and "fundamental movements" (Kondratievs). Clement Juglar was the first to iso-

Like Kondratiev, Schumpeter accepted that long waves (in Arthur Burns's words, "lopsided surges of development that mark economic progress" ["Business Cycles" (1968), p. 227]) were not externally caused, but were the *internal* regulators of capitalist development. He had already concluded that savings and investment were mere quantitative expressions of demographic growth, and what he sought was an explanation for the qualitative shifts that define development. Technical innovation embodied his notion of qualitative change: innovation as "the setting up of a new production function" (*Business Cycles,* p. 87). Almost as an echo came the remarks of Robert McCormick Adams in his 1988 essay "Contexts of Technological Advance": "It is difficult to escape the view that technological change has a focussed, non-random, and episodic or wavelike character" (p. 43). Such "technological change is not an isolate, but a set of material and behavioral manifestations deeply embedded in a social and cognitive system. . . . There is a perception that it is an independent causative agent because of massive second-order effects [or] revolutions" (p. 63).

In Schumpeter's view (*Business Cycles,* pp. 93–101) major innovations require non-negligible time and outlay. They tend to be embodied in "new firms" and to be associated with the rise to leadership of "new men." Old firms are conservative; innovations emerge primarily with new and less conservative firms. And new men insert "a class of facts of the behavioristic type." Old businessmen work within a limited horizon, making decisions about profitability with the foresight provided by well-worn channels: "the repetition of acts of routine." Innovations have to come from new men working outside these channels: "a new frame has to be constructed." Thus, whenever there is evidence that a major breakthrough has been made, it becomes much easier for others to do the same thing and to improve upon it: "They are driven to copying it if they can . . . and it becomes easier to do similar things in similar lines . . . when certain innovations such as the steam engine, directly affect a wide variety of industries. . . . *First . . . innovations do not remain isolated events, and are not evenly distributed in time. . . . they tend to cluster, to come about in bunches, simply because first some, and then most, firms follow in the wake of successful innovation; second . . . innovations are not at any time distributed over the economic system at random, but tend to concentrate in certain sectors and their surroundings*" (italics added).

Disturbances from equilibrium arising from innovation cannot be smoothly absorbed. The "disturbances must necessarily be big, in the sense that they will disrupt the existing system and enforce adaptation" (ibid., p. 101). "For actions

---

late the 7-to-11-year business cycle, averaging 9–10 years. Schumpeter said that three Kitchin cycles occur within each Juglar, and that each Kondratiev long wave was composed of six Juglars. See Joseph Kitchin, "Cycles and Trends in Economic Factors," *Review of Economic Statistics* 5 (1923): 10–16; Clement Juglar, *Des crises commerciales en leur retour périodique en France, en Angleterre et aux États-Unis* (1862); and Schumpeter, *Business Cycles.* See also Arthur F. Burns and Wesley C. Mitchell, *Measuring Business Cycles* (1946).

which consist in carrying out innovations we reserve the term Enterprise; the individuals who carry them out we call entrepreneurs" (p. 102). (The contrasting view is that of the planned innovation that takes place in the R&D facilities of the large modern corporation.) But entrepreneurial activity upsets the equilibrium of the system. This increases instability and risk. Thus, after the initial burst of enterprise, it is necessary for a new equilibrium to be established. As new products stream into markets, the agenda switches to the predictability of a new routine and entrepreneurial activity ceases (p. 176). Economic change or evolution thus "goes in units separated from each other by neighborhoods of equilibrium" (p. 138). Moreover, "one cyclical solution produces the next. . . . Recession is a reaction to prosperity. . . . Windfall gains, rising prices and so on produce waves of optimism" (pp. 140–142). And "if innovations are being embodied in new plant and equipment, additional consumers' spending will result practically as quickly in new producers' spending. Both together will spread from the point or points in the system on which they first impinge, and create prosperity. Two things are then practically sure to happen. First, old firms will react to this situation and, second, many of them will speculate on this situation. . . . New borrowing will then no longer be confined to entrepreneurs, and deposits will be created to finance general expansion, each loan tending to induce another loan, each rise in prices another rise. . . . This is what we call . . . the Secondary Wave, which superimposes its effects on the Primary Wave" (p. 145). "The phenomena of this secondary wave may be and generally are quantitatively more important than those of the primary wave. . . . This is one reason why the element of innovation has been so much neglected" (p. 146).

The booms caused by the bunching of innovations will come to an end. New entrepreneurs' demands for labor, capital, and raw materials drive up their prices. New products come on the market and compete with the original innovations; receipts decrease as costs increase. The appearance of new products favors a fall in prices—the timing of which depends on how soon the new products appear—which terminates the boom and leads to a depression.

Schumpeter thus argued that economic development is a discontinuous process, appearing in clusters of entrepreneurial activity that changes the structure of the economy: new techniques, new products, new markets, and new raw materials. Concentrations of entrepreneurial fervor are separated by long periods of consolidation of the new advances, without major new entrepreneurial activity. Major innovations sparked Britain's first Industrial Revolution in the downwave from the stagflation crisis of 1763 and helped spark the upwave of the 1790s: Watt's rotary-motion improvements to Newcomen's steam engine came between 1769 and 1784; the period 1765–1769 saw the introduction of Hargreave's spinning jenny and Arkwright's water frame, followed by Cartwright's machine loom in 1787; in 1761 the Bridgewater canal was built to move coal, and by 1815 Britain had 2,200 miles of canals and 2,000 miles of improved rivers; in the 1790s John L. McAdam introduced his hard-packed road surface that became standard for turnpikes. Railroads were introduced in the downwave of the 1820s (Stockton and Darlington, 1825; Liverpool and Manchester, 1829). The invention was proved by the success of 6,500 miles of track before the depression of the Hungry Forties, and was a major element of the steam-railroad-iron expansion of the 1850s and 1860s that followed.

But what was involved simultaneously, Schumpeter said, was a process of *creative destruction*. Economic development involves the periodic destructive disruption of the capitalist production system and its creative renewal by innovations that lift the economy to a higher plane of development: "Capitalism, then, is by nature a form or method of economic change and not only never is but never can be stationary. . . . The fundamental impulse that sets and keeps the capitalist engine in motion comes from the new consumers' goods, the new methods of production or transportation, the new markets, and the new forms of industrial organization that capitalist enterprise creates. . . . The opening up of new markets, foreign or domestic, and the organizational development from the craft shop and factory to such concerns as U.S. Steel illustrate the same process of industrial mutation. . . . That incessantly revolutionizes the economic structure *from within*, incessantly destroying the old one, incessantly creating a new one. This process of Creative Destruction is the essential fact about capitalism" (*Capitalism, Socialism, and Democracy* [1942 (1976)], pp. 82–83).

Mensch's Metamorphosis Model

Schumpeter-inspired research has multiplied. Recently, a neo-Schumpeterian, Gerhard Mensch, proposed a *metamorphosis model,* attempting to set Schumpeter's ideas more squarely in a long-wave frame.[4] Mensch's key concept is that of a *technology stalemate* out of which an economy is ultimately eased by clusters of innovations taken from a reservoir of investment opportunities formed by a continuing stream of scientific discoveries. This produces a *structural metamorphosis* as old activities are cast off and replaced by revolutionary new ones.

Mensch postulates the following causal sequence:

1. A cluster of basic innovations (introducing new branches of industry) and radical-improvement innovations (which rejuvenate existing branches) occurs in response to a technology stalemate. Venture capital is attracted to the new lines of business. New demands are awakened.

---

4. Gerhard Mensch, *Stalemate in Technology* (1979). See also J. J. van Duijn, *The Long Wave in Economic Life* (1983); John Clark, Christopher Freeman, and Luc Soete, "Long Waves, Inventions, and Innovations," *Futures* 15 (1981); Christopher Freeman, ed., *Long Waves in the World Economy* (1984); Christopher Freeman, *Design, Innovation, and Long Cycles in Economic Development* (1986). See also Alfred Kleinknecht, *Innovation Patterns in Crisis and Prosperity: Schumpeter's Long Cycle Reconsidered* (1987). Kleinknecht, a major figure in the neo-Schumpeterian revival of the 1980s, argues that "waves of important innovations are an endogenous element of the long-wave process. The wave-like occurrence of major innovative breakthroughs is a decisive cause of the fairly simultaneous rise of new branches of industry which foster the long-wave theory" (p. 206).

2. Parallel S-shaped innovation-growth cycles, some of which substitute for older goods or services, characterize the new branches of industry. Initial entry is followed by rapid upswing and by accelerated growth.

3. During the new-product upswing, investment, employment, and incomes increase rapidly, well ahead of prices and inflation. This is the period of disinflation or deflation.

4. Basic and radical-improvement innovations are followed by routine-improvement innovations that rationalize production and increase capital intensity. But these innovations are subject to diminishing returns on the demand side. The growth curve grades over from acceleration to deceleration. This is a natural phase of the product life-cycle of manufactured goods.

5. Corporate growth overestimates domestic markets and produces excess supply and heated competition. Markets become saturated. Almost inevitably, an industrial economy tends to overinvest in any new technology—capital goods in particular.

6. There are two responses to excess supply: attempts to reduce competition by product differentiation and industrial mergers, and attempts to segment domestic and foreign markets, "dumping" excess output. Overinvestment breeds "pseudo-innovation," which benefits neither buyer nor seller. Rather, existing industries attempt to protect their market shares by means of product differentiation in which the "image" or "packaging" of the product is changed, but no longer are any of its basic qualities altered. The economy then enters a period in which output stagnates. Limits to growth are encountered, markets are flooded, key resources may be scarce and their prices rise, and there is a slowdown in income and employment growth. Rates of return decline, and capital is therefore not reinvested in existing lines of business. Instead, money moves into speculation.

7. The end result is a technology stalemate in which growth is replaced by stagnation, and in which large-scale organizations seek to maintain the appearance of growth by controlling output and raising prices, thereby inducing stagflation. During this period, one sees increasing protectionism, yet overconcentration in leading industries sets the price spiral into gear. Large-scale industry and large-scale labor push up wages and prices. Large-scale organizations that grow in the period of pseudo-innovation require and promote conservative patterns of investment: risk-taking in new ventures is minimized.[5]

5. In this context Carlota Perez argues, in "Structural Change and the Assimilation of New Technologies in the Economic and Social System" (1981), that old technologies are perpetuated after new technologies are introduced, due to institutional forces such as the formation of special-interest groups and the protection of specialized labor by trade unions. There is also a merger-wave literature, which says that mergers have come in cycles in the United States. Martin Schnitzer (1987) argues that mergers afford a way of protecting against decline, for if a firm can gain control over competing plants, it has a better opportunity to fix prices and control output. The first great wave of mergers occurred between 1887 and 1904; these mergers took place in such industries as petroleum, iron and steel, copper, sugar, lead, and salt, and their common feature was the drive toward

8. The price spiral ends in a sharp collapse. But because returns in older, established industries were eliminated during the period of stagflation, and the prospect of speculative profit vanishes in the ensuing collapse, new venture capital becomes available, seeking high-growth investment opportunities. The appearance of venture capital at this time results in a rush of attempts to convert many of the inventions that have appeared since the preceding period of basic innovation into useful techniques or products—that is, into a cluster of basic innovations that precipitates another long-term growth upswing. New industries attract capital and labor from stagnant sectors, circumvent older resource scarcities, stimulate demand for new kinds of goods and services, and generally introduce the reinvigorating effects of a structural transformation of the economy. Another cycle begins.

The key to Mensch, then, is the technology stalemate that occurs in a stagflation crisis, and the emergence of a pool of venture capital that seeks out innovative alternatives in the ensuing era of declining prices. But as we shall see later, Mensch's formulation has several critical weaknesses. He does not allow for intervening depressions, nor does he recognize that the growth impulses come in Kuznets-cycle bursts. Because he, like so many other authors, treats Kondratiev waves as growth cycles, he confuses growth with the S-shaped technology successions that do have Kondratiev periodicity.

Mensch writes that he has discerned three major innovatory clusters since 1800—in 1814–1828, 1870–1886, and 1925–1939. See Figure 32. These coincide with the European growth accelerations from the inflationary crises of 1814 (Britain), 1873 (Britain, France, Germany), and 1920 (Britain)/1923 (Germany). The comparable U.S. crises occurred in 1814–1815, 1864–1865, and 1920, each followed by a decade of deflationary growth. But several authors have suggested that Mensch failed to include a full record of innovations and that this is why he found clusters that fit into the European timing. Certainly, if his clustering notion has merit, the proof should be demonstrable by comparing the United States with Europe, since the timing of the inflation crises and the ensuing growth accelerations is somewhat different in each. I know of no such proof.

Mensch also errs because the bandwagon effect he postulates is not immediate, but takes off well after the innovations have been put into place and their viability has been established. Christopher Freeman notes that the diffusion time

---

monopoly—the consolidation of producers into firms dominating the market. The second cycle of mergers occurred between 1916 and 1929; these mergers—primarily in the mass-production and entertainment, automobile, automobile parts, motion picture, movie theater, and appliance industries—took the form of vertical integration by oligopolists. A third cycle of mergers occurred between 1954 and 1968; this wave was characterized by a movement toward conglomerates. A fourth cycle of mergers—of the conglomerates—began in the 1980s; this cycle resembles the third one in the sense that it has witnessed mergers across different kinds of industries, but on a larger scale. See Martin Schnitzer, *Contemporary Government and Business Relations* (1987); George Bentson, *Conglomerate Mergers* (1980); Yale Brozen, *Mergers in Perspective* (1982); and Ralph L. Nelson, *Merger Movements in American Industry, 1895–1956* (1959).

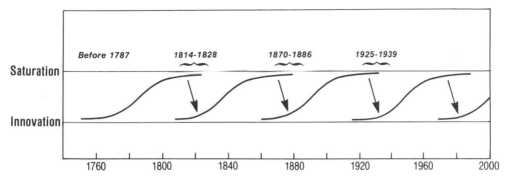

Figure 32. Mensch's Metamorphosis Model Showing "Innovatory Clusters" That Accompany the Structural Metamorphosis in Which a Saturated Growth Wave Is Succeeded by the Growth of the Next Technologies

for all groups to benefit from adopting a new technology is approximately thirty years. If there is "bunching," Freeman says, it arises from imitation and from a clustering of technically related inventions that is "rather more likely [to be] related to breakthroughs in fundamental science and technology, to bursts of invention, and to periods of very strong demand (including booms and wars)" than to "explosive bursts of imaginative entrepreneurs [and] a swarming of innovative behavior" (Freeman, Clark, and Soete, *Unemployment and Technical Innovation* [1982], p. 321). A related criticism appears in Solomos Solomou's 1986 paper "Innovation Clusters and Kondratieff Long Waves in Economic Growth": "Mensch's ideas are faulted on a number of counts, the two most important being the use of an unrepresentative innovation selection and the use of an inappropriate statistical test. An examination of the Mensch, Van Duijn and Kleinknecht innovation selections rejects the idea of *regular* innovation clusters during long wave depression phases. The evidence also rejects the weaker hypothesis of Van Duijn that innovation flows have followed a long wave path; *structural changes in the twentieth century have been confused with long waves.* The evidence presented here vindicates the Freeman et al. conclusion that the flow of innovation is not responsive to long-wave phases" (p. 111).

MARXIST LONG-WAVE THEORY

The initial Marxist reaction to Kondratiev was spearheaded by Leon Trotsky, who formulated a "curve of capitalist development" in his "Report on the World Crisis" to reinforce the argument that long-wave cycles are not internally regulated. Rather, he argued, long waves are periods of growth and decline that lie between capitalist crises—turning-points with external causes, such as wars and revolutions. He reasoned that each epoch of revolution eroded the mainstays of capitalist equilibrium—"a dynamic equilibrium, one which is always in the process of either disruption or restoration" (p. 226). At clearly defined turning points, the external forces changed the slope of the dynamic equilibrium, producing a curve of capitalist development that moved inevitably toward the final crisis and collapse.

The Profit Cycle

Trotsky was forced out of the Soviet Union and was ultimately murdered, but Marx and Engels had already argued that changes in the rate of profit on both new and replacement investments lay at the root of long swings in capitalist countries. The Belgian Trotskyite Ernst Mandel drew together his hero's notion of the crisis-prone tendencies of capitalist development and Marx's profit cycles to produce the contemporary Marxist theory of long waves. Mandel argues in his 1975 book, *Long Waves of Capitalist Development,* that long waves have their roots in long-term fluctuations in rates of profit. For Marxists, profit arises from the surplus value over that received by workers in the productive process. Profits provide capital. But competition forces capitalists to use capital to mechanize the productive process, replacing labor. The rate of profit $r = s/(c + v)$, where s is surplus value, c is fixed capital in machines, etc., and v is variable capital items used in the productive process. If s and v remain static, as capital c is increased, r, the rate of profit, must decline, leading to Marx's "Law of the Tendency for the Rate of Profit to Fall." If profits fall, so does the possibility for further capital accumulation. Hence an expansionary phase of growth necessarily must give way to stagnation. During an upswing, demands for means of production in the consumer-goods sector raise the output and profits of capital-goods producers. Investment funds flow to that sector, where above-average rates of profit can be earned. But competitive capital intensification forces profits down. As this occurs, investment funds flow back to the consumer-goods sector. These movements in the rate of profit drive the capitalist industrial cycle through a sequence of accelerated capital accumulation, overaccumulation, decelerated accumulation, and underinvestment in the capital-goods sector as investment drives growth in the consumer-goods sector. Others are not so sure. In his 1987 treatise, *Phases of Economic Growth,* Solomos Solomou rejects Kondratiev phasing for prices, investment, and productivity between 1850 and 1973.

A new cycle can only begin, Mandel says, when some *externally generated* change permits a new round of above-average surplus profits to be earned; a capitalist crisis occurs because the profit possibilities of the old industries have been exhausted. Capitalism would fail if it were not for external stimuli that ease it out of crisis and change its character. Examples include: (1) the sudden flight of capital to other countries, (2) a rise in the surplus value of capital as a result of increased exploitation of the working class by entrepreneurs, (3) a fall in the price of fixed capital, and (4) innovation.

Thus, Mandel says, the British long wave from 1790 to 1848 was fueled by the access of new manufacturing industry to pre-capitalist-agricultural regions that provided cheap labor and raw materials. The late-nineteenth-century long wave drew surplus profits from the imperialist expansion of developed capitalist economies into colonial regions. The boom following World War II was fueled by the surplus profits of giant corporations that monopolized the most productive techniques within their own countries. The curve of capitalist development moved from competitive capitalism to imperialism to monopolistic late capitalism. Each stage involved a new wave of technical change. The succession of long waves was produced by the dialectic of endogenous (profit cycle) and exogenous (surplus profit opportunity) factors.

In this light, Mandel (*Late Capitalism* [1975], pp. 131–132) advances the following time-line. It bears little relationship to other long-wave chronologies, and I can find little empirical support for it, save Andrej V. Poletayev's recent essay "Long Waves in Profit Rates in Four Countries" (1989), in which peaks in the rate of return are identified in the early 1870s, soon after 1900, and in the 1950s.

Long Wave	"Main Tonality"	Origins of This Movement
1793–1825	Expansive; rate of profit rises.	Artisan-produced machines; agriculture lags behind industry; rising prices for raw materials. Fall in real wages with a slow expansion of the world market (South America).
1826–1847	Slackening; rate of profit stagnates.	Dwindling of profits made from competition with precapitalist production in England and Western Europe. Expansion of the World Market decelerates.
1848–1873	Expansive; rate of profit rises.	Transition to machine-made machines. Massive expansion of the world market following the growing industrialization and extension of railway construction in the whole of Europe and North America as a result of the 1848 Revolution.
1874–1893	Slackening; rate of profit falls, then stagnates, then rises slightly.	Machine-made machines are generalized. The commodities produced with them no longer produce a surplus profit. The increased organic composition of capital leads to a decline in the average rate of profit. In Western Europe real wages rise. The results of the growing export of capital and the fall in the prices of raw materials only gradually permit an increase in capital accumulation. Relative stagnation of the world market.
1894–1913	Expansive; rate of profit rises, then stagnates.	Capital investments in the colonies, the breakthrough of imperialism, and the generalization of monopolies profiting even further from the notably slow rise in the price of raw materials (promoted by the second technological revolution, with its accompanying steep rise in the productivity of labor and the rate of surplus-value), permit a general increase in the rate of profit, which explains the rapid growth of capital accumulation. Vigorous expansion of the world market (Asia, Africa, Oceania).

| 1914–1939 | Regressive; rate of profit falls sharply. | The outbreak of World War I, the disruption of world trade, and the regression of material production, determine growing difficulties in the valorization of capital, reinforced by the victory of the Russian Revolution and the narrowing of the world market it provoked. |
| 1940/1945 | Expansive; rate of profit first rises, then slowly starts to fall. | The weakening (and partial atomization) of the working class determined by fascism and World War II permits a massive rise in the rate of profit, which promotes the accumulation of capital. This is first thrown into armaments production, then into the innovations of the third technological revolution, which significantly cheapens constant capital and thus promotes a long-term rise in the rate of profit. The world market shrinks through autarky, world war, and the extension of non-capitalist zones (Eastern Europe, China, North Korea, North Vietnam, Cuba). |

Without a secure empirical footing, Mandel's profit-cycle model remains an ideologically preformed construct rather than a useful contribution to long-wave theory.

Political Business Cycles

Notwithstanding the lack of a firm empirical footing, Marshall takes Marxian long-wave analysis a step beyond Mandel in his 1987 monograph, *Long Waves of Regional Development*. He writes: "The development of industrial capitalism can be divided into three historical periods. These are the period of *competitive capitalism*, consisting of the long waves from the late eighteenth to the late nineteenth century; the *imperialist long wave* from the late nineteenth century to the Second World War; and the post-war long wave of *late capitalism*" (p. 19). "Cyclical crises during each wave are indecisive in the sense that they are of insufficient impact to sweep away social, economic and political obstacles to capitalist regeneration. The upward turning-points of the long waves presume a decisive crisis which has the function of transforming the social and economic structure, preparing the path for a fresh and durable phase of renewed economic expansion. These *decisive crises* involved social upheavals hinging upon the transformation of the capitalist labor process" (p. 70, italics added). But then Marshall provides a very confusing diagram (Figure 33). His curiously selected turning points—1790, 1825/1826, 1847/1848, 1873/1874, 1893/1894, 1913/1914, 1940/1945, 1966/1967—reveal how heavily he relies upon Mandel's construct as he attempts to develop "a historical framework for economic and social analysis by weaving together the perspectives of the course of the long waves, the overall periods of capitalist development . . . and the evolution of the labor process which marks each phase of industrial and technological transformation" (p. 97).

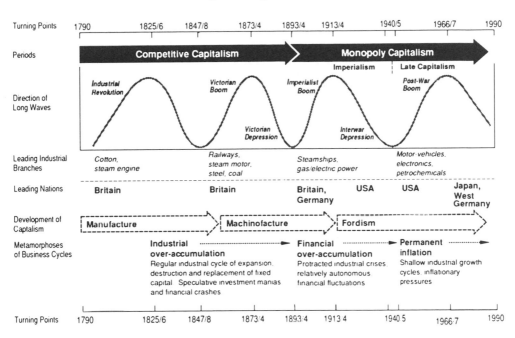

Figure 33. Marshall's Neo-Marxian Schematic of the Major Features of Long Waves

Figure 33. Marshall's Neo-Marxian Schematic of the Major Features of Long Waves
Marshall relies on Ernst Mandel's profit-cycle construct to develop this image of long waves. But the chronology bears little resemblance to the evidence on price movements presented by non-Marxist investigators and is even more curious as a concept of economic growth. The long waves depicted are indeed figments of the Marxists' wishful thinking; for them, the "facts" must fit their preformed notions of crises in capitalism.

Marshall does break with Mandel in one respect, however, by introducing the alternative causation proposed by Michal Kalecki in his notion of political business cycles. According to Kalecki (1939, 1943), the capitalist and working classes both place demands upon government. At the end of a boom phase, under conditions of full employment, capitalists cannot tolerate the greater bargaining power of labor and thus exert pressure for governments to enact deflationary policies leading to recession and rising unemployment. Recessionary conditions, on the other hand, stimulate labor to put pressure on government through militancy and the ballot box to adopt reflationary policies to increase employment and wages. The dialectic is sufficient, Kalecki argues, to produce the oscillation of boom and recession. But other Marxists, such as David M. Gordon (1978), argue that the intervention by government is unnecessary: rising unemployment in the downswing disciplines labor and facilitates the ensuing upturn. As Glyn and Sutcliffe (1980) note, rising wages resulting from improved bargaining positions drive down profits and ultimately lead to the scrapping of old lines of production. This, they feel, is a better explanation of the profit cycle.

What remains important, Marshall says, is the classic Marxist concept of capitalist crisis (revealing thereby that his ideology shapes his "facts"). He says that one element of the crisis is the profits squeeze. Each long wave has been generated by a new way to create surplus profits and reverse that squeeze. But the boom-crisis cycle has led to the progressive concentration of capital in fewer hands, and the future of capitalism depends upon how the next decisive crisis is handled by the key actors: multinational corporations, international bankers, and nation-states. Whether we accord this argument credibility depends upon whether we are comfortable with Marshall's ideologically shaped view of what drives long waves, the facts of the case notwithstanding. I prefer to get my facts straight first, *and the facts of growth cycles are quite different,* as I will show in Chapter 3.

THE KUZNETS QUESTION:
HAVE THERE BEEN LONG CYCLES OF GROWTH?

Seduced by their interest in technology-driven revolutions, many economic historians, not simply the Marxists, have tended to assume that long waves are not simply waves of prices, but are also waves of economic growth. Hartman and Wheeler (1979), for example, say that "the macroeconomic effects of innovational and infrastructure clusters fit neatly into the time periods identified by the Kondratieff price cycle," and offer the following contrasts of economic performance during the long-wave periods of rising and falling prices:

1. Kondratiev upswings (the periods of rising prices 1790–1813, 1849–1873 in Europe, 1849–1865 in the United States, 1896–1920):

    • aggregate demand shifting out more rapidly than aggregate supply
    • smaller increases in national product
    • low unemployment
    • real consumption above trend
    • low levels of infrastructure development
    • real gross domestic capital formation below trend
    • low innovational activity, low rate of patents
    • technical progress below trend

2. Kondratiev downswings (the periods of falling prices 1813–1849, 1865–1896 in the United States, 1873–1896 in Europe, 1920–1940):

• aggregate supply shifting out more rapidly than aggregate demand
• greater increases in national product
• high unemployment
• real consumption below trend
• higher levels of infrastructure development
• real gross domestic capital formation above trend
• high innovational activity, high rate of patents
• technical progress above trend

The Kondratiev downswings, Hartman and Wheeler note, were characterized by waves of innovation and infrastructure development. High rates of technical progress generated aggregate supply shifts that were greater than shifts in demand, and this drove prices down as long as the money supply was steady. There was rapid growth of industrial production and national product. In spite of falling prices, business expectations were raised in the sense of competing for future markets: in the periods 1815–1850 and 1873–1896, for example, competition was intense, prices fell, and profit margins were low. Yet unemployment increased as labor shifted from old to new technologies, and real total consumption was low because unemployment was high. The limit was reached when the new technologies were unable to shift aggregate supply out faster than aggregate demand. This evidence, they say, "lends support to the hypothesis that long waves of innovation have long-run cyclical effects" (p. 69).

Others contest Hartman and Wheeler's view: "Little support," Roger Lloyd-Jones wrote in 1987, "has been found for the notion of innovatory clusters acting as a key mechanism of economic change nor do such clusters appear to phase with the temporal sequence of the Kondratieff long-wave" (p. 333). This view, also expressed by Maddison in *Phases of Capitalist Development* (1982), was supported by Solomou in his 1987 monograph *Phases of Economic Growth*. Goldstein concludes (*Long Cycles*, pp. 186–187) that it has been mostly Marxist scholars of the "capitalist crisis" school (such as Thomas Kuczynski in 1980) who have claimed to show that economic growth rises and falls with the long wave's upswing and downswing phases. Among other researchers, support has been weak.

To resolve the matter, what is needed is input of the kind of graphical analysis presented in Chapter 1, but this time focused upon fluctuations in economic growth. That is what follows, again in the form of a sequence of graphs with accompanying text—first the growth rates (in this case, growth of real per capita gross national product as the measure of U.S. economic growth in the period 1790–1988), next the moving averages, then the chaos diagrams, and finally the synthesis. Again, I ask the reader to proceed sequentially, graph by graph, starting with Figure 34. *Those who want to skip over the details and go right to the conclusions should turn to Figure 43, which shows that growth has fluctuated with 25-to-30-year rhythms—two Kuznets cycles per Kondratiev wave.*

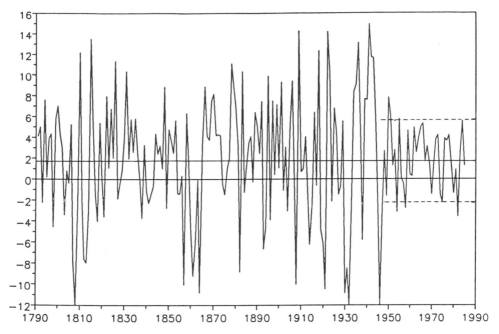

Figure 34. Oscillations of the Annual Growth Rate of Real Per Capita GNP in the United States, 1790–1988

As in Figure 7, annual growth rates are plotted. The base information on real GNP is derived from B. R. Mitchell (1983) and several U.S. Department of Commerce publications: *Historical Statistics of the United States* (1976), *Statistical Abstract of the United States* (1987), and *Survey of Current Business* (1986). The fluctuations reveal the same wide year-to-year oscillations as did growth rates of prices. The pattern will once again pass all of the standard tests for randomness. The average growth rate around which these oscillations have occurred has been quite consistent over the entire 1790-1988 timespan: 1.79 percent annually. This is consistent with Duncan K. Foley's observation that "a path of exponential growth at a constant rate arises naturally in theories of capitalist economies in which some part of profit (or, indeed, of income in general) is reinvested in production" ("Endogenous Financial-Production Cycles in a Macroeconomic Model" [1989], p. 89). Whereas in the aftermath of the Great Depression the growth rate of prices moved from a lower to a higher regime, nothing happened to the long-run growth rate of real per capita GNP. Instead, the *oscillations* of growth rates were dampened. A number of reasons have been advanced for this dampening: the shift in the composition of output from manufacturing to services has made total GNP less volatile (the demand for services is less sensitive to income than the demand for goods); public sector employment has grown, and such employment does not shrink in recession (in the United States the increase in the past century has been from 4 percent to 20 percent); automatic fiscal stabilizers have become more important (in recession, taxes fall more than income, and transfer payments that cushion income increase); active Keynesian fiscal programs have stabilized the oscillations of economic growth, forcing them to fluctuate within narrower bounds; wages and prices are less flexible than heretofore; the aggravating force of financial panics wiping out assets has been offset by deposit insurance and cooperation among central banks; better inventory control has helped soften downturns; and expectations may have been altered (people now expect milder recessions and act accordingly). See V. Zarnowitz, *Facts and Factors in the Recent Evolution of Business Cycles in the U.S.* (1989). If the Keynesian goal was to combat the deflationary depression, it was accomplished by moving the entire price regime to a higher level and putting in place a floor beneath which the growth rate would not fall: future depressions would become merely disinflationary, and the depths of the crisis would be controlled. Yet the essential rhythms of economic growth remain.

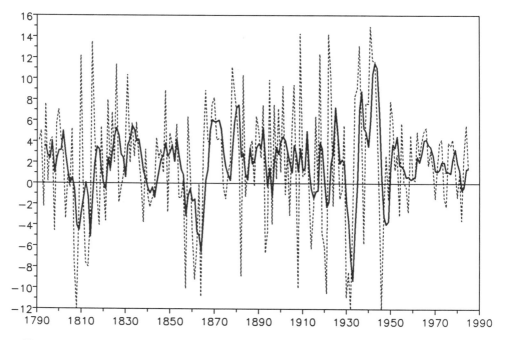

Figure 35. Four-Year Moving Averages, Computed Annually (*solid lines*), Superimposed on the Annual Growth Rates of U.S. Real Per Capita GNP (*dotted lines*), 1790–1988

Are there underlying rhythms, as there were in the case of prices? As in the case of Figure 8, four-year moving averages can be used to smooth the annual seesaw of growth rates as a first step in this search for more fundamental motions. As before, each four-year average is plotted in the end-point year for every year from 1793 to 1988. What quickly emerges are the upswings and downswings of the familiar 7-to-11-year business cycle. This is the well-known Juglar investment cycle, which describes the rhythms of office and factory building, purchases of machinery and other capital equipment, etc.

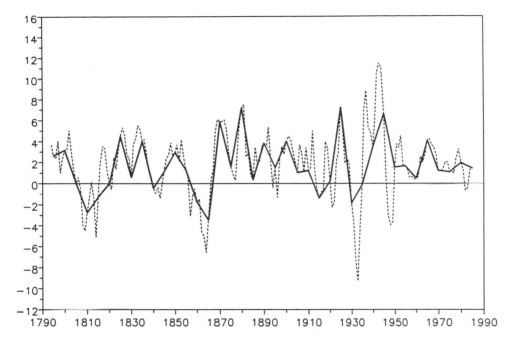

Figure 36. Four-Year Averages, Computed Every Fifth Year (*solid lines*), Superimposed on the Four-Year Moving Averages of the Growth Rates of U.S. Real Per Capita GNP (*dotted lines*)

That the Juglar cycles are not artifacts of the smoothing technique is shown in this comparison of the four-year moving averages and the four-year averages decoupled by being computed every fifth year. As in the case of price oscillations, no Slutsky propagation results from the smoothing technique. We are not dealing with statistical artifacts. The Juglar cycles peak and crash where both Schumpeter (1939) and Burns and Mitchell (1946) said they should. The moving average once again tracks underlying movements in the growth rates, separating signals from the noise.

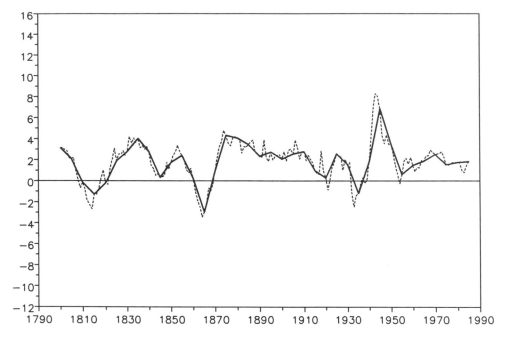

Figure 37. Ten-Year Moving Averages of the Growth Rates of U.S. Real Per Capita GNP Computed Annually (*dotted lines*) and Once Every Fifth Year (*solid lines*)

As Kuznets and Schumpeter suspected, however, the underlying signals of the economic growth process are more complex than those for prices. Here, as in Figure 10, ten-year moving averages computed annually and once every five years are charted. A second growth rhythm is suggested, but it is longer than that of the Juglar cycles in Figure 36. Major troughs occur in conjunction with each of the inflation crises shown in Figure 10, revealing that "stagflation" episodes have repeated themselves in U.S. history—in 1814–1815, in 1864–1865, in 1919–1920, and most recently in 1980–1981—contrary to the assertions of some economists that the stagflation episode of 1980–1981 was unique in the nation's experience.

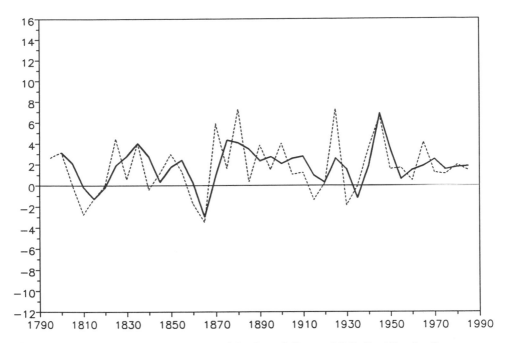

Figure 38. Ten-Year Moving Averages of the Growth Rates of U.S. Real Per Capita GNP, Computed Every Fifth Year (*solid lines*), Superimposed on the Four-Year Averages, Computed Every Fifth Year (*dotted lines*)

In contrast to Figure 11, which shows a single underlying rhythm of accelerating and decelerating growth rates of prices, when the ten-year averages are superimposed on the four-year averages, a pair of rhythms of accelerating and decelerating rates of economic growth is revealed. The question of whether the different cycles are "real," one embedded within the other in the manner suggested by Schumpeter (1939), or are artifacts of the different lengths of the smoothing period, as suggested by Bird et al. (1985), must be resolved. The proof is in the chaos formulations that follow: there are two scales of loops around the same "strange attractor," indicating that economic growth has cycled in a pattern of rhythms within rhythms.

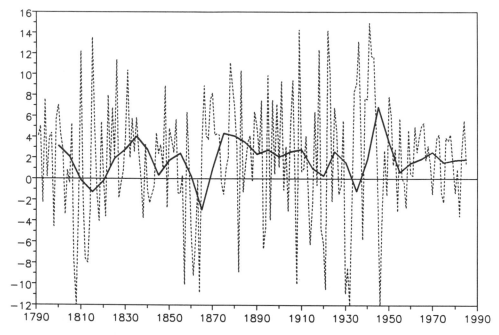

Figure 39. Ten-Year Moving Averages of the Growth Rates of U.S. Real Per Capita GNP, Computed Every Fifth Year (*solid lines*), Superimposed on the Original Annual Growth Rates (*dotted lines*)

Anticipating the chaos formulation, this diagram summarizes, in the manner of Figure 12, the longer-term rhythm within the very noisy annual growth rates of real per capita gross national product. The annual oscillations ratchet the growth rate up to higher levels, but the rate peaks, and sharp dips pull it downward.

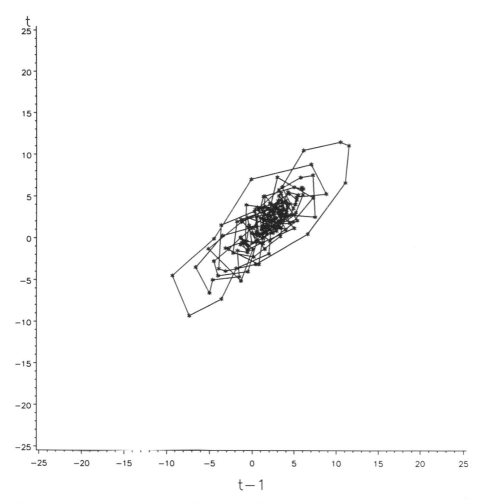

Figure 40. Convergence of Growth Rates on a "Strange Attractor": Four-Year Moving Averages of the Growth Rates of Real Per Capita GNP in Year _t_ Plotted as a Function of the Growth Rates in Year _t − 1_

Is the pattern random or chaotic? In the manner of Figure 14, this illustration shows how the four-year moving averages cycle around a strange attractor, suggesting chaos. We see the same pattern of long loops and shorter whirls that we noted in the case of the price oscillations. Evidently, the same acceleration-deceleration and critical-limit mechanisms are at work in a complex system marked by the same boom-and-bustiness that is produced by self-reinforcing endogeneity. On the one hand, the economy moves to its average level of moderate growth (Haubrich and Lo, _The Sources and Nature of Long-Term Memory in the Business Cycle_ [1989]). On the other hand, there is pressure to accelerate. The economy ratchets upward from one stable growth rate to another until a critical rate of acceleration is reached, collapsing downward thereafter to maximum rates of decline before beginning the long climb back upward. The repetitions of this pattern in each long wave are, I believe, clear evidence that deterministic chaos has been at work. Some recent support for this belief comes from Scheinkman and Le Baron's analysis of these same U.S. real per capita

GNP data for the period 1870–1986 using the demanding BDS tests. They conclude that the tests "failed to reject the [chaos] model after dummies for the great depression (1930–1939) and World War II (1940–1945) were introduced. . . . the results certainly buttress other evidence of nonlinearities in macroeconomic data" ("Nonlinear Dynamics and GNP Data" [1989], pp. 225–226).

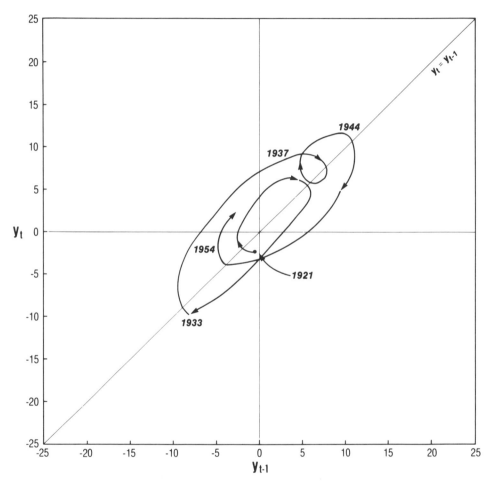

Figure 41. Interpretation of the Period 1920–1954: Chaotic Cycling of the Four-Year Moving Averages along an Acceleration-Deceleration Path

How have the rhythms moved between peaks and troughs? As in the case of Figure 17, this diagram depicts the chaotic behavior that occurred during a particular period of time, illustrating thereby a cyclical pattern of peak-to-trough movements. Beginning in 1921, growth accelerated until 1929 and crashed in 1933, spiraled upward in the New Deal recovery and again in World War II, and then crashed in 1954. What we see are Juglar cycles set within longer rhythms. What are these longer rhythms? The answer is provided in Figure 42.

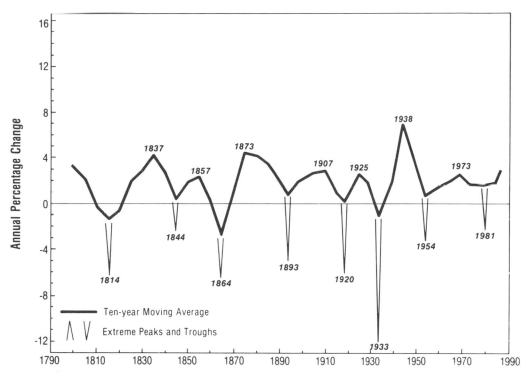

Figure 42. The Longer Growth Cycles, Summarized from Figures 36–38

We are thus able, in the manner of Figure 20, to summarize the longer growth cycles suggested by the moving averages: 1814-1837-1844, 1845-1857-1864, 1865-1873-1893, 1894-1907-1920, 1921-1925-1933, 1934-1938-1954, 1955-1973-1981, 1982-1988-(?). This finding is reiterated for other countries in separate 1989 conference papers by Solomos Solomou and Hans J. Gerster: "During 1850–1913 a long swing pattern of 20 to 30 year growth cycles best describes economic growth for many economies, including the four dominant countries, Britain, France, Germany, and America" (Solomou, "Long Waves in National and World Economic Growth, 1850–1973"). "The majority of the long waves are closer to the Kuznets range" (Gerster, "Econometric Tests on Long Savings in Price and Volume Series from 16 Countries"). Gerster bases his conclusions on applications of modern digital filter methods that assure that cycles are not produced by the smoothing process and that thus enable him to reject the Slutsky effect. There is, he says, "a predominance of Kuznets cycles in industrial production and gross investment." Have these cycles been similar? What is their relationship to the Kondratiev waves? The answer is provided by slicing them into trough-to-trough segments (as from Figure 20 to Figure 21) and overlaying them (again, as in the manner of Figure 21) by centering them on a common vertical axis corresponding to the 1814–1815, 1864–1865, 1919–1920, and 1980–1981 inflationary peaks. The result is shown in Figure 43, anticipating the synthesis that is presented in Chapter 5.

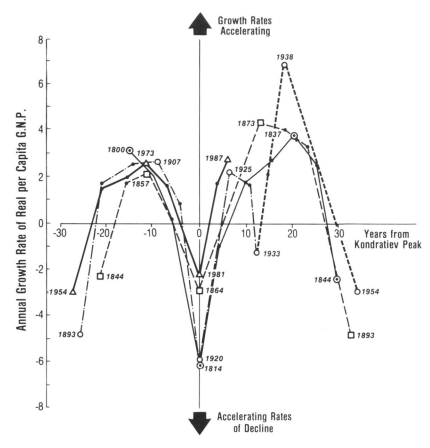

Figure 43. Pairs of Kuznets Growth Cycles Centered on Kondratiev Inflation Peaks

The outcome is quite startling: *economic growth accelerates and decelerates between the Kondratiev peaks and troughs with the 25-to-30-year periodicity suggested by Simon Kuznets*. Specifically:

• There are two *Kuznets cycles* per Kondratiev wave.

• The Kondratiev inflation peaks of 1814–1815, 1864–1865, 1919–1920, and 1980–1981 coincide with growth troughs in major *stagflation crises*.

• When the Kondratiev price troughs coincide with growth troughs, as in 1844 and 1893, major *depressions* result.

• *Stagflation crises and depressions alternate* at 25-to-30-year intervals.

• Financial crises have also occurred at the turning points of the Kuznets-cycle growth peaks: 1857, 1907, and 1973 on the first set of cycles, and 1837 and 1929 on the second.

The "wild card" in the latter groupings is, of course, the Great Depression, which, unlike 1837 and 1873, was not merely a recessionary turning point on a growth cycle. The U.S. economy collapsed, began to recover during the New Deal, was given a major boost by World War II, and slowed again before the postwar boom took off, producing a pair of "mini-Kuznets" growth waves where in other cycles there had been but one, a pattern not seen in other countries. This pair of shorter growth cycles was undoubtedly the reason that Abramovitz, in his 1968 article, "The Passing of the Kuznets Cycle," claimed that the Kuznets cycle was a distinctively American post-1870 phenomenon that ceased to function after 1914. I reject his view, which was supported by Rostow in "Kondratieff, Schumpeter, and Kuznets" (1975). The shorter pair of growth cycles resulted from the special American experience in the Great Depression. The graph shows that Kuznets cycles occurred before 1870 and that the rhythms have continued since 1914, exemplified no more clearly than by the 1954-1973-1981 postwar boom cycle, and by the 1982–1989 Reagan-era upswing following the 1980-1981 stagflation crisis. Far from having passed, the Kuznets cycle is alive and well. And if Gerster is to be believed, it is not a distinctively American cycle, but probably is, like the Kondratiev wave, global.

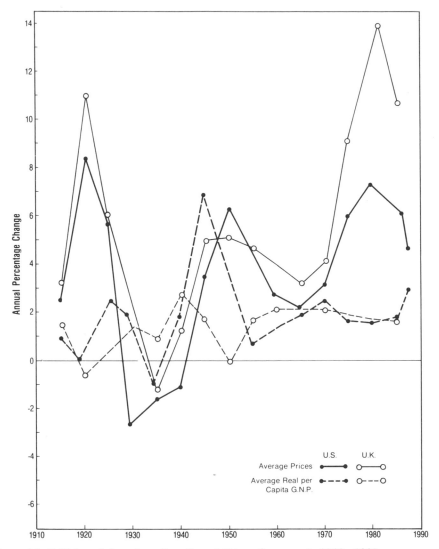

Figure 44. British and American Growth and Prices Compared, 1910–1985

This special nature of the U.S. growth experience in the Great Depression and the New Deal needs to be amplified because the issue is clearly controversial. The differences are revealed by comparing British and American growth and price movements for the period 1910–1985. Both Britain and the United States experienced the high inflation and sagging growth of the stagflation episodes of 1919–1920 and 1980–1981. Both experienced the collapse of prices in the Great Depression. Both experienced the post-World War II boom. But Britain did not experience the extreme collapse of growth rates that the United States did in the 1930s; nor did it have a New Deal. The main sag of British growth came at the long-wave turning point of the early 1950s, in the continuing aftermath of World War II. As was suggested at the end of Chapter 1, special factors resulted in the transformation of a primary vortex into the Great Depression in the United States, and the advent of the New Deal produced a second mini-Kuznets cycle between the stagflation crisis of 1919–1920 and the Kondratiev trough of the early 1950s, whereas in other countries there was only one. The world economy had moved back onto a synchronized track by 1954.

CHAPTER 4

EXPLANATIONS OF GROWTH CYCLES: KUZNETS AND KIN

What is deficient about many of the theories discussed in Chapter 2 is that they treat economic growth as if it fluctuates with the same rhythms as the Kondratiev wave. A few investigators, such as Solomos Solomou, have cautioned against this assumption ("Non-balanced Growth and Kondratieff Waves in the World Economy, 1850–1913" [1986] and *Phases of Economic Growth, 1850–1973* [1987]). Between 1850 and 1913, Solomou says, there were waves of irregular length and amplitude in each of the sixteen countries he studied. He preferred the explanation that the waves resulted from structural changes and different national growth paths. I prefer the Kuznets cycle. Technology transitions do occur with 55-year Kondratiev-wave frequency, but growth accelerates and decelerates with 25-to-30-year Kuznets periodicity. As both Klotz and Neal (1973) and Richard M. Goodwin (1986) have affirmed, growth rates of real GNP, the labor force, family formation, residential construction, and capital formation all have oscillated in harmony near the 25-year, not the 55-year, waveband, a point made by Arthur F. Burns in *Production Trends in the United States since 1870* (1930) and by W. Arthur Lewis and P. J. O'Leary in, "Secular Swings in Production and Trade" (1955).

What appears to have confused many authors is that while 25-to-30-year oscillations of investment—Kuznets cycles—provide the essential growth impulses, they put into place long-lived physical infrastructure that has a lifespan of more than one Kuznets cycle. It is the *accumulation* of this infrastructure, and its ultimate replacement, that displays Kondratiev phasing. Indeed, as I will show in Chapter 5, there have been alternating periods of accelerating infrastructure accumulation during deflationary growth cycles and periods of decelerating accumulation during the succeeding inflationary growth cycles: *technology, energy, and resource transitions occur with Kondratiev periodicity, driven by acceleration- and deceleration-phase Kuznets growth cycles that are embedded within the Kondratiev waves.* Deflationary growth cycles establish Schumpeter's technological alternatives; inflationary growth cycles push established alternatives to market saturation. After the stagflation crisis, the older technologies decline and the new technologies take over, offering investment opportunities that have been exhausted in the older lines. The market-domination crossover comes in the following depression, when the newer technological alternatives substitute for the old.

THE KUZNETS GROWTH CYCLE

The harmonious pattern of acceleration and deceleration of growth in 25-year cycles is named for another Russian-born economist, Simon Kuznets, who received the Nobel Prize for his pioneering work on the measurement of national income and economic growth. Kuznets left the Ukraine in 1920, and in 1926 received his Ph.D. from Columbia University for a dissertation on "Cyclical Fluctuations in Retail and Wholesale Trade." As a Harvard professor, he became the intellectual "father" of modern methods of national income accounting. While he was analyzing economic growth, he became the first economist to thoroughly document the 25-year-long cycle.

In his 1930 book, *Secular Movements in Production and Prices: Their Nature and Their Bearing upon Cyclical Fluctuations,* and his 1958 article, "Long Swings in the Growth of Population and in Related Economic Variables," Kuznets showed that production and price series, with primary trends eliminated and the influence of shorter business cycles attenuated or smoothed by moving averages, exhibited pronounced wave-like undulations. In his 1940 article, "Schumpeter's Business Cycles," he reaffirmed that these growth cycles were not Kondratiev waves: "The prevalence of fifty-year cycles in volumes of production, either total or for important branches of activity, in employment, in physical volume of trade, has not been demonstrated" (p. 267). The real growth impulses come in periods "of an average length of slightly more than twenty years for a complete swing." Concurring with Alvin Hansen's remarks in his 1941 book, *Fiscal Policy and Business Cycles,* Kuznets said the swings are investment or building cycles, calling them secondary secular movements. His measurements suggested that the average duration of the cycles had been about 22 years in the production series.[1]

What was particularly notable about Kuznets's approach was his ability to reveal new facts and new relationships using common sense, clear thinking, and sensible data analysis (qualities that I value), with a minimum of the abstract mathematical modeling that most economists place highest in their hierarchy of attainment. Models are only as useful as the factual base of their assumptions is well founded.

WHAT THE LITERATURE SAYS ABOUT CAUSAL AGENTS

Why are there 25-year oscillations? Much of the literature has dealt with the American experience in the late nineteenth century, following Kuznets in arguing that the driving force was the immigration-driven surges of population that produced city-building and other population-sensitive development booms, including transport-building cycles that accounted for large shares of capital investment.

In one early study, Walter Isard (1942) identified six transport-building cycles between 1830 and 1933:

Trough	Peak	Trough	Source of Growth
Before 1830	1836	1843	Canal construction
1843	1853	1864	Railroads 1
1864	1871	1878	Railroads 2
1878	1890	1900	Railroads 3
1900	1909	1918	Street and electric railways
1918	1925	1933	Automobile 1

The first witnessed the emergence of the canal. Construction surged around 1825 with the completion of the Erie Canal, reached a peak in the early thirties, and continued until the early forties. The next three cycles were associated with

1. Kuznets was not the first to publish empirical evidence suggesting the existence of general long swings of 20–25 years' duration. Three years before Kuznets's book appeared, C. A. R. Wardwell announced the discovery of fluctuations in economic time series with a duration longer than business cycles but definitely shorter than the Kondratiev cycles ("An Investigation of Economic Data for Major Cycles" [Ph.D. diss., 1927]). Wardwell's evidence was less elaborate than Kuznets's, in that it included fewer periods and fewer countries. Although Kuznets apparently believed that the swings he observed in the output of individual commodities appeared at about the same time in many different activities, he made no systematic attempt in his early work to establish the existence of long swings in aggregate economic activity. This matter was settled, at least for the United States, when Arthur F. Burns published the results of his study of a large sample of U.S. production series for the years 1870–1930 (*Production Trends in the United States since 1870* [1934]). The principal effort to extend the major findings of this study to international scale was undertaken by Burns in the 1930s as part of an overall inquiry into the cyclical characteristics of the building and construction industry, and resulted in a paper calling attention to the "longer cycles" in residential and urban building, and parallel long cycles in immigration and real estate trading ("Long Cycles in Residential Construction" [1935]).

the irregular emergence of the railroad network in the United States. Railways were in an embryonic state from 1830 to 1843, but beginning in 1843, construction of railway track increased rapidly, reached a peak in 1856, then slumped and touched bottom in 1861. The next peak and trough were in 1871 and 1875, and the final surge of track mileage took place in the 1880s.

The next transport innovation was the street and electric railway, which started to develop rapidly in the late 1880s, was checked by the depression of the 1890s, and accelerated after 1897, reaching a peak around 1906 and declining thereafter. The last cycle before the Great Depression was the first wave of automobile growth, which began in 1918, peaked in 1923, and fell to a trough in 1932. Extending Isard's analysis, the immediate post–World War II era saw yet another wave of automobile growth, construction of the Interstate Highway System, and development of the airline system in the form we now know it. The succeeding growth acceleration of the 1980s has seen the rapid development of telecommunications and computer networks for the transport of voice and data.

Similar swings are found in many related series. There were strong waves of foreign immigration between 1830 and 1930:

Trough	Peak	Trough
1844	1854	1862
1862	1873	1878
1878	1892	1898
1898	1907	1918
1918	1921	1933

City-building was not smooth and uniform, but occurred in a similar series of growth impulses, as evidenced by composite indexes of construction and real estate activity:

Trough	Peak	Trough
1825	1837	1843–1844
1843–1844	1852–1853	1861–1864
1861–1864	1871–1872	1878
1878	1889–1891	1897–1899
1897–1899	1905–1907	1918–1919
1918–1919	1925	1933

The literature on these building cycles is substantial. Edward R. Dewey and Edwin F. Dakin's *Cycles* (1947) is a handy source on the rhythms of real estate and city-building (pp. 115–125), but it should be handled with a delicate touch because of the authors' overenthusiastic search for cycles in almost everything. Also important are Long's *Building Cycles and the Theory of Investment* (1940), pp. 145, 149; Gottlieb's *Long Swings in Urban Development* (1976); E. W. Cooney's "Long Waves in Building in the British Economy of the Nineteenth Century" (1960); and J. Perry Lewis's *Building Cycles and Britain's Growth* (1965). Gottlieb charts building cycles running from trough to trough in the periods 1843–1864, 1864–1878, 1878–1896, 1896–1918, and 1918–1933. Long says that the cycles occurred in all cities, and the agreement on the

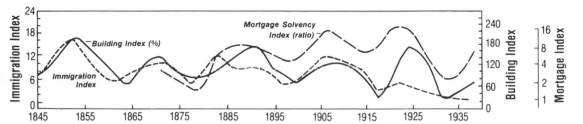

Figure 45. Kuznets Cycles of Immigration and Urban Development, 1845–1940
This figure is adapted from Norman J. Silberling's 1943 book, *The Dynamics of Business* (pp. 189–190). The *immigration index* is the five-year smoothing of the ratio of gross immigration to estimated annual total population. The *building index* is the Riggleman index for urban construction, described in detail in Silberling (p. 186). The *mortgage-solvency index* is the reciprocal of per capita urban foreclosures. The clear Kuznets-cycle rhythmicity can be seen by comparing this graph with Figure 42.

turning points of these cycles is surprisingly high, especially with respect to the troughs. Indeed, as Isard argued, "Throughout data on basic investment, production of basic industrial commodities, and population, there has been remarkable consistency of movements, with coincident troughs in the years 1825–1830, 1840–1844, 1860–1864, 1875–1879, 1894–1900, 1914–1918, and 1932–1934" (p. 156). *Throughout, the periodicity of growth has been that of the Kuznets cycle, not the Kondratiev wave,* as Figure 45 shows clearly enough. Isard said that he "accepts the existence of the Kondratieff cycle in the price data for the United States. However, save for a few monetary series intimately related with price movements, *the writer can find no evidence of Kondratieff cycles in other data for this country*" (p. 165, italics added). *The upswings and downswings in growth* of real per capita GNP that we saw in Figures 42 and 43 *have thus been marked by waves of transport- and city-building, population growth and industrial production, moving in harmony and synchronized by periodic depressions.*

The Rhythms of Transport Development

The greatest share of transport investment was devoted to railroad construction. It required immense capital commitments and had the most pervasive economic and geographical impacts. The necessary capital was forthcoming only when potential profits were high. Profits were dependent on the ratio of traffic to installed capacity. Investment booms began in the rebound from recessions. A quickening of the economy increased traffic on existing capacity, and therefore profits. Rising profits were the signals for new investors to move in, stimulating a construction boom that created jobs, tightened labor markets, increased incomes, and resulted in multiplier effects that spread throughout the economy.

But lags between capital commitments, contracts, construction, and completion led to false signals of the demand yet to be satisfied and the profits to be made. As a result, there was "overshoot" in construction decisions. In the gap between increasing demand for and completion of new capacity, soaring profits pulled in even more investors; soon speculation took over in an atmosphere of rising expectations. Substantial capital overcommitment resulted. But once the new capacity came on line, the traffic-capacity ratio sagged, and along with it, profits. In the resulting crisis of confidence, new commitments ceased, the construction boom ended, labor markets softened, and the economy weakened. Failure to meet profit targets, and resulting sags in asset values, led to defaults and to the banking crises that have occurred in every depression and stagflation crisis.

New growth cycles began only when entrepreneurs were able to identify unmet needs or new investment opportunities. That these cycles would emerge was guaranteed by the pessimistic withdrawal from the railroad investment arena that occurred as growth came to a halt each quarter-century. The essential mechanism producing the cycles was the interaction of lag and overshoot.

The Dynamics of Overshoot in Myopic Capital Markets

Jay Forrester realized that capital-lifespan theory had to include the psychological and speculative forces that cause overexpansion, just as Rostow found it necessary to use notions of lag and overshoot in his attempt to explain long waves. The first systematic attempt to build these ideas of the mass psychology of overshoot into cycle theory was that of A. C. Pigou in his 1927 book, *Industrial Fluctuations*. In this book Pigou formulated what he called the *theory of uncompensated errors*: "When expected facts are substituted for accomplished facts as the impulses to action, the way is open for a second group of causes of industrial fluctuations, namely, psychological causes. . . . These causes consist in variations in the tone of mind of persons whose action controls industry, emerging in errors of undue optimism or undue pessimism in their business forecasts" (p. 66).

Pigou believed that three influences worked to promote these errors: "First, among business men . . . there often exists a certain measure of psychological interdependence. . . . An expansion of business confidence propagates itself by . . . epidemic excitement. . . . Secondly, . . . an error of optimism on the part of one group of businessmen itself creates a justification for some improved expectation on the part of other groups. . . . Thirdly, yet another connection is set up . . . by the debtor-creditor relation. . . . As the tide of profits advances, credits do in fact tend to become larger and longer. . . . It follows that interdependence of fortunes carries with it some degree of interdependence of forecasts. . . . The three links . . . act as conducting rods along which an error of optimism or pessimism, once generated, propagates itself about the business world. By their joint action they exert a powerful influence, in favor of action in droves" (ibid., pp. 79–82).

On the other hand, these "errors of optimism and pessimism . . . have the characteristic of generating, after a while, errors of the opposite sort. . . . There is some period of gestation, the conclusion of which brings forecast to the test of fact. When this test has been applied to a fair number of things and found wanting . . . confidence is shaken. . . . As a consequence, the flow of business activity is checked. This leaves [businessmen] in no mood for further errors of optimism. . . . In consequence of financial interdependence . . . they are apt to fall into a strong reaction. . . . A fairly general liquidation of bad business sets in" (ibid., pp. 83–84).

"The dying error of optimism gives birth to an error of pessimism [that] implies an unduly depressed view in all industries of the prospective demand of other industries for their products. . . . [But] after an interval . . . the error of undue pessimism, like the previous error of undue optimism, is discovered. . . . In these circumstances certain of the bolder spirits in industry begin to make preparations for an enlarged output. The pioneers . . . are further encouraged by the fact . . . that, during the preceding period of depression, there has probably been an accumulation of technical improvements of which new plants can take advantage, and therefore the greater becomes the inducement to invest in new equipment" (ibid., p. 85).

In other words, *the optimism that arises from successful growth leads to speculative excess. The pessimism bred by a turn of fortunes leads to mass depression.* In both cases, there is overshoot that is ultimately self-correcting. Pigou's is the important insight that enables us to link the 25-year Kuznets growth cycle and the 55-year Kondratiev price wave.

In a more recent essay, Sahlman and Stevenson (1985) call the phenomenon *capital-market myopia*, a situation in which participants in capital markets ignore the logical implications of their individual investment decisions. Viewed in isolation, each decision seems to make sense, but when taken together the set of decisions is a prescription for disaster. Capital-market myopia leads to overfunding of industries and unsustainable levels of valuation in the stock market. What happens on the upswing is a self-fulfilling "chain of success": projected growth produces increased valuation that leads to access to capital, which makes new technological and human resources available. In turn, technological and manufacturing innovation produces price reductions that lead to new uses for products, which leads to reassessments of projected growth, and a new cycle begins.

The crunch comes when risky investments in innovations fail to pay off. A "chain of failure" ensues: as risky investments fail and expose both consumers' and suppliers' financial weaknesses, investor disappointment produces a more conservative stance. The basis of competition switches from innovation to price, which lowers margins and reduces capital availability and expenditures on future development, which further reduces risk-taking.

The problem arises because during growth, professional investors fail to take account of the emergence of numerous well-financed competitors, the existence of multiple competing technologies, and the need for continuing research-and-development expenditures, even though the information is readily available. Instead, they continue to invest. Individual pursuit of excessive valuation increases, based in part on a "greater fool theory." Such capital-market myopia inevitably breeds overinvestment, turning growth opportunity into disastrous overshoot.

City-building Booms

A similar overshoot-collapse mechanism has occurred in each of the nation's city-building booms. Each boom originated in the rebound from either a depression or a stagflation crisis, beginning as increasing employment opportunities drew down the pool of unemployed workers, labor markets began to tighten, and wages rose, signaling opportunities to migrants, predominantly young adults. As migrants streamed in, rates of labor force participation rose and rates of household formation increased. This response produced further economic growth. Demands for housing and urban services stimulated urban development, financed in part by foreign capital. The resulting increase in both consumer spending and private and public investment induced further growth in aggregate demand through an accelerator-multiplier effect, and this spurred growth of the capital-goods industries needed to meet that demand.

The capital-goods response was lagged, however. In each boom, speculative homebuilders overestimated demand. Expectations built on rising profits in the earlier stages of tightened markets were dashed as new developments were completed and new productive capacity came on line. Unrealized expectations resulted in an inability to repay loans. As Easterlin noted in *Population, Labor Force, and Long Swings in Economic Growth* (1968), defaults produced a banking crisis, triggering the onset of stagflation or depression. Because rising unemployment signaled hard times, the wave of immigration slackened.

It was the terminal banking crises that brought the transport- and city-building cycles into phase with each other. Each cycle lasted up to 25 years because of the long lead times involved in major infrastructure investment.

The Importance of Money-Supply Variables

This synchronization highlights the importance of money-supply variables, but in their *Monetary History of the United States* (1983), Milton Friedman and Anna Schwartz demonstrate that two relationships are at work: at the level of the Kuznets and shorter cycles, money supply is an important causal variable in economic growth; at the level of the Kondratiev wave, money-supply variations pass directly into prices.[2]

2. The key sources on money supply-long wave relationships are Milton Friedman and Anna J. Schwartz, "Money and Business Cycles" (1963), and their subsequent *Monetary History of the United States* (1983). See also Irving Fisher, "The Business Cycle Largely a 'Dance of the Dollar'" (1923); and Richard G. Davis, "The Role of Money Supply in Business Cycles" (1968). An effective

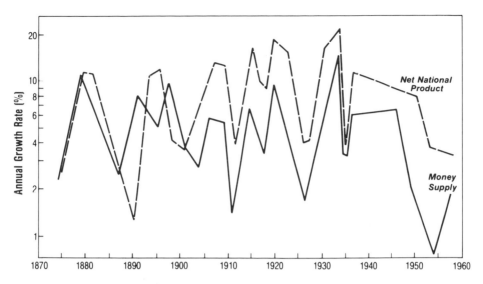

Figure 46. Relationship between the Growth Rate of Money Supply and the Growth Rate of Net National Product

The source of the data in this graph is Friedman and Schwartz's *Monetary History of the United States* (1983). Compare these oscillations with those in Figure 45: the rhythms are those of the cycles of urban development; that is, they are Kuznets cycles. Barnett and Chen's 1986 essay, "The Aggregate-Theoretic Monetary Aggregates Are Chaotic and Have Strange Attractors," apparently supports the conjecture of Figures 40 and 41.

Friedman and Schwartz argue that while the *stock* of money has increased during both cyclical expansions and contractions, the *rate of change* of money supply closely conforms to long swings in business, and the *amplitude* of changes in the rate of change correlates with the severity of the cyclical movements. Figure 46 is an adaptation of their graphical summary: *the oscillations are quite clearly those of the Kuznets cycle.* Up to this scale of oscillation, they say, changes in the growth of the stock of money are capable of exerting a sizable influence on the rate of growth of output via availability of credit.

───────────

summary of much of the literature is found in Gaston Imbert, *Des Mouvements de Longue Durée Kondratieff* (1959). Among the advocates of money supply and/or gold supply as key determinants of the long wave were Joseph Kitchin, "Production et consommation de l'or dans le passé et dans l'avenir" (1930); W. Woytinski-Lorenz, "Das Rätsel der langen Wellen" (1931); G. Cassel, *Theoretische Sozialökonomie* (1932); F. Simiand, *Les Fluctuations économiques à longue période et la crise mondiale* (1932); L. H. Dupriez, "Einwirkungen der langen Wellen auf die Entwicklung der Wirtschaft Seit 1800" (1935); and George F. Warren and Frank A. Pearson, *Gold and Prices* (1935). On the war/inflation hypothesis see E. Wagemann, *Struktur und Rhythmus der Weltwirtschaft* (1931); Alvin H. Hansen, *Economic Stabilization in an Unbalanced World* (1932); S. Von Ciriacy-Wantrup, *Agrarkrisen und Stockungsspannen sur Frage der lange Welle in der Wirtschaftlichen Entwicklung* (1936); E. M. Bernstein, "War and the Pattern of Business Cycles" (1940); and Kenneth L. Fisher, *The Wall Street Waltz* (1987).

With respect to the major price fluctuations that characterize Kondratiev waves, Friedman and Schwartz's story is different, however. At this scale, they say, there has been a one-to-one relationship among monetary changes, changes in money income, and changes in prices. Appreciable changes in the rate of growth of the stock of money have resulted in appreciable changes in the rate of growth of money income; in turn, changes in money income have been reflected in different price behavior rather than in different rates of growth of output. Indeed, each major inflationary upsurge that has occurred in the United States has been driven into a final spiral by the government's use of the printing press to help finance the nation's military expenditures.

During the Civil War, "greenbacks" were printed by the Union to finance the war, resulting in an increase in the inflation rate. But from 1868 to 1878 a small rise in the stock of money was converted into a sharp decline in prices by a rapid rise in output. In 1879 the country went back on the gold standard after being on a "greenback standard" from 1862 to 1879. From 1879 to 1897 the stock of money grew at a steady rate of 6 percent per year, but there was a secular decline in the world price level measured in gold, and also in interest rates, as this growth progressed. Between 1897 and 1914 the stock of money grew at an annual rate of 7.5 percent and prices rose 50 percent, part of a worldwide movement, due to a doubling of the world stock of gold from new discoveries in South Africa, Alaska, and Canada in the same period. The U.S. Federal Reserve opened its doors in November 1914, and promptly became involved in increasing the nation's money supply to help finance World War I. For a comparably rapid and extended rise in prices and in the stock of money, one must either go back to the Civil War or forward to World War II. But then a massive contraction in the money supply in 1920–1921 led to a brief but deep primary postwar trough. Between 1921 and 1929 the United States experienced rapid economic growth and a stable rate of money growth, so that prices were on a declining trend. The twenties were, in the main, a period of high prosperity and stable economic expansion. The bull market in stocks mirrored soaring American optimism about the future. The stock market crash of October 1929 precipitated "The Great Contraction, 1929–1933." Between 1929 and 1933 the stock of money fell by a third and the number of commercial banks fell by a third. The contraction was capped by the March 1933 banking holiday. With the New Deal came reorganization of the structure of banking, increases in stocks of money, and decreasing interest rates. Wholesale prices rose rapidly between 1933 and 1937, the result of a devaluation that had differential impact on the level of wholesale prices plus a number of explicit measures to raise prices with government assistance and encouragement, among them the Agricultural Support Act, the Guffey Coal Act, and the National Labor Relations Act. By 1941, money incomes were 17 percent lower than they had been in 1929, but real incomes were 3 percent higher. During World War II, the stock of money tripled due to the rapid rise in government expenditures, money incomes increased two and a half times, and wholesale prices doubled. Although the war ended in 1945, the price peak did not occur until 1948.

In all, Friedman and Schwartz conclude, between 1867 and 1960 there were two major episodes of price inflation: 1914–1920 and 1939–1948. In both, a doubling of prices accompanied a doubling of the stock of money. In both, the money supply initially increased with inflows of gold from belligerents using their reserves to finance the war and later expanded as a result of government decisions about financing war expenditures. There were five periods of sharp price contractions, each accompanied by a decline in the stock of money as a consequence of banking or monetary disturbances:

1875–1878: Political pressure for resumption of the gold standard led to the banking crisis in 1873 and subsequent bank failures, to a shift by the public from deposits to currency, and to a fall in the deposit-reserve ratio.

1892–1894: Agitation for silver produced fears of imminent abandonment of the gold standard by the United States and an outflow of capital which trenched on gold stocks. Those effects were intensified by the banking panic of 1893, which produced a sharp decline, first in the deposit-currency ratio and then in the deposit-reserve ratio.

1907–1908: The banking panic of 1907 led to a sharp decline in the deposit-currency ratio and a protective attempt by banks to raise their own reserve balances, and so to a subsequent fall in the deposit-reserve ratio.

1920–1921: Sharp rises in Federal Reserve discount rates in January 1920 and again in June 1920 produced a sharp contraction in Federal Reserve credit outstanding, and thereby in the stock of money.

1929–1930: An initial mild decline in the stock of money from 1929 to 1930, accompanying a decline in Federal Reserve credit outstanding, was converted into a sharp decline by a wave of bank failures beginning in late 1930. Those failures produced widespread attempts by the public to convert deposits into currency and hence a decline in the deposit-currency ratio, as well as a scramble for liquidity by the banks and hence a decline in the deposit-reserve ratio. The decline in the money supply intensified after September 1931 as a result of deflationary actions on the part of the Federal Reserve System in response to England's departure from gold, which led to still further bank failures and even sharper declines in the deposit-reserve ratios.

But according to Friedman and Schwartz, these major movements in the stock of money did not cause a long wave; rather, they were caused by developments in an already existing one. Silver agitation was intensified by a long period of declining agricultural prices. The financial boom in the early 1900s was encouraged by the speculative activities that led to the failure of the Knickerbocker Trust. In neither peak nor panic was monetary policy a cause per se. The expansions were used to finance wars. The contractions accompanied banking crises. A monetary theory, Friedman and Schwartz conclude, is insufficient to explain the long swings; *money supply reinforced the major episodes of instability, but cannot be said to have caused them.*

Demographic Factors Shaping Kuznets Cycles: Is the Cycle Dead?

In "The Nature and Significance of Kuznets Cycles" (1961), Moses Abramovitz pointed out that several demographic factors helped shape Kuznets cycles in the United States up to World War I. America permitted relatively unrestricted immigration, had a growing farm population, and was experiencing a steadily declining rate of natural increase. As Jerome noted in *Migration and Business Cycles* (1926), each upswing signaled economic opportunities that pulled in waves of foreign immigrants and investment, as well as urbanward migrants from rural America. (On waves of domestic urbanward migration, see Dorothy S. Thomas, "Some Aspects of the Study of Population Redistribution in the United States, 1870–1950" [1956–1957], and Thomas and Zachariah, "Some Temporal Variations in Internal Migration and Economic Activity, United States, 1880–1950" [1963].) Figure 47 presents the pattern for 1855–1910.

During this period, U.S. fertility rates did not rise and fall with the upswings and downturns of economic opportunity, however, as economic demographers have suggested they should. Instead, the responsiveness of immigration to the increased demand for labor helped steady the birth rates of the native-born American population. Although the economic position of all workers increased

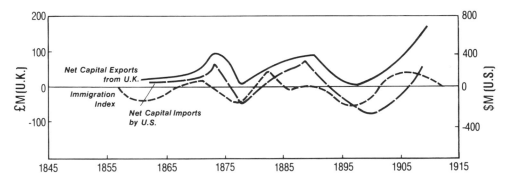

Figure 47. Cycles of Immigration and Foreign Investment in the United States, 1855–1910

This figure was prepared using data on foreign investment in the United States tabulated by Arthur I. Bloomfield in *Patterns of Fluctuation in International Investment before 1914* (1968). The immigration index is from Norman J. Silberling, *The Dynamics of Business* (1943).

in booms, encouraging more and earlier marriages and births, the influx of young adult immigrants enlarged the supply of labor in the most marriageable and fertile age groups.

Thus, the effect of good economic times on native-born Americans was less than it might have been. Native birth rates kept on a steadily declining trend without major cyclical swings. "Immigration was a cushion which protected the native population from fluctuations in demand for labor and muffled its own latent responses to changing economic conditions" (Abramovitz, "The Passing of the Kuznets Cycle" [1968], pp. 360–361).

Because immigration was seen as one of the driving forces of U.S. growth, the end of unrestricted immigration in the 1920s led observers such as Abramovitz and Rostow to proclaim in the 1960s that the Kuznets cycle was dead. Echoing Abramovitz, Van Duijn wrote: "The Kuznets cycle is an 'American' cycle. It was discovered by American economists; the United States is also the country in which the Kuznets or building cycle is most visible, or perhaps we should say: was visible. This last addition is necessary because in the present period the existence of a Kuznets cycle is no longer commonly accepted. Rostow argues that it is restricted to the period between 1840 and 1914 and therefore has no general validity: I propose, therefore, to set aside the twenty-year Kuznets cycle" (*The Long Wave in Economic Life* [1983], p. 15). Van Duijn's notion is belied by the evidence presented in Figures 42 and 43, however. That the Kuznets cycle is alive and well is reinforced by Figures 49 and 50.

Alleged Inversion of the U.S. and European Cycles

Before these figures are discussed, the issue of causation must be considered. Jerome argued that conditions in the United States determined the cycle of European emigration to the United States, a thesis that was accepted by Kuznets and Rosen in *Immigration and the Foreign Born* (1954) and by Easterlin in *Population, Labor Force, and Long Swings in Economic Growth* (1968). But the linkage of capital and labor markets has led some—for example, Brinley Thomas in *Migration and Economic Growth* (1954) and *Migration and Urban Development* (1973), building on A. K. Cairncross's *Home and Foreign Investment, 1870–1913: Studies in Capital Accumulation* (1953)—to argue that the Kuznets cycles experienced by the United States and Britain were inverted throughout much of the period 1840–1914, thereby raising the question of whether British or American growth was the driving force. Brinley Thomas noted that there were four major outflows of population and capital from Europe—in 1845–1854, 1863–1873, 1881–1888 and 1903–1913. He said that the upward phases of these swings in transatlantic migration and foreign lending coincided with upswings in capital construction in the United States and downswings in capital construction in Britain; the downward phases coincided with downswings in capital construction in the United States and upswings in capital construction in Britain. W. Arthur Lewis offered a somewhat different interpretation in *Growth and Fluctuations, 1870–1913* (1978): that the key driving element was the shift in the relative prices of industrial products on the one hand and of agricultural commodities and raw materials on the other, leading to inverted rhythms of growth in industrial core and peripheral regions and producing the rhythms and waves of migration.

There are, in fact, two interpretations of what was happening in the "Atlantic Economy," however. American scholars argue that employment opportunities in the United States drew off workers who were potential migrants from Europe's farms and villages to its cities. This cut the growth of the European labor supply and reduced the demand for city-building in Europe at a time when city growth was booming in the United States. The boom conditions in the United States attracted European capital, thereby depressing European domestic capital formation. The consequences rippled worldwide: reductions in British domestic investment reduced British demands for imports and slowed down growth elsewhere in the British-centered world economy.

The second interpretation comes from the other side of the Atlantic. Brinley Thomas, in particular, has argued that the British economy generated long swings in this era, and that the inverse cycles in the United States (and in other settlement countries) occurred in response to the push and pull of the British economic engine that drove trade within the Atlantic community. According to Thomas's interpretation,

• As much as half of the Atlantic economy's capital formation was "population sensitive"—that is, involved residential and railroad construction as opposed to industrial plant, store, and office construction—in this period.

• The homeland exported labor, goods, and "population sensitive capital" to the hinterland ("settlement countries" or "periphery") on a 20-year cycle, trough to trough. Labor followed capital out of the homeland in the export periods.

• The homeland imported materials from the hinterland for "infrastructure" growth on a 20-year cycle, the peak of which occurred at the trough of the homeland export cycle.

An accompanying consequence of these developments was the inversion of the growth cycles of agricultural countries such as Rumania and Hungary. As Allen Kelley noted in "Demographic Cycles and Economic Growth: The Long Swing Reconsidered" (1969), when the industrial countries boomed, they experienced waves of immigration, family formation, city-building, etc. When their economies sagged, potential migrants stayed in the agricultural regions and married there (Gottlieb presents dramatic graphical evidence of this inversion in *Long Swings in Urban Development*). Migration waves shifted the locations of marriage and household formation.

Maurice Wilkinson helps resolve the issue in his 1970 paper, "European Immigration to the United States: An Econometric Analysis of Aggregate Labor Supply and Demand." He points out that in many cases, growth in U.S. output resulted in increased emigration from Europe (the exceptions being Germany and the United Kingdom); that without exception, expansion of output in the European country reduced emigration to the United States; but that overarching these two, the most significant force influencing emigration was the wage differential between the United States and the European country in question.

What was the outcome of these forces in the case of the United States and the United Kingdom? Were the growth cycles in the two countries inverted? The issue cuts to the heart of the question of whether the global economy was synchronized in the nineteenth century, and if so, how. Figure 48 compares the long-term annual growth rates of per capita GNP in the United Kingdom and the United States from 1840 to 1914. The four major outflows from the United Kingdom are evident in the low rates of British growth that accompanied them, but I cannot see countercyclicality. I am willing to concede that the U.S. economy experienced fluctuations of greater *amplitude* than Britain because in Britain movements of domestic investment were counterbalanced by opposite movements in foreign investment (they were substitutes). But this is an argument for greater *stability* of the British growth rate rather than for countercyclicality. In the United States a wave of prosperity or depression was contained within the domestic economy; in Britain, where the export and home construction sectors

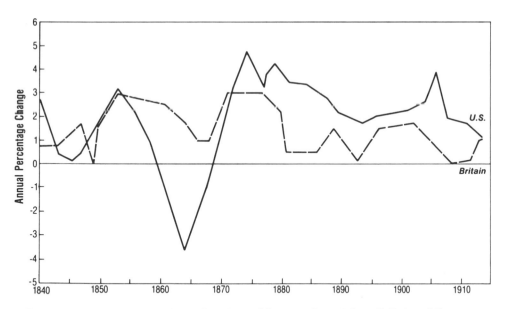

Figure 48. Accelerations and Decelerations of Average Annual Growth Rates of Per Capita GNP in the United Kingdom and the United States, 1840–1914

The rates are ten-year moving averages, plotted like those in Figure 7. There is no evidence of the countercyclicality of rates of economic growth proposed by Brinley Thomas or A. K. Cairncross. Their idea of the inverted growth rhythms of Britain and the United States is not supportable.

were more evenly balanced, a wave of prosperity was partially offset by an opposite swing in the export sector. Growth at home meant more investment overseas to expand markets and gain access to new sources of raw materials. But countercyclicality? I think Thomas and Cairncross were mistaken.

End of the Immigration-driven Dynamic

What happened when U.S. immigration controls were instituted in the 1920s? Did fertility, "unmuffled," begin to fluctuate with economic growth? As Figure 49 shows, there certainly was a change in behavior of the birth-rate curve from very modest accelerations and decelerations around a steady rate of decline from 1810 to 1920 to strong cyclicality thereafter. But what happened ran counter to the muffling hypothesis.

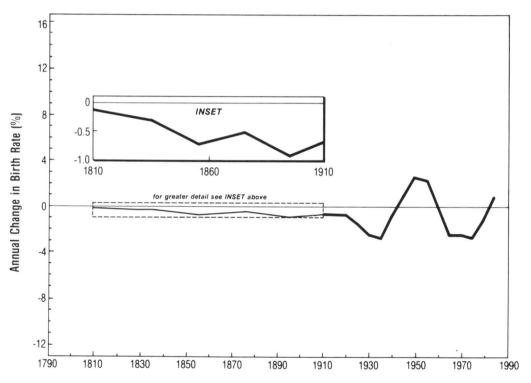

Figure 49. Accelerations and Decelerations in the Average Annual Rate of Change of the U.S. Birth Rate

The inset shows only modest fluctuations around a secular trend of decline in the U.S. birth rate before 1910. But observe the massive oscillations that begin with the accelerating decline of the rate as World War I ended. The graph supports the idea that waves of immigration "muffled" the domestic fertility response in good economic times during the nineteenth century; but the decline in the birth rate after World War I, in a period of accelerating economic growth and restricted immigration, belies the predicted consequences of "unmuffling" domestic fertility.

The "unmuffling" idea is that, absent immigration, expanding job opportunities bring a rapid improvement in the economic position and occupational mobility of young native adults. Age of marriage should therefore be younger in good economic times, and both family-formation and fertility rates should increase. *But there is simply no evidence that this kind of fertility response occurred during the 1920s; in fact, the opposite is the case.*

As seen in the upper panel of Figure 50, the U.S. birth rate went into accelerating decline during the growth epoch of the Roaring Twenties, turned around in the mid-1930s in the heart of the Great Depression, and then accelerated, ultimately increasing from 1940 to 1950, a period of slack economic growth. From 1954 to 1975, while economic growth was accelerating, there was deceleration in the birth rate (with an accelerating decline after 1960). From the 1975 trough, declines decelerated while the economy slackened and then stagnated from 1973 to 1981. But since 1981 the birth rate has started to accelerate again while the economy has grown. *Contrary to the procyclical fertility of the "muffling" hypothesis, changes in the U.S. birth rate appear to have run counter to the Kuznets cycle until 1981.*

The first dip in birth rates occurred after World War I in an increasingly urbanized society in which women began to move into the labor force in substantial numbers, and after effective means of contraception had diffused sufficiently to make limitation of family size a reality; many young men learned about condoms when they served in the army in World War I. Yet, contrary to conventional wisdom, the upturn in birth rates that produced the baby boom in fact preceded the main post–World War II Kuznets cycle of economic growth. As the lower panel of Figure 49 shows, the baby boomers entered the labor market during the postwar economic boom.

There is a good argument, then, that from World War I to 1981, the U.S. birth rate was countercyclical. But since 1981, as "birth dearthers" have entered the labor force, the birth rate has increased. Of course, much of this increase is an "echo" of the baby boom. The general fertility rate has remained relatively constant, while the size of the cohort of women in their child-bearing years has increased.

This suggests a fascinating new dynamic: *baby-boom generations enter the job market in one Kuznets growth cycle, and the fertility rate falls; birth dearthers enter the job market during the next growth cycle, and the birth rate increases.* As I will show in Chapter 5, the baby-boom-entry growth cycle is characterized by inflationary growth; the birth-dearth-entry growth cycle is a deflationary epoch. What factors are at work to produce this alternation?

The New Linkage between Birth and Fortune

Richard Easterlin asserts in *Birth and Fortune* (1987) that "the recent behavior may be largely explained as a Kuznets-cycle phenomenon," arguing that the key link is between birth and fortune. The fortunes of children born into a "baby

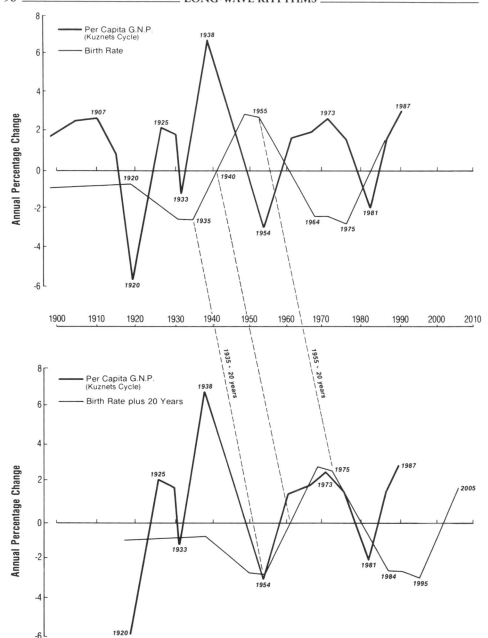

Figure 50. Relationships between the Kuznets Growth Cycle and Changes in the U.S. Birth Rate

In the upper panel, accelerations and decelerations in the rates of economic growth and in birth-rate changes are compared. In the lower panel, the fluctuations of GNP growth are the same, but the birth-rate curve has been shifted 20 years to the right to suggest fluctuations in the rate of growth of new entrants to the labor force. Note the coincidence between labor-force entries and the upswings of the 1954-1973-1981 Kuznets cycle, but the continuing post-1981 declines in labor-force entries, even as the 1981–1987 economic boom unfolded. Also note the declining birth rates throughout much of the same Kuznets cycle, but the upturn of birth rates in the 1981–1987 boom.

boom" generation differ from those of a "baby bust" generation. Since the size of the baby-boom birth cohort is large, twenty years later, when baby boomers begin to enter the labor market,

- Earnings, occupational mobility, and employment prospects will be adversely affected.
- Young adults will be hesitant to marry.
- Families will put off having children.
- Young women who choose motherhood will often have to combine a job outside the home with child-rearing.

Tough labor-market conditions produce a birth dearth. When the birth-dearth children reach the labor market two decades later, they will be confronted by a much different set of opportunities; for them, the labor market will be more benign and fertility rates will increase. For each cohort, opportunity is driven by the fertility and family decisions of their parent's cohort—decisions that biologically require a generation to unfold. As Gary Becker remarks in "Family Economics and Macro Behavior" (1988), "Although family behavior presumably has only a small part in the generation of ordinary business cycles, it is likely to be crucial to long cycles in economic activity" (p. 7).

Does this relationship show up in Figure 50? The data certainly illustrate alternating birth dearths (1920–1940, 1960–1980) and baby booms (1940–1960, 1980–2000). The Kuznets-cycle linkage is more complex than that envisaged by Easterlin, however, even though a link to the cycle does exist. The children born in the birth dearth between 1920 and 1940 entered the labor market during World War II, the slack economic times right after the war, and in the early 1950s. It was their fertility decisions that produced the major baby boom. Their offspring flooded into the labor market between 1960 and 1980, during a major transport- and city-building boom reminiscent of the nineteenth-century effect of an immigration wave. But despite these good economic times, the baby boomers' fertility response resulted in a baby bust. These decades witnessed, in combination, the most rapid rates of labor-market entry by baby boomers, the most rapid rates of economic and employment growth, and growth of real per capita GNP, and the most rapid declines in birth rates. And in turn, as the baby boomers' children have entered the labor market since 1981, despite a massive new wave of immigration, the nation's birth rate has increased. *There is a powerful alternation of Kuznets cycles at work. In one, baby boomers enter the labor market and fertility plummets. In the next, birth dearthers enter the labor market and the birth rate rises.*

One reason for this pattern (advanced by Butz and Ward in "The Emergence of Countercyclical U.S. Fertility" [1979] and by England and Farkas in *Households, Employment, and Gender* [1986]) is that the increase in female participation in the labor force has introduced a tension between men's and women's earnings: when men's earnings increase relative to those of women, the de-of men, the opportunity cost of fertility increases and fertility rates go down. Growth in the cycle when baby boomers enter the labor force is broad-based: all rise on the elevator of growth, women's fortunes alongside those of men. But growth is much more selective when birth dearthers enter the job market: participants in high-technology industries flourish, but those employed in activities that have saturated their markets lose. Downward pressures on wages affect the relative economic standing of women most adversely. The link between baby boom—baby bust and alternating-growth-cycle cyclicality is thus the relative economic standing of women, and *far from having passed away, the Kuznets cycle may thus have been reinforced by this powerful engine of intergenerational interdependence.*

CHAPTER 5

THE SYNCHRONIZED MOVEMENTS
OF GROWTH AND PRICES

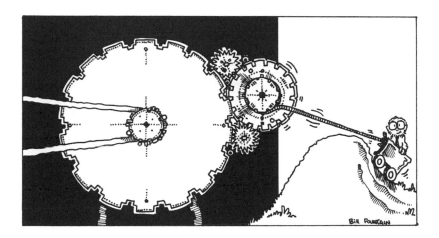

Separate threads in Chapters 1 and 3 now can be drawn together. Chapter 1 concluded with Figure 21, in which the repetitive rhythms of long-wave price behavior were summarized. At the end of Chapter 3, the repetitive rhythms of growth were captured in Figure 43, which revealed that there are two Kuznets cycles per Kondratiev wave. Acceleration-phase and deceleration-phase Kuznets growth cycles put into place the technologies that accumulate with Kondratiev periodicity, displaying S-shaped life cycles. Successive pairs of Kuznets cycles also are linked via labor-market relationships into a structure of intergenerational interdependence. Long waves and growth cycles are synchronized in a combined Kondratiev-Kuznets chronology. I will examine that chronology in this chapter. How might the chronology enable us to periodize American economic history into phases of development? Is there sufficient basis for a long-wave theory?

I begin with Figures 51 and 52. Figure 51 superimposes a schematic summary of the pairs of Kuznets cycles that appeared in Figure 43 upon a similarly schematic summary of the Kondratiev long waves that appeared in Figure 21. It would be worth reexamining Figures 21 and 43 at this time, to establish that

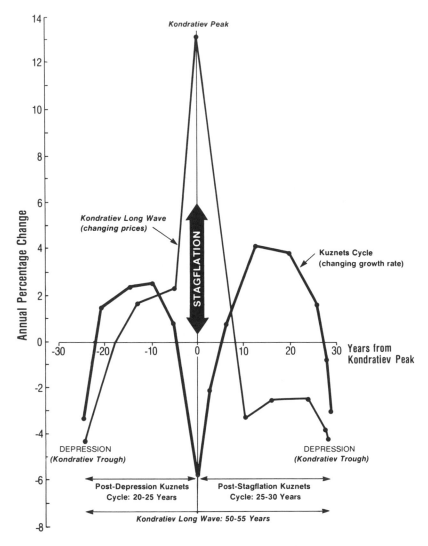

Figure 51. Relationship of Growth Cycles to Price Waves, Centered on Stagflation Crises

This schematic draws together Figures 21 and 43, showing how pairs of Kuznets growth cycles are nested within the rhythms of long waves of prices, using the stagflation crises as the common central axis. Beginning in a depression, an inflationary growth wave leads into the stagflation crisis. After the crisis, there is a deflationary growth epoch, a secondary price recovery, and the final sag of stagnation into the deflationary depression.

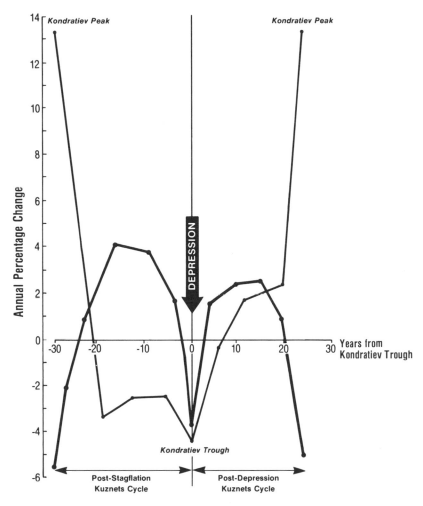

Figure 52. Relationship of Growth Cycles to Price Waves, Centered on
Deflationary Depressions

This schematic contains the same data as Figure 51. The difference is that the deflationary
depressions serve as the common central axis. Following a stagflation crisis, an epoch of
deflationary growth acceleration occurs, followed by collapse into a deflationary depression. The growth acceleration out of the depression is inflationary, and culminates in a
stagflation crisis.

Figure 51 is a reasonable and fair summary of the long-wave and growth-cycle
rhythms. As before, the vertical axis in Figure 51 is that of the Kondratiev-peak
stagflation crises, and the graph runs horizontally approximately 55 years from
depression to depression. Figure 52 provides an alternative view of the same
overlay, superimposing the Kuznets cycles on the Kondratiev waves using the

Kondratiev-trough depressions as the common vertical axis, so that the curves run horizontally for 55 years from stagflation crisis to stagflation crisis.

The behavior of growth and prices during the post-depression/pre-stagflation growth cycles (hereafter referred to as *Type A* or *Inflationary Growth Cycles*) differs from that during the post-stagflation/pre-depression cycles (*Type B* or *Deflationary Growth Cycles*):

- In *Type A/Inflationary Growth Cycles*, which on average are 20–25 years long, accelerating growth is accompanied by accelerating prices in an initial decade of reflationary recovery. Growth rates then peak at a turning point. Thereafter, growth decelerates, but the rate of acceleration of prices accelerates, driving toward a stagflation crisis. Part of the mechanism is the rapid increase of interest rates, which turns portfolio choices to shorter term instruments, and as the final spiral begins, to speculatory profits.

- In *Type B/Deflationary Growth Cycles*, which on average last for 25–30 years, the stagflation crisis is followed by a deflationary growth period in which the growth rate accelerates to a turning point while prices plummet into a primary vortex. The growth rate then turns downward toward the following depression while prices cycle through a secondary recovery before dipping into the depression. During deflationary growth epochs, as prices and interest rates fall, portfolio choices shift to longer-term instruments and to the profit potentials afforded by investment in innovative technologies.

In Figure 53 the Type B/Deflationary Growth Cycles have been replotted on the common vertical axis of their growth peaks to enable the reader to assess their similarities. While there is some consistency, behavior does vary from one cycle to the next, and there is the exception of the Great Depression, when the primary vortex was kicked downward into a deep deflationary downspin, resulting in a pair of cycles when otherwise there might have been just one. It is, of course, the individuality of growth cycles that excites many economic historians, rather than what the cycles have in common.

The pattern of growth in deflationary cycles can be captured by graphing the chaos relationship. Figure 54 is an example for the period 1815–1844. Note how growth ratchets up from 1815, lags as prices sag into the primary trough of the mid-1820s, cycles up again to a turning-point peak in 1837 when a major financial crisis occurred in conjunction with overheated expansion, and sags thereafter into the deflationary trough of 1844. In deflationary growth cycles, most of the ratcheting takes place on the upward move to the growth-peak turning point.

This contrasts with the Type A/Inflationary Growth Cycles. Figure 55 plots the set of such cycles, again superimposing them on a common vertical axis at their growth peaks. The curves are much more tightly aligned here than in Figure 53. There is evidently much more consistency in inflationary growth cycles than in deflationary cycles.

A chaos plot of the 1844–1865 cycle reveals the underlying behavior: the

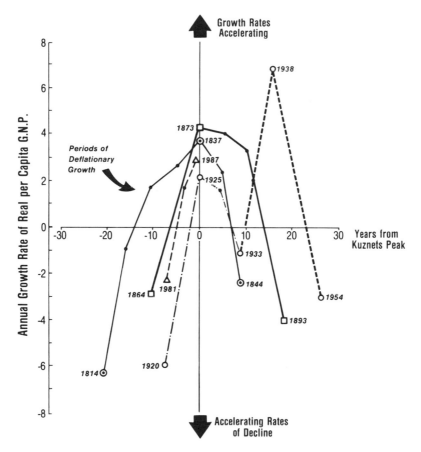

Figure 53. Kuznets Type B/Deflationary Growth Cycles Superimposed at Their Growth-Rate Peaks

In this diagram the growth cycles that have run from stagflation crises to deflationary depressions are compared: 1814-1837-1844, 1864-1873-1893, 1920-1925/1938-1954, and 1981-1988-(?). The waves have differed in the length and intensity of their acceleration phases and in the speed of their decelerations into the Kondratiev trough. Note in particular the long, leisurely deceleration of the so-called Victorian Depression from 1873 into the 1890s.

acceleration to peak (1844–1857) is quick and smooth, but after the growth rate has peaked in another turning-point crisis (1857), a long downward spiral ratchets growth rates down into the stagflation crisis. In deflationary growth cycles there is long ratcheting upward to peak and a smoother descent to trough; in inflationary growth cycles there is a smooth ascent from trough to peak, and the ratcheting is downward to trough.

The *combined Kondratiev-Kuznets chronology* indicated in Figures 51, 54, and 55 is summarized in Table 1.

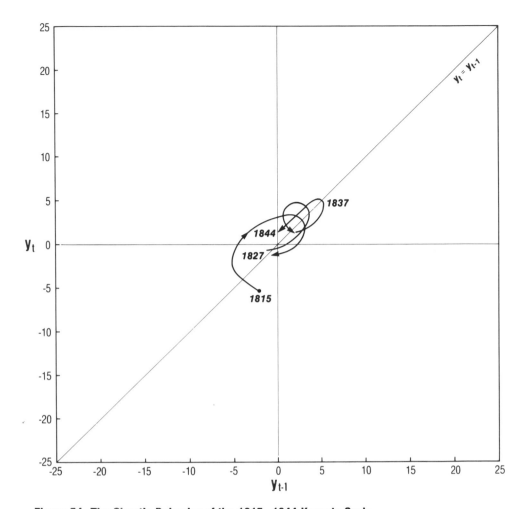

Figure 54. The Chaotic Behavior of the 1815–1844 Kuznets Cycle
The deflationary growth cycles do evidence longer periods of ratcheting upward out of the stagflation crisis to the growth-rate peak, and a shorter slide into the ensuing deflationary depression, than inflationary growth cycles (Figure 56), but as Figure 53 reveals, there is considerable variability in the timing of the phases.

No one, to my knowledge, has previously shown that *pairs of growth cycles are embedded within each long wave, and that there are alternating inflationary and deflationary growth environments.* Likewise, no one has previously demonstrated that *stagflation crises and depressions alternate systematically, or that some of the nation's historic financial crises have been of a third kind, the turning points when growth rates peak.* The differences prove to be extremely important to an understanding of why there have been higher rates of technical progress in the decades following stagflation crises.

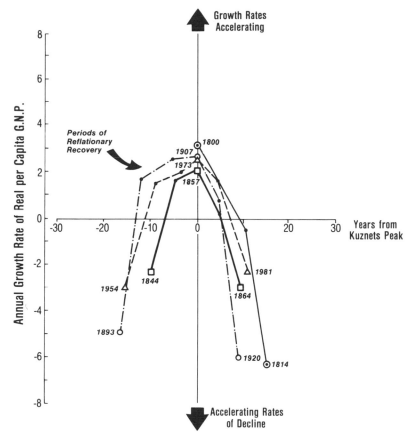

Figure 55. Kuznets Type A/Inflationary Growth Cycles Superimposed at Their Growth-Rate Peaks

Growth cycles running from depressions to stagflation crises—the 1844-1837-1864, 1893-1907-1920, and 1954-1973-1981 inflationary growth cycles—show much more consistent behavior than their deflationary counterparts.

Table 1. The Combined Kondratiev-Kuznets Chronology

Kondratiev Wave	Kuznets Cycle	Trough	Peak	Trough	Length (No. of Years)
I	1	c. 1789	c. 1807	1814	c. 25
	2	1814	1837	1844	30
II	3	1844	1857	1864	20
	4	1864	1873	1893	29
III	5	1893	1907	1920	27
	6a	1920	1925	1933	34
	6b	1933	1938	1954	34
IV	7	1954	1973	1981	27
	8	1981			

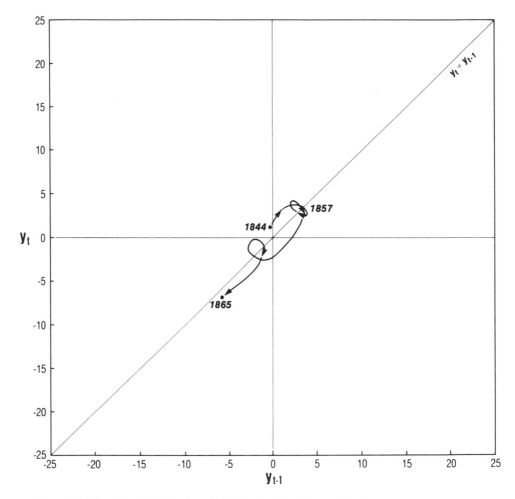

Figure 56. The Chaotic Behavior of the 1844–1865 Kuznets Cycle

This consistent behavior of the inflationary growth cycles includes a sharper, more consistent acceleration-to-peak from the deflationary depression and a longer downward deceleration into the stagflation crisis.

This is to run ahead of ourselves, however. First, we should explore the synchronized Kondratiev-Kuznets chronology revealed by Figures 51 and 52. To accomplish this, I have constructed a series of *cobweb* diagrams, beginning with Figure 57, and a series of *trend-period* diagrams, beginning with Figure 62. As in Chapters 1 and 3, the figures should be examined in sequence. They provide the additional insights into the combined Kondratiev-Kuznets rhythms and the key phases of American economic development that are needed for the synthesis presented in Chapter 6.

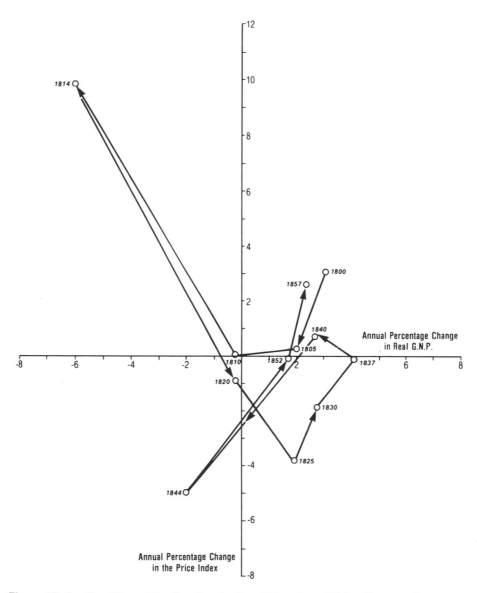

Figure 57. Another View of the Synchronization of Growth and Price Movements: The "Cobweb" from 1800 to 1857

I begin with the synchronized movements of growth and prices in the first half of the nineteenth century. If change in prices is plotted on the vertical axis and change in real per capita GNP runs along the horizontal axis, the synchronized movements are revealed by the resulting "cobweb" pattern. Follow the time sequence that begins in 1800. The rate of price increase declines and growth decelerates until 1810, after which a stagflationary spiral begins. There are accelerating rates of increase of prices and declining rates of growth until the 1814 stagflation crisis is reached. The trend then reverses. Prices fall and growth accelerates, rushing into the deflationary growth of the early 1820s. The primary vortex is in 1825, after which growth continues to accelerate but the rate of price decline decelerates until the turning-point crisis of 1837. After this turning point, growth rates begin to decelerate and prices begin to increase. The secondary recovery of prices is, however, weak, and both growth and prices soon rush downward into the deflationary depression beginning in 1844. The second Kondratiev wave begins in this trough. A period of reflationary recovery soon turns into an inflationary growth acceleration that lasts until the turning-point crisis of 1857. By 1857 the growth rates are again close to those of 1800. The double-spiked pattern reveals the synchronized motions of prices and growth—two growth cycles within a price wave—and it is this synchronization that produces distinctive trend periods of inflationary and deflationary growth, marked off by different kinds of crises and turning points: the stagflation crisis (1814–1815), the deflationary depression (the ''Hungry Forties''), the primary vortex when prices collapse (1825), and the peak turning-point (1837).

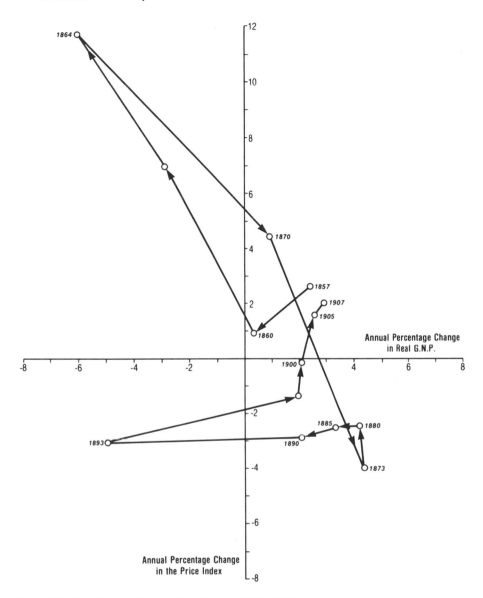

Figure 58. The Cobweb Pattern Continued: 1857–1907

The double-spiked rhythms of Figure 57 are repeated in Figure 58. Stagnation after 1857 leads into the stagflationary spiral of 1864, there is an ensuing period of deflationary growth to the primary vortex of 1873, and after 1880 there is decline into the deflationary depression beginning in 1893. The third Kondratiev wave begins with a period of inflationary growth which lasts until the turning-point crisis of 1907, when the rates of growth are once again close to the first cobweb's starting point (1800).

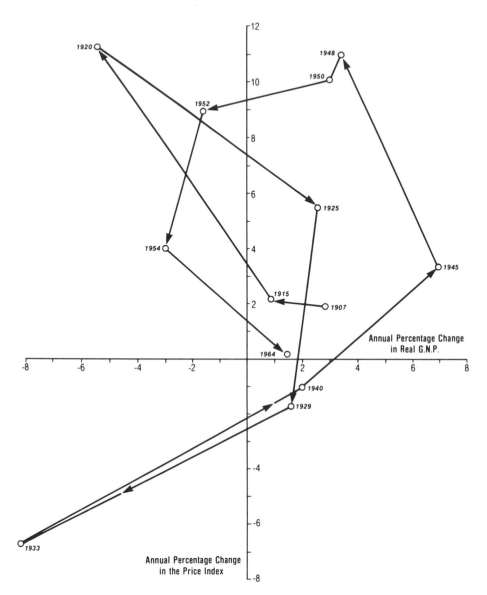

Figure 59. A More Complex Cobweb, 1907–1964, Embodying the New Deal Transition

The rhythms repeat from 1907 to the 1919–1920 stagflation crisis and down into the primary vortex of 1929, but then a change occurs. There is rapid collapse into the Great Depression, followed by the New Deal's reflationary recovery and World War II. After World War II, increased government spending prolongs the period of inflation while growth decelerates. After the Korean conflict ends, growth resumes during the postwar boom. The Great Depression and the New Deal did introduce an extra beat to the rhythm: a second growth cycle.

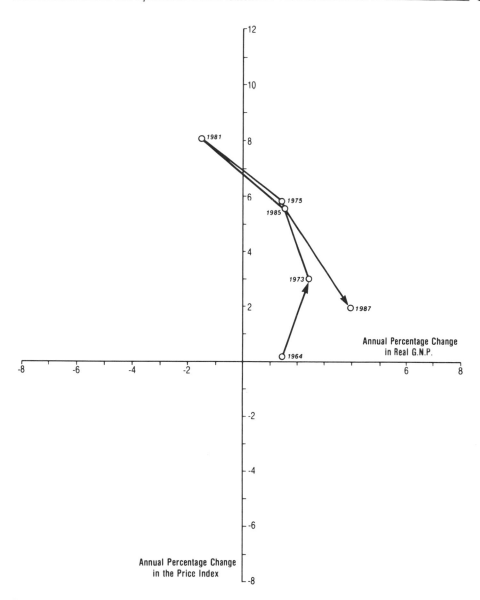

Figure 60. Back on Track: Cobweb Behavior since 1964

The historic long-wave rhythms move back "on cycle" after the turning point of 1973, however. In the graph, this year is not that far from the growth-peak turning points of the previous inflationary growth cycles in 1857 and 1907 (see Figures 55, 58, and 59). Growth decelerates and inflation increases into the stagflation crisis of 1980–1981, followed by the disinflationary growth epoch of the Reagan years. The pattern of previous waves and cycles is repeated, but the effect of anti-inflationary government actions is reflected in the fact that the 1980–1981 stagflation crisis is not as pronounced as previous stagflation episodes.

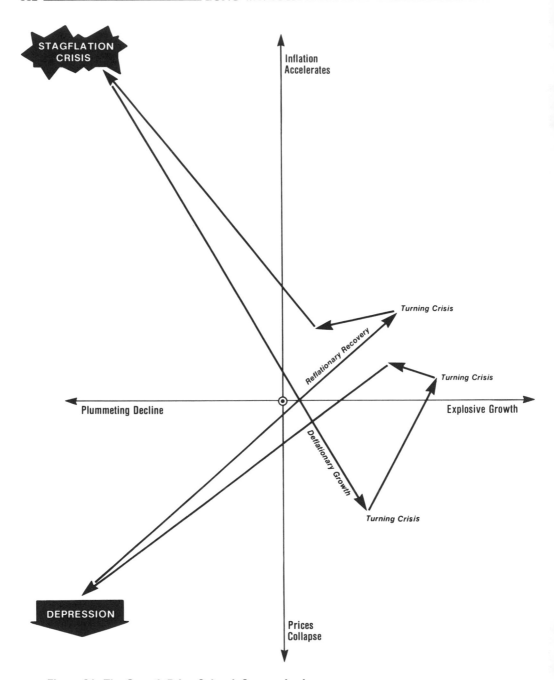

Figure 61. The Growth/Price Cobweb Summarized

The long-wave rhythms have repeated themselves. This schematic summarizes the synchronized movements of growth and prices seen in the preceding diagrams, suggesting
distinctive types of trend periods between equally distinctive types of crises: stagflation
crises, deflationary depressions, and the turning-point crises of the primary price vortex
and the two growth-rate peaks. The trend periods are described in Figures 62–69.

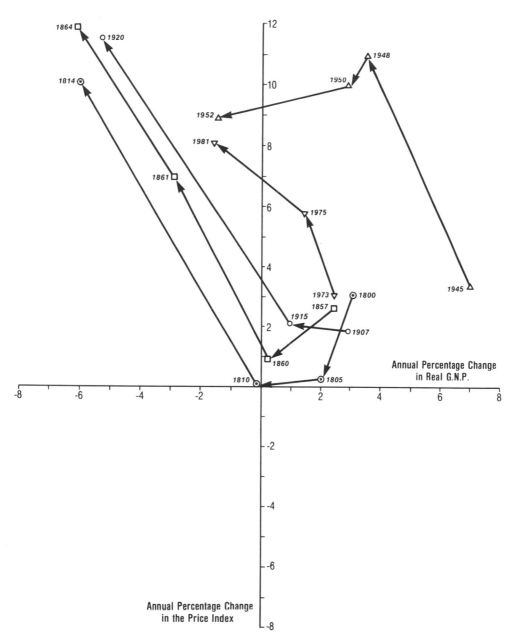

Figure 62. Episodes of Stagnation Leading to Stagflation Crises

Repetitive trend periods have common characteristics because the growth and price cycles are synchronized. This can be shown graphically in two ways. In this figure the phases of stagnation leading into stagflation crises are isolated, as they appear in the four cobweb diagrams (Figures 57–60). Figure 63 shows how these phases appear in a time-series graph that charts the smoothed-average growth and price movements. There appears to have been a secular move to successively higher rates of inflation in each of the stagflation eras. The lines are aligned one above the other, and only the last inflation peak is different; it was prevented from moving as far as in previous crises by the drastic interventions of Republican supply-siders after the election of Ronald Reagan.

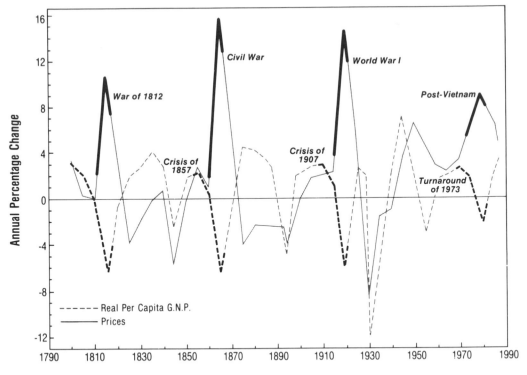

Figure 63. Stagflation Crises

This diagram of two centuries of economic history is reminiscent of a cardiogram: the stagflation crises "beat" with a distinctive regularity in which inflation peaks coincide with growth troughs at roughly 55-year intervals. Note the confused rhythm in the years immediately after World War II, the outcome of the New Deal and Keynesianism in government. It was in this period of confusion that Abramovitz declared that the Kuznets cycle was dead.

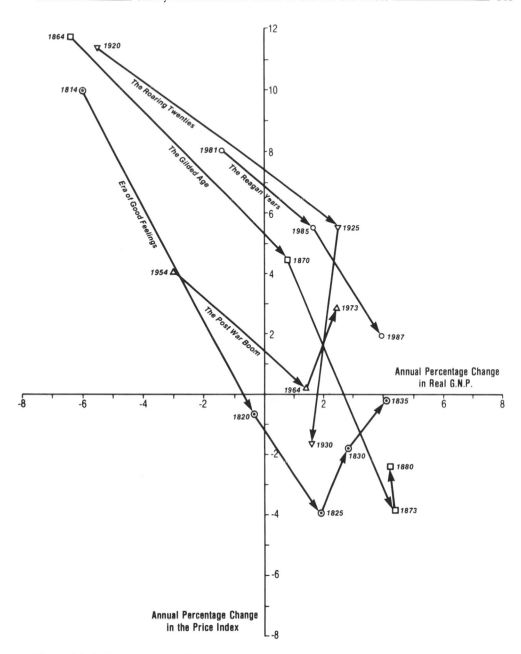

Figure 64. Deflationary Growth Epochs

Figures 64 and 65 illustrate the phases of development that follow stagflation crises: epochs of deflationary (now disinflationary) growth. American economic historians have given these epochs distinctive names: "The Era of Good Feelings," "The Gilded Years," and "The Roaring Twenties." New Deal intervention had as its consequence a postwar boom with an initial disinflationary phase to 1964; the U.S. economy recently experienced the sustained disinflationary boom of the Reagan years. The defining characteristic of these growth epochs is accelerated growth as prices plummet toward a primary vortex.

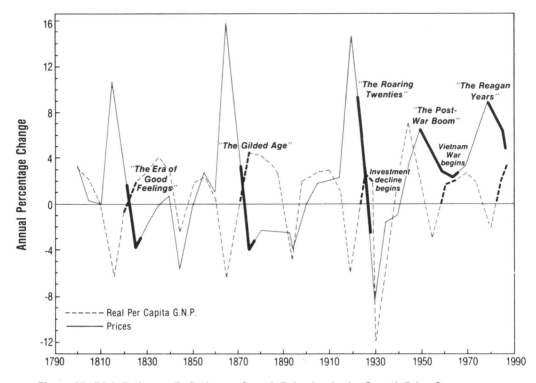

Figure 65. Disinflationary/Deflationary Growth Episodes in the Growth/Price Sequence

This chart reveals the opposing movements of growth and prices in these trend periods: prices fall into a primary deflationary vortex, while growth accelerates to a turning-point peak. Note that the postwar boom took off in a brief disinflationary period before inflationary growth asserted itself as the long-wave rhythms reestablished themselves.

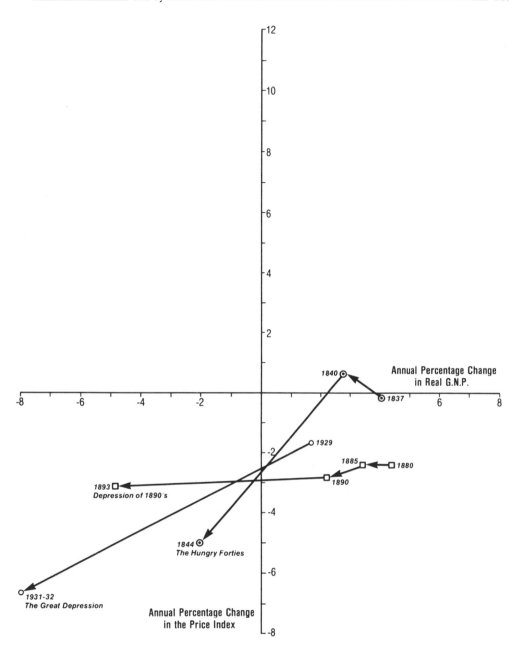

Figure 66. Periods of Decline Culminating in Depression

After deflationary growth cycles peak, prices continue their downward slide, and are joined by growth. Deceleration shifts to decline, and growth and prices then begin their downward plunge into a deflationary depression.

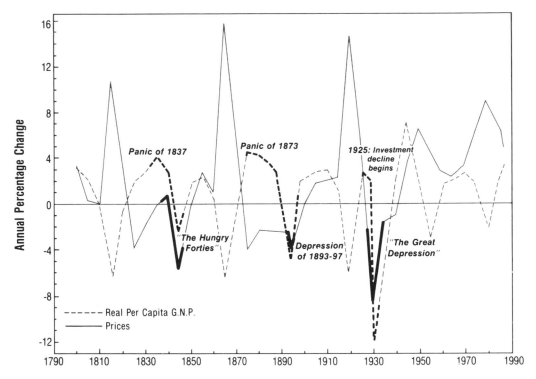

Figure 67. Episodes of Deflationary Depression

Deflationary depressions synchronize the growth cycles and price waves in common troughs. These troughs also have been given distinctive names by economic historians: "The Hungry Forties," etc. Like the stagflation crises in Figure 63, the deflationary depressions "beat" with a regular 55-year rhythm.

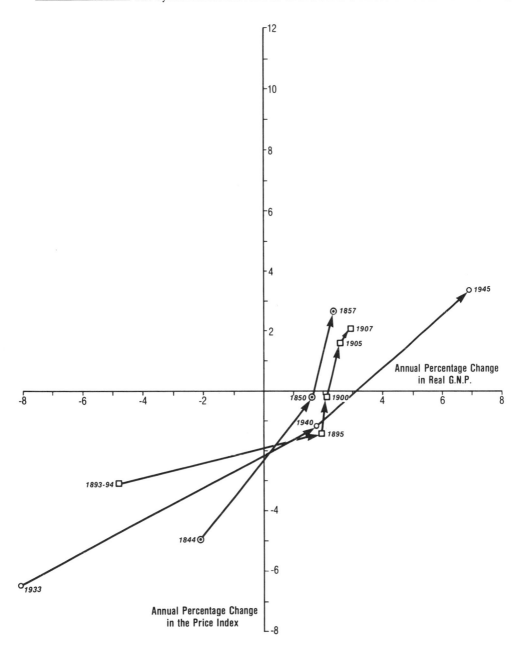

Figure 68. Phases of Reflationary Recovery from Depressions

The final trend period is the epoch of reflationary recovery from a deflationary depression. Such recovery grades into inflationary growth acceleration until a turning-point peak is reached. The peaks include 1857 and 1907.

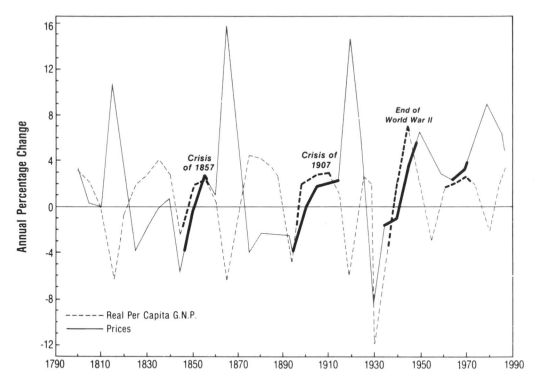

Figure 69. Reflationary Recoveries

The parallel upward acceleration of rates of increase of prices and economic growth is the defining feature of reflationary recovery and the ensuing period of inflationary growth acceleration.

CHAPTER 6

PHASES OF DEVELOPMENT
AND THE LONG-WAVE CLOCK

Some critics who read the manuscript have said that I am guilty of overkill in Chapter 5, but I will not apologize. I want the evidence to drive the message home. While we are not dealing with a completely deterministic periodic system, neither are we dealing with a "random walk." There are underlying rhythms within the noise of economic history. There has been a repetitive sequence, which is as it should be if, as suggested by the chaos formulation, an underlying deterministic process embodies endogenous causation (dependence upon prior conditions).

Crises of three different types have succeeded each other in a regular sequence in American economic history (Table 2). These crises divide that history into distinct phases of development (Table 3). While the oscillations are not mathematically perfect cycles, it is clear that both sequence and repetition of trend periods and crises have occurred. The synchronization of long waves and growth cycles is more than a figment of some overactive imagination.

To be sure, the substance of each phase varies; economic history is cumulative and irreversible. Yet it is equally true that there is a systematic element to modern economic history. I know that there are many economic historians who will

Table 2. Crises in American Economic History: A Typology

Price Crises			Growth Crises		
Inflation Peaks	Primary Troughs	Kondratiev Troughs	Growth Rate Peaks	Growth Rate Troughs	Type of Crisis
1814				1814	Stagflation crisis
	1825				Primary vortex
				1837	Growth peak crisis
		1844–		1844–	Depression
			1857		Growth peak crisis
1864				1864	Stagflation crisis
	1873				Primary vortex
			1878		Growth peak crisis
		1893–		1893–	Depression
			1907		Growth peak crisis
1920				1920	Stagflation crisis
	1929				(Primary vortex)
		1954		1954	(Depression)
			1973		Growth peak crisis
1980				1980	Stagflation crisis
			1988		Growth peak crisis

say "So what? The noise is the essential reality." The "so what" is discussed in Chapters 11 and 12. If all were noise, policy analysis would be for naught. If all were noise, historians would forever describe the forest leaf by leaf, and never understand the ecosystem of which the forest is a part—the mechanisms by which economies grow and economic development takes place.

The Long-Wave Clock

How might the rhythms be captured in a representation that effectively summarizes the sequences and repetitions? I tussled with this problem for a long time before deciding that the simplest synthesis I could construct was a *long-wave clock*. In 1987, Pierre Allan wrote of the desirability of building a clock of this kind, a clock in which the succession of social phenomena is timed against

Table 3. Phases of American Development: The Trend Periods

1. The Kondratiev Troughs

   1844–1847: "The Hungry Forties" was a period of rock-bottom growth and prices, high unemployment, and great poverty.

   1893–1897: The onset of the depression was the February 1893 market crash and the bank panic that followed: altogether 568 banks failed and 125 railroads went into receivership. The depression of the 1890s rivaled that of the 1840s. See Charles Hoffman, *The Depression of the Nineties* (1970).

   1949–1954: There was a recession in 1949 as the economy moved from a wartime to a peacetime footing, but the Korean conflict soon followed and government spending kept price increases positive, even though the rate of decrease was declining. The turning point was 1954.

2. Inflationary Growth Cycles: Acceleration Phase

   1847–1857: Growth resumed, led by an eightfold expansion of the railroads and the rapid development of the iron industry, and helped by a "trough war," the Mexican War of 1848. The first major wave of European immigrants arrived—2 million in 1850–1855. California gold helped push up prices after the 1849 discoveries.

   1897–1907: Growth resumed, along with price increases pushed upward by government spending during another "trough war," the Spanish American War. There was increasingly diversified manufacturing growth.

   1954–1973: The "postwar boom" began in earnest as growth accelerated, but the slackening of the rate of price increase ended with the onset of the Vietnam war, when government spending surged, and prices then spiraled upward. Deficit spending produced progressively higher levels of inflation.

3. Turning-point Crises at Inflationary Growth Peaks

   1857: The crisis was brought on by intense speculation. Land was mortgaged to buy more land, which was remortgaged. Easy credit expansion was fueled by California gold. Finance companies were established, promoting low down payments and large speculative gains. Inflation accelerated. But bad loans led to the failure of the Ohio Life Insurance Company, the effects of which cascaded outward. Small banks failed. Larger banks restricted credit. Bankruptcies followed. Railroad construction stopped. The growth rate began to decelerate and the stock market plunged. See George W. Van Vleck, *The Panic of 1857* (1957).

   1907: On October 22, 1907, the Knickerbocker Trust failed, after it had been used in promoting a variety of pyramiding speculative schemes. A money panic ensued. The economy began to retract as manufacturing growth edged down and interest rates went up. See Kenneth L. Fisher, *The Wall Street Waltz* (1987, pp. 76–77).

   1973: Growth acceleration peaked in 1973, when the 1965–1973 Vietnam war ended, and a sharp recessionary curtailment of growth occurred.

4. Inflationary Growth Cycles: Deceleration Phase

   1857–1861: Decelerating growth resumed until the onset of the Civil War, but prices began an upward spiral.

   1907–1914: Growth resumed, but at a decelerating rate; the electricity, chemicals, and petroleum industries were among the leading sectors. There was rapid immigration, but momentum was lost, prices continued upward, and the stock market sagged.

   1973–1981: Stagnation turned into stagflation as prices surged upward, in part impelled by OPEC. Stock prices initially declined, but then began a long, slow recovery.

(*continued*)

Table 3 (*continued*)

5. The "Peak Wars" and Stagflation Crises
   1812–1814: War of 1812. Government borrowing to finance the war fueled an inflationary spiral accompanied by wartime speculation.
   1814–1815: Inflation rose to a peak and growth halted as the country adjusted from wartime spending to a peacetime economy.
   1861–1865: The Civil War. The Union issued greenbacks to finance its operations during the war, driving up inflation as too much money chased too few goods.
   1864–1865: Wartime inflation reached its peak, and as the economy adjusted from wartime spending to a peacetime economy, the growth rate bottomed out.
   1914–1918: World War I. Initially, the United States benefited from the outbreak of the European War, but then came the need to finance U.S. involvement. Government spending pushed up prices.
   1919–1920: The inflation rate peaked at the war's end. The growth rate bottomed out as the economy shifted from a wartime to a peacetime footing.
   1980–1981: Stagflation Crisis. The peak of inflation and the trough of growth combined in another stagflation crisis.

6. Deflationary Growth Cycles: Acceleration Phase
   1815–1825: "The Era of Good Feelings" unfolded as growth accelerated, prices decelerated, and the stock market boomed. Southern cotton production led the expansion, accompanied by growth of the New England textile industry and by canal-building. The deflation was compounded by the retirement of government debt incurred in the Louisiana Purchase.
   1865–1873: "The Gilded Age." The cash accumulated during the period of war and stagflation made possible loans that financed rapid output growth during the period of reconstruction. Prosperity increased rapidly in an atmosphere of accelerating deflation. There was another wave of immigration, and a prolonged bull market.
   1921–1929: "The Roaring Twenties" began with the rapid growth of the automobile industry, petroleum, chemicals, electricity, and consumer electronics. The new Federal Reserve System, after the panic of the 1920 crisis, pursued an easy-money policy. New techniques of mass production and scientific management increased output, reduced prices, and led to another great wave of prosperity. There was a massive building boom, and a strong bull market unfolded.
   1982–1987: "The Reagan Era" was marked by the rapid growth of new information technologies. As in previous episodes, an era of disinflationary growth began in 1982. A strong bull market pushed stock prices upward, culminating in another historic high, but ending in the crash of 1987.

7. Turning-point Crises in a Primary Vortex
   1825: Deflation ended in 1825 in a monetary crisis produced by "wildcat" banks that had made too many bad loans to Mexico and South America. The turn was signaled by the stock exchange panic of 1825, itself fueled by overenthusiastic speculation.
   1873: A money panic caused by speculation in gold brought the period of growth to an end. Banks suspended payments. There were many business failures. According to one estimate, there were 3 million tramps in the winter of 1873–1874. The stock market slid.
   1929–1934: The crash came in 1929, followed by the deepest deflationary depression the nation had known, with widespread bank, business, and personal failures and massive unemployment. The trough was reached in 1932–1933, but the stock market sagged until the eve of World War II. See John Kenneth Galbraith, *The Great Crash, 1929* (1954), and Charles P. Kindleberger, *The World in Depression, 1929–1931* (1973).

Table 3 (*continued*)

1987:	The overheated stock market crashed, bringing to an end wild speculation in land and property markets and in resources, and precipitating a major crisis in the Savings and Loan industry, which had made too many loans secured by over-valued assets.

8. Secondary Recovery of Prices with Continuing Growth

1825–1837:	Major investments were made in the first several thousand miles of railroads and in infrastructure. Expansion of the textile industry continued apace. The U.S. debt was retired. Banking and credit expanded. Prices increased.
1873–1878:	Prices recovered somewhat, but the country remained locked in a severe recession.
1934–1938:	Franklin D. Roosevelt came to office in 1933 and initiated his New Deal policies to alleviate distress. Federal deficits helped stimulate recovery. Prices began to move up again, and government spending took over as the lever for further growth.

9. Turning-point Crises at Deflationary Growth Peaks

1837:	The stock market peaked, but expansion was too heated. Too much improperly secured debt had accumulated, especially in excessive land and stock specula-tion. Rising U.S. interest rates had attracted much British investment, which the British began to withdraw in 1836. The government withdrew its deposits from the Second Bank of the United States in July 1836, setting off a panic. In May 1837 the market crashed as banks suspended payments, growth stopped, the Bank of the United States failed, and highly mortgaged speculative land invest-ments collapsed. See Reginald G. McGrane, *The Panic of 1837* (1965).
1878:	As prices turned, there was a stock market recovery that had begun in 1877.
1938–1939:	New Deal recovery peaked on the eve of World War II in Europe.

10. Deflationary Growth Cycles: Deceleration Phase

1837–1843:	Prices, growth, and stock market averages declined as purchasing power and land prices fell. Continuing bank failures culminated in the Panic of 1843.
1878–1893:	Prices continued their downward slide, and although railroad construction re-sumed, steel replaced wrought iron, and the first electric lights began to be in-stalled, growth rates continued to slacken. Speculation pushed the stock market to another historic high before the Panic of February 1893.
1949–1954:	Post-World War II readjustments were curtailed by the outbreak of the Korean conflict. As that was scaled down and ended, the country eased down into a low-growth trough.

its own internal dynamic rather than on a fixed natural time scale. Figure 70 is such a formulation.

In constructing the clock, I placed the Kondratiev-peak stagflation crisis at the 12 o'clock position. Now follow the movements. As the stagflation crisis ends, a Type B/Deflationary Growth Cycle begins, accelerating during the next decade to a peak that follows the bottoming-out of prices in a primary vortex. As growth rates top out, there is a financial crisis accompanied by a turning-point recession that shifts the economy from acceleration to deceleration. Dur-

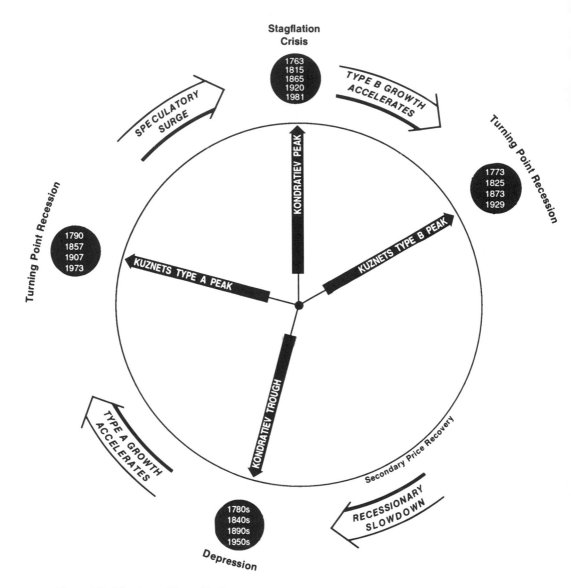

Figure 70. The Long-Wave Clock

ing the deceleration, a secondary price recovery occurs, but when this secondary recovery runs out of steam, growth and prices slide into a deflationary depression. The time from stagflation peak to depression trough is 25–30 years.

With the end of the depression, growth and prices accelerate upward with the onset of a Type A/Inflationary Growth Cycle. The acceleration phase of this cycle again culminates in a financial crisis and a turning-point recession as growth rates peak and the economy shifts from acceleration to deceleration. But at this juncture, prices begin a speculatory surge as growth sags. High and unpredictable interest rates push portfolio choices toward short-term instruments, and many investors seek quick speculatory gains. The forces leading to another stagflation crisis are set in motion. That crisis occurs some 20–25 years after the trough depression. The clock has reached noon again, completing a rotation that has lasted an average of 55 years. It is time for another sequence to begin.

Hans Mark wrote me, after hearing me present some of my conclusions, that what is revealed is that the U.S. economy behaves like a complex driven oscillator, with frequencies that are harmonics of the Kondratiev wave. In the same vein, Paul Ove Pedersen wrote, after reading the manuscript, that he "thinks of a complex system in which different parts of the economy fluctuate with different inherent frequencies; in such interdependent systems, only one set of harmonic cycles will be realized, e.g. 11, 27 and 55 years." The chaos idea suggests that the clock captures the underlying rhythms, which may often be clouded to the casual or short-term observer because of the amount of noise in the system.

Long-Wave Rhythms: Multiple Endogenous Causality

In an essay that was highly critical of the innovation-wave theorists, Nathan Rosenberg and Claudio Frischtak argued in 1983 that there are four logically interdependent requirements for any long-wave theory: *causality, timing, recurrence*, and *economy-wide repercussions*. Have these requirements been met? Do we now have a sufficient basis for a long-wave theory?

Insofar as *causality, timing,* and *recurrence* are concerned:

- Long waves are internally driven by a repetition of increase and expansion, overshoot and collapse: *each phase of the long wave is a consequence of the cumulative sequence of phases which has preceded it*; each new cycle follows its predecessors with the same regularity with which the successive phases follow each other. The cumulative sequence implies multiple causation: the systematic element in the unfolding of modern economic history is the product of simultaneous, endogenous, multiple forces.

- Kondratiev waves are not growth cycles. Embedded within each 55-year Kondratiev wave are two *infrastructure-investment and city-building Kuznets cycles that provide the growth impulses*. Pairs of these growth cycles put into place new energy and transportation technologies whose epoch of dominance extends from one Kondratiev peak to the next.

- The Kondratiev waves and the Kuznets cycles are synchronized when they collapse, in concert, in deflationary depressions, as well as when prices spiral and growth collapses in stagflation crises.

- Scarcity followed by speculation is what drives prices in an inflationary upswing, made possible by an expansion of credit and an increase in the money supply. War translates each upswing into a final spiral.

• The link between Kondratiev waves and Kuznets cycles is provided by *psychological factors* that take over and drive prices up after an inflationary growth cycle has peaked, and down after a stagflation crisis, producing overarching price upwaves and downwaves that end in stagflation crises or depressions.

• Price waves differentiate inflationary from deflationary growth cycles, setting the necessary conditions for the higher rates of technical process (characterized by Schumpeter's clusters of innovations) that occur in Type B/Deflationary Growth Cycles.

• The concentration of innovativeness in periods of deflationary growth acceleration results in technology and materials successions and in distinctive growth epochs that display, and are repeated with, Kondratiev synchronicity.

• Inflationary and deflationary growth cycles are linked by demographic dynamics: deflationary growth epochs are periods in which "baby bust" cohorts enter the labor market and the fertility rate increases; during inflationary growth epochs, "baby boom" cohorts enter the labor market and the fertility rate declines.

Technically, *there are long waves and cycles because the process is endogenous:* the essence of a cycle is an internal dynamic that gives rise to repetition. The motions result in *timing against an internal clock,* timing that is only approximately scaled to natural time. Ample evidence of *recurrence* has been provided. Inflationary growth cycles accelerated in 1848–1857, 1897–1907, and 1955–1973. The acceleration phases ended in the turning-point banking and financial-market crises of 1857, 1907, and 1973. Stagflationary spirals occurred in 1812–1815, 1861–1865, 1915–1920, and 1973–1981 after an intervening period of slackening growth and rising prices. Type B/Deflationary Growth Cycles accelerated in the years 1818–1825, 1868–1873, 1920–1925, and 1982–1989. Turning-point recessions followed the primary vortexes of 1825, 1873, and 1929 as growth acceleration turned to deceleration. There were secondary price recoveries in 1827–1837, 1877–1893, and 1933–1948, each of which ended in further turning-point crises that pushed the economy down to the depressions of the 1840s and 1890s and the slack growth of the early 1950s.

These movements were *economy-wide.* To be sure, both within nations and globally, new growth has favored new industries in new regions, and technology successions have borne down with greatest severity on regions with the heaviest reliance on older technologies or materials output; but these movements have been interdependent, and substantial evidence has been produced that the price movements and economic growth of many of the world's nations have been tightly synchronized. I thus conclude that each of the Rosenberg-Frischtak requirements has been met: there is a sufficient basis for a long-wave theory. Because the mechanisms are endogenous, however, such a "theory" will surely have an unfamiliar form, with cause and consequence reversing roles at different times in a system of feedback loops that result in extreme boom and bustiness.

Rather than attempt to specify the relationships in symbolic form, I have chosen to describe the "natural history" of long waves. It will remain for others more technically adept than I am to take this next step. Where such a description might begin is really immaterial, because the rhythms are driven endogenously. For me, the easiest place to start is the period when growth and prices are synchronized at their maximum rates of decline in the depths of a severe depression. (Even the Marxists are correct in their argument that long waves end in capitalist crises, although they are wrong when they argue that only exogenous influences can propel capitalism out of these crises.) In such depressions, industries that have been in decline since the last stagflation crisis see their excess capital pruned through plant closures and physical depreciation. Simultaneously, excess debt load in new-growth industries is cleared out by defaults and bankruptcies of those least able to survive extreme price competition. Commodity prices and land values are at their nadir. Unemployment soars, real estate markets are saturated, rents and property values decline, and real wealth shrinks along with the value of assets.

The turnaround comes as those who have survived the crash see assets that can be acquired at bargain-basement prices and market opportunities that have been created by the pruning and failures. As orders increase, existing machines are put back into operation, resources available at rock-bottom prices are brought back into use, and the slack in the economy is reduced. With portfolios and asset values at their nadir, little capital is available for venturing. Investors disavow the search for new alternatives, preferring the security of the products and technologies proven by earlier innovators and entrepreneurs. The growth that occurs is in the sectors for which there are proven markets, but for which growth opportunities have not been exhausted.

Increased utilization of existing capital stock results in rising profits, and the prospect of future profits attracts credit and produces orders for new capital equipment. As empty space is filled, rents rise and plans are laid for new building. Rising fortunes signal opportunities to migrants, and a building boom begins, reinforced by the arrival of a baby-boom generation in the job market.

As the upsurge continues, consumer-goods industries expand and further stimulate growth of the capital-goods sector. But gradually demand begins to move out ahead of supply, and pressure on resources begins to push up prices and wages. Prosperity returns to agriculture and to raw-materials producers as relative prices shift in their favor. With further price increases, competition heats up for control of higher-cost resources contained in inferior deposits or located in more remote areas. Wage pressure produces filtering. More workers are drawn into the labor market, and occupational mobility increases. Rising labor costs promote adoption of labor-saving technologies and stimulate growth among producers of these technologies. Labor-intensive industries relocate to low-wage areas and contribute to their economic growth. Even though a baby-boom generation enters the labor market, the improving bargaining power of labor pushes up wage and benefit packages and increases women's labor-market opportunities. As women's earnings increase relative to those of men, so does the cost of a child, measured in lost wages, and the fertility rate decreases. This ensures a birth dearth a quarter-century hence.

The boom is a lengthy one, generalized among industrial, agricultural, and raw-materials-producing areas, reaching down the skill ladder to draw increasing numbers of participants into the labor market. Such inflationary growth cycles last for about 20 years, the initial 15 of which see progressive acceleration of the rate of economic growth. Stimulus is provided by a general expansion of credit, justified by growth and rising asset values. Unfortunately, however, lags between capital orders and completions produce profit signals that result in excessive investment. The growth acceleration comes to an end as this new capital stock comes on line and begins to erode profits. Rising interest rates begin to distort markets by biasing portfolio choices toward short-term investments. As relative prices shift, urban real wages come under pressure.

Capital orders are cut back. In the intensity of competition, companies whose investments were financed by more expensive capital are unable to meet their commitments, and the bad loans result in a banking crisis and turning-point recession. Yet the boom psychology persists. A change in upwave dynamic occurs as mass psychology takes over as the driving force behind aggrandizement. Optimism about investment opportunities switches from the growth industries and the stock market to credit-financed profits in commodities and in physical assets such as land. Profits are assured by rising prices driven by the demand pressures made possible by easy credit. The stage is set for a speculatory surge, even as real growth lags.

As speculative gains become self-fulfilling prophecies, inflation is kicked into full gear, fed by additional borrowing justified by inflationary gains. Speculators leverage to the limit. Contention for loanable funds drives up interest rates, and this in turn drives up the cost of capital and dries up investment. In each of the last four Kondratiev waves, it has been at this point that the world has gone to war. With the printing presses running at full capacity, the money supply shoots up and a full-blown stagflationary spiral results.

The end comes as the war ends. There is a stagflation crisis and the economy grinds to a halt. Before the war, the growth industries had saturated their markets. Cost- and wage-inflation had driven up prices and eroded the value of fixed incomes and of many assets. There was nothing left in which to speculate. As the war ends, there is a sharp contraction of money supply and credit. Bank failures accompany the crisis. With the economy in the doldrums, prices and wages come tumbling down. Unemployment shoots up. Speculatory profits in commodities and land vanish. Relative prices shift again, and agricultural regions and raw-materials producers are severely affected. Defaults mount in housing and property markets. As opportunity vanishes, increasing numbers of families drop beneath the poverty line and homelessness increases.

The solution comes because many investors' bank accounts are full. As interest rates fall, the search for investment alternatives turns back to the longer term. As Rostow pointed out (1978), prices shift away from raw materials and agriculture in favor of industry. But the main industrial growth sectors of the just-ended cycle are no longer profitable; saturated markets and excess physical capital result in plant closings and bankruptcies. A venture-capital industry emerges as investors look for profit opportunities in new and untried industries: the available pool is the accumulated stock of unexploited inventions, experiments, and early trials. Declining costs, including the lower capital costs made possible by falling interest rates, permit experiments that hold out the possibility of substantial gains, even though venture capitalists know that perhaps one in ten of their carefully selected investments will succeed. The growth that begins to unfold is concentrated in the newer technologies that effectively substitute for older industries, overcoming infrastructure constraints or resource scarcities, or opening up new markets. The stage is set for one of Schumpeter's innovational revolutions.

The initial products are experimental and high cost. Turbulence and change characterize high-technology markets. Supply-side marketing dominates the early stages: companies deliver what they can make, and customers can hardly demand something they know nothing about. The innovations that attract attention are quickly routinized and imitated, however. Costs and prices come tumbling down as supply moves out more rapidly than demand. Almost the entire 10–12 year period of growth acceleration is also one of disinflation or deflation. Demand increases first for technically sophisticated workers who can design and maintain the new systems. With deskilling, demand also increases for minimum-wage workers who can perform the tasks left for the human participants. A dual labor market results. At the first sign of pressure on the minimum wage, labor-intensive industries move to low-wage regions.

The investment sequence is repeated: high profits attract investment; there are lags between capital orders and deliveries, and ultimately cumulative investment decisions overshoot demand. Meanwhile, new jobs and rising incomes in new regions signal opportunities to prospective migrants. There is an infrastructure- and property-building boom that also ends in overshoot. And despite the entry of a birth-dearth generation into the labor market, the earnings of female workers relative to those of males decrease, and the fertility rate increases. A baby boom is assured for the next inflationary growth cycle.

The entire period of growth acceleration is led by an enthusiastic bull market that gets caught in its own speculative frenzy before a crash that signals the bottoming-out of price declines and the topping-off of the growth upswing. There is the usual banking and financial market crisis at the turning point as growth turns from acceleration to deceleration. Absent panic intervention, decline is not immediate, however. The transition is gradual. Another 10–15 years of slackening economic expansion lie ahead. A secondary recovery of prices begins as initial resource contention develops for the materials demanded by the new-growth technologies, but finally, downwave psychology takes over and declining growth pulls down prices and the market in a synchronized descent from the doldrums into a depression. The final *coup de grâce* is administered to those older industries and technologies for which substitutes have emerged. For them, the gradual erosion of markets is followed by collapse in the depression. And these are the most severely pruned industries and technologies as the newly adopted set of mutually supportive infrastructure and energy technologies rejects alternatives. This is what Schumpeter meant by the gales of *creative destruction* that are central to economic development. It is in these new technologies that the succeeding demand-driven inflationary growth acceleration will begin. For them, major corporate entrants and general industry shakeouts signal the transition to demand-driven markets. The cycle is complete: the clock has gone full circle. Growth and prices are synchronized once again at their maximum rates of decline, and the stage has been set for the next long wave.

CHAPTER 7

THE QUESTION OF ELLIOTT WAVES: ANOTHER LONG-WAVE RHYTHM?

Now the focus changes. We move to shifting sands. Scratch the surface, and you will find people attempting to structure the phenomena that interest them in a long-wave context—the stock market, voting behavior, incidence of wars, even the rise and fall of the great powers. The problem is to separate substance from illusion. Claims of the long-wave systematicity of practically everything—most based on wishful thinking rather than hard evidence—weaken the credibility of the more basic propositions that have just been developed. What is mirage, and what might possess a long-wave dynamic? I will start by assessing the so-called Elliott Wave, of which many stock market numerologists are enamored. Chapters 8 and 9 deal with politics, parties, and international relations, and Chapter 10 discusses even more suspect literatures.

If growth and prices move in synchronized rhythms, are there also 55-year long waves in the stock market? Ralph N. Elliott believed he was able to discern such long waves (see Alfred J. Frost and Robert R. Prechter, Jr., *The Elliott Wave Principle* [1985]; Robert R. Prechter, Jr., ed., *The Major Works of R. N. Elliott* [1986]). I decided to test for the presence of such waves and obtained from Prechter's Foundation for the Study of Cycles its listing of monthly stock market averages from 1789 through 1988. From these, I calculated the annual averages, deflated them to be able to study the movements of the real market averages, and computed the annual growth rates and the smoothed averages in a manner identical to the procedures used in Chapters 1 and 3. As in those chapters, the evidence I developed is laid out in a series of graphs, beginning with Figure 71. These should be studied in sequence.

Briefly, the graphs show extreme volatility in the annual rates of change in market prices (Figure 71). If there are Elliott Waves, they must therefore be very weak, and an underlying boom and bustiness must characterize much shorter term behavior. Indeed, one may quite reasonably ask whether there is any pattern at all, at any level of generalization. Only when the 10-year moving averages are used do the chaos graphs suggest some 55-year rhythmicity, plus something not identified by previous observers, loops in the phase space indicating cycles *within* Elliott Waves (Figure 74). Follow-up segmentation of the 10-year moving averages in the manner of Figure 21 led me to conclude that the most consistent signal was one of *triplets of "DJ Cycles,"* not 55-year Elliott Waves (Figure 76—the "bottom line" illustration). The peaks and crashes of these DJ cycles evidently anticipate the turning-point crises of the inflationary and deflationary growth cycles, plus the end of the secondary price recovery before prices and growth plunge into a deflationary depression. These signals are very weak, however, and the essential stock market reality may be the shorter-term boom and bustiness that produces wide, and often wild, noisy oscillations.

There is a moral to this story. Elliott evidently imposed his 55-year long waves on the data, making his numerology fit the preformed idea that the stock market should rise and fall with Kondratiev periodicity. Careful data analysis reveals that within the overriding noisiness of this behavior there are some weak rhythms, but the most persistent of these are not Elliott Waves. Facts *can* be stubborn things. The problem with so much of the long-wave literature is exactly what emerges in this case: long waves have been *imposed upon* the data regardless of what the underlying dynamics may be. Unsupportable long-wave assertions based on dubious evidence are what have led many serious scientists to reject the long-wave idea out of hand. Because overenthusiasm bred overreaction, everyone lost: the baby was thrown out with the bath water!

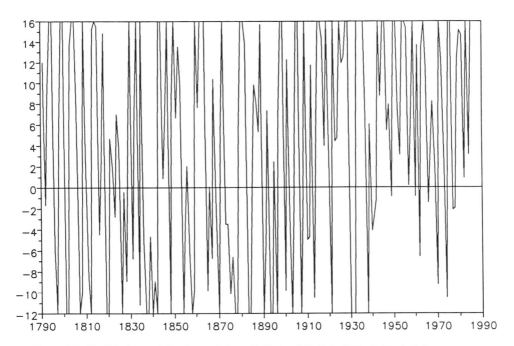

Figure 71. Oscillations of the Annual Growth Rate of Deflated Stock Market Averages, 1790–1988

The extreme oscillations are evidence of a high noise-to-signal ratio. The long-term average growth rate was 5.24 percent annually from 1790 to 1930, and has been 6.78 percent annually since 1930.

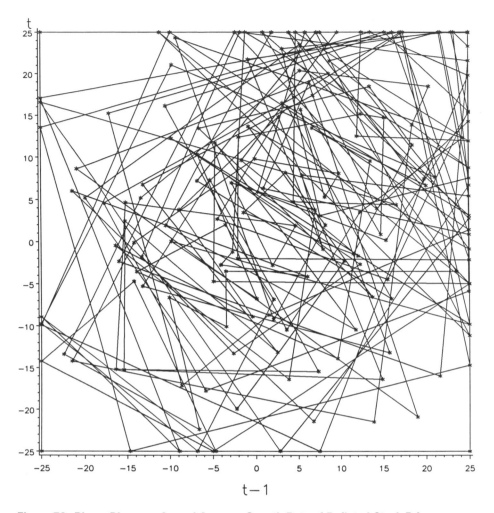

Figure 72. Phase Diagram: Annual Average Growth Rate of Deflated Stock Prices, 1790–1988

The wide dispersion in the phase space is further evidence of the extreme volatility of the stock market. It is only when ten-year moving averages are used to smooth the seesaw that signals of weak underlying rhythms appear, as in Figures 73 and 74. These extreme oscillations are undoubtedly the reason why J. A. Scheinkman and B. Le Baron's claim to have found weak evidence of chaos in their 1987 paper, "Nonlinear Dynamics and Stock Returns," failed to survive what Charles Dale (1989) terms the "NYU Meat Grinder" test. See Ramsey, Sayers, and Rothman (1988).

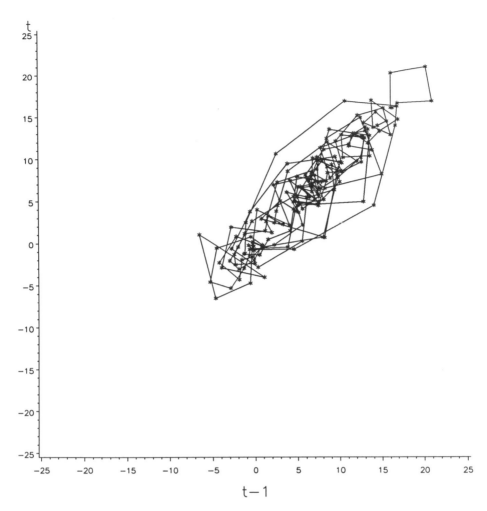

Figure 73. Phase Diagram: Ten-Year Moving Averages of the Growth Rates of Deflated Stock Prices, 1790–1988

Only when the ten-year moving averages are plotted in a phase diagram do the deflated stock prices appear to cycle along an acceleration-deceleration path similar to that of whole-sale prices. This suggests that the "strange attractor" is again that of a constant growth rate pushed by growth pressures into an acceleration-deceleration ratchet, in a system marked by extremely short-term as well as long-term boom and bustiness. To reiterate once again, however, this is a very weak signal in a very noisy environment.

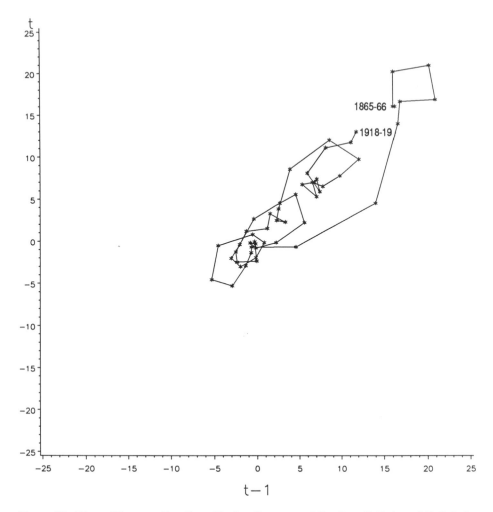

Figure 74. Phase Diagram: Ten-Year Moving Averages of the Growth Rates of Deflated Stock Prices, 1865–1919

Ten-year moving averages, traced in the phase space between two stagflation crises, show a similar pattern of behavior to that appearing in Figure 16, thereby supporting the idea that the weak Elliott Wave of *deflated* stock prices tracks Kondratiev price movements, with a similar collapse from maximum-acceleration peak to deflationary trough, followed by the gradual upward ratchet. But there are also well-defined inner loops that require closer examination.

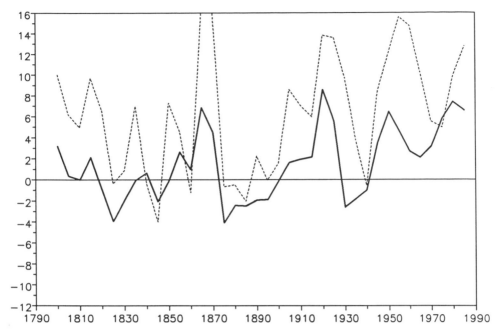

Figure 75. Ten-Year Moving Averages of the Annual Growth Rates of Deflated Stock Prices (*dotted lines*) Compared with Similar Averages of the Annual Growth Rates of U.S. Wholesale Prices (*solid lines*), 1790–1988

The weak consistency between Kondratiev waves and deflated stock-price movements provides the best available evidence for the existence of Elliott Waves, but the deflated Dow Jones stock averages show a supplementary rhythmicity that was first seen in the inner loops of Figure 74. By slicing the series into trough-to-trough segments and overlaying the segments, in the manner of Figures 21 and 43, we can isolate this rhythmicity.

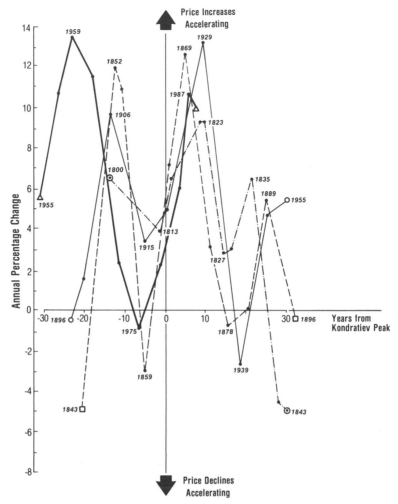

Figure 76. Depression-to-Depression Segments of the Ten-Year Moving Averages of the Stock-Price Growth Rates Superimposed at Stagflation Crises

What suddenly becomes clear is that we are dealing with *triplets* of "DJ Cycles" per Kondratiev wave: to the extent that the stock market has longer-term rhythmicity, admittedly weak, there is a three-cycles-per-Kondratiev-wave consistency. Strong bull markets accompany the acceleration phases of both the inflationary and deflationary growth cycles, and a lesser one tracks the secondary price recovery during the period of deflationary growth deceleration. Beginning in the trough of a depression, the long-term stock market averages accelerate to a turning point and decelerate to a trough in a first cycle that lasts approximately 18 years. A quick turnaround follows and the averages increase again, accelerating through and beyond the Kondratiev peak to another stock market peak-acceleration rate that occurs 8–10 years after the stagflation crisis. The market then crashes and the stock averages decelerate into the primary trough. There is a secondary recovery from that trough to another peak, a turnaround, and a slump into the next depression. The second cycle takes an average of 22 years and the third cycle perhaps 12. The triplet of stock market cycles—hereafter called DJ (Dow Jones) cycles—fits neatly into the 55-year depression-to-depression timing of the Kondratiev wave. Yet this rhythmicity should not be overstated; it is overwhelmed by the day-to-day reality of the wide oscillations and extreme volatility of the market.

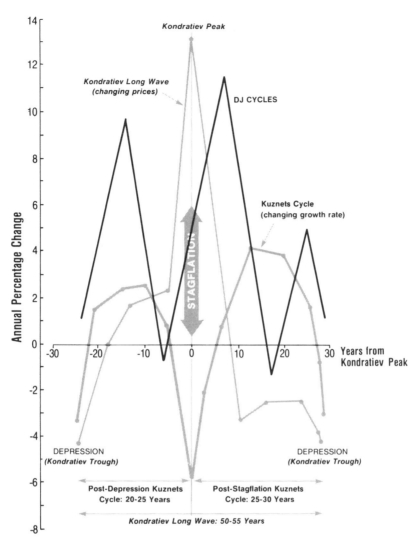

Figure 77. Kondratiev Waves, Kuznets Cycles, and DJ Cycles Superimposed at Stagflation Crises: A Schematic Summary

How are the weak DJ cycles, the Kondratiev waves, and the Kuznets cycles synchronized? What stands out in the schematics of Figure 77 is the synchronous acceleration of growth, prices, and DJ averages out of a Kondratiev-trough depression as a new long wave begins to unfold. The DJ acceleration is the first to peak, signaling a financial panic as the inflationary growth cycle peaks. The panic's end coincides with the DJ trough. Growth then decelerates and prices spiral into the Kondratiev stagflation crisis, but the DJ averages begin a long acceleration to a peak occurring 8–10 years after the crisis. This peak is followed by a stock market crash that initiates an era of decelerating averages to a primary trough. It is in this era that the deflationary growth cycle peaks. Next comes a decade-long secondary recovery of prices and DJ averages before growth, prices, and DJ averages all begin their synchronized slide into the next depression.

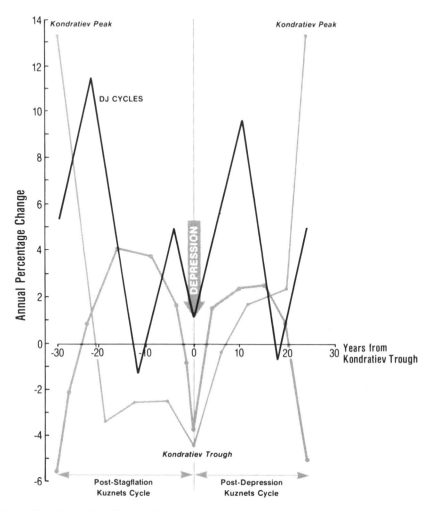

Figure 78. Kondratiev Waves, Kuznets Cycles, and DJ Cycles Superimposed at Depressions: A Schematic Summary

Figure 78 emphasizes this synchronization of the triple troughs in depressions and reveals that in contrast to the synchronization of economic, price, and DJ-average acceleration which occurs in an inflationary growth cycle following a depression, the period of deflationary growth acceleration is one of price deceleration and DJ-average acceleration:

- Within a Kondratiev wave, the peak of the first DJ cycle signals the financial crisis during which the inflationary growth cycle peaks, and the DJ trough signals the end of the crisis.

- The peak of the second DJ cycle and the following market crash signal the turnaround of the deflationary growth cycle in a primary recession. The DJ trough occurs at the end of that recession.

- The peak of the third DJ cycle signals the synchronized deceleration of growth, prices, and stock averages into a depression; the DJ averages are in a trough at the end of this depression.

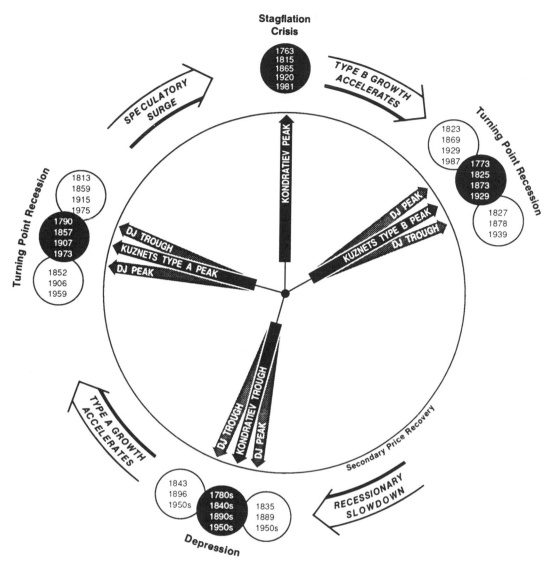

Figure 79. The Long-Wave Clock Showing Stock Market Signals

The whole may be summarized by adding the DJ-cycle peaks and troughs to the long-wave clock presented at the end of Chapter 5 (Figure 70). Each Kondratiev long (price) wave embraces two Kuznets (growth) cycles and a triplet of DJ (stock) cycles. DJ-cycle peaks signal peaks on the growth cycles (when turning-point recessions occur) and the end of secondary price recoveries before the plunge into the troughs of Kondratiev depressions (in which all three cycles are synchronized); DJ-cycle troughs occur at the end of the turning-point recessions and depressions. The weak, but repetitive, sequence of DJ cycles is, I submit, a better-founded view of the long-wave dynamic within an extremely noisy stock market than is the idea of a 55-year Elliott Wave. That, however, provides little solace for those who have invested heavily in the considerable superstructure of stock market numerology which has been erected upon that supposed foundation. There is one consolation. This new view eliminates from further consideration a literature that has more than its share of crackpot contributions.

CHAPTER 8

WHAT ABOUT CYCLES IN AMERICAN POLITICS AND THE TIMING OF CRITICAL ELECTIONS?

Enthusiastic long-wavers in political science argue that American political life also has seen recurring shifts that are consonant with the long wave. According to Joshua S. Goldstein, "Results from a number of research projects that search for 50-year cycles in war, foreign policy, and social values consistently support the presence of long waves at the level of society, and not just in economics" (*Long Cycles* [1988], p. 110). Among the rhythms that have been proposed are those of "mood cycles," alternations between public purpose and private interest, the timing of political realignments, and liberal-conservative transitions in the White House. It is easy to be turned off by these proposals. The claimed "results" are more often rhetorical than statistical, but the fact that active research communities exist is reason enough to examine these ideas. What I will attempt, therefore, is to evaluate the proposals in the context of the long-wave rhythms presented in Chapters 5 and 6, and to attach some strength of belief to the hypotheses that have been advanced concerning the relationships between economic development and political life.

Where do the *mood* cycles in America's involvement in world affairs hypothesized by Frank L. Klingberg in 1952 and reaffirmed by Jack E. Holmes in 1985 fit? Klingberg argues that a succession of introvert and extrovert public moods has dominated American foreign policy, constituting the "collective unconscious" that has shaped and limited government actions. During the extrovert phase, presidential leadership is widely supported, while during the introvert phase Congress reasserts its constitutional prerogatives. In extrovert periods (e.g., 1844–1871 and 1891–1919), the nation has been both willing and eager to bring its influence to bear on other nations, exerting direct military and diplomatic pressure to achieve its ends. In periods of introversion (1824–1844, 1871–1891, 1919–1940), the reaction to wars that comes at the end of an era of great bellicosity produces a collective unwillingness to become involved in foreign adventures and a desire to concentrate on internal problems. Klingberg's extrovert phases run from depressions to stagflation crises, and his introvert phases extend from stagflation crises to depressions, synchronized with Kondratiev "upwaves" and "downwaves." "Why these phases of around 25 years," Klingberg said in his 1983 book, *Cyclical Trends in American Foreign Policy Moods,* "should apply to the introvert-extrovert alternation . . . is not apparent. . . . it may be related to the 50-year long economic wave identified by . . . Kondratieff" (p. 20). Klingberg did not say how or why.

Support for the idea that extrovert-introvert switches accompany long-wave peaks comes from those who have examined *liberal-conservative transitions in the White House:* "Certain things that have happened in American politics do seem to bear a relationship to the long wave. . . . If we look at the Presidents who took office on the upswing side of each long-wave peak and were still President at the time of each peak war, we find three things: all were liberals; all were important in terms of what their administrations did or how their thinking influenced future generations; all were succeeded by conservatives" (Shuman and Rosenau, *The Kondratieff Wave* [1972], pp. 112–113):

> *Madison*   Elected 1808 and 1812; liberal; succeeded by *Monroe,* who was elected in 1816 and was conservative.
> *Lincoln*   Elected 1860 and 1864; liberal; succeeded by *Grant,* who was elected in 1868 and was conservative.
> *Wilson*   Elected 1912 and 1916; liberal; succeeded by *Harding,* who was elected in 1920 and was conservative.

Extending this view, Robert Beckman says in *The Downwave* (1983): "At the beginning of the upwave there is usually a shift from right wing to left wing politics. At the end of the upwave, there is a shift back to the right. . . . During the later stages of the upwave, there is a distinct tendency toward left wing politics. At the end of the upwave, the left is ousted and a right wing government usually takes over" (pp. 34ff.).

To Beckman, a City of London market analyst writing from a British perspective, the key to the interaction lies in mass psychology: as prices accelerate in the Kondratiev upwave but growth fails to keep up with rising expectations, there are increasing demands on government to satisfy both have-nots and special interests. Those who promise that the government will deliver are elected.

But in the end, even those who make the biggest promises cannot satisfy—or survive—the speculative mania. There is political disarray, and with the crash those who are in power are ousted in favor of more conservative leaders who act against inflation, and who try to reduce the role of government and encourage new investment and business expansion. Downwave politics move to the right until the depression hits. There is then a shift back to the left as calls for government action become more strident. The normal routines of party politics, Beckman says, are disrupted during both mania-and-crash and depression; it is at these times that the interjection of powerful new issues can lead to a reshaping of the parties. Indeed, it is only at such times that significant change occurs. As Anthony Trollope opined, "It is the necessary nature of a political party . . . to avoid, as long as it can be avoided, the consideration of any question which involves a great change." Great changes are precipitated by crises.

Another rationale for the nation's mood switches is offered by psychologist David C. McClelland in his book *Power: The Inner Experience* (1975). McClelland believes that three motives shape human behavior: the desire for *power* (to have status above, and to control, others), the desire for *achievement* (to accomplish measurable results), and the desire for *affiliation* (to acquire security via the affection and approval of others). During periods in which the need for power dominates the need for affiliation, people tend to be outwardly aggressive and competitive. The need for power produces a collective desire for strength, as manifested in charismatic leaders—empire-builders with a high propensity to lead the nation to war. This need for power dominates the need for affiliation in expansionary growth epochs. The need for affiliation dominates during periods of retrenchment, when people seek security. Activist presidents have been elected to power in extrovert periods. Much more passive presidents have been preferred by the electorate in introvert periods. (See, for additional insights, James David Barber, *The Presidential Character: Predicting Performance in the White House* [1977]).

What about the switching points? It is in the depths of depressions that religious revivalism and the reformist spirit that asserts itself in the upswing have jelled. It is at the heights of the speculative frenzy that inflation erodes personal wealth and the need for security reasserts itself. The strongest empirical support for these mood-cycle ideas is that of Holmes in 1985. Robert S. Erikson ("Economic Conditions and the Presidential Vote" [1989]) adds that the state of the economy and the electorate's evaluations of the candidates together but independently drive presidential election outcomes: the best predictor is the growth rate of per capita income.

Another idea, with another timing, is that of *alternations between public purpose* (the desire to better society) *and private interest* (the desire to better oneself), advanced by Arthur M. Schlesinger, Jr., in *The Cycles of American History* (1986). Public action, Schlesinger says, is impelled by the mystical vision of America as a nation of destiny. In an atmosphere of public morality, idealism, reform, and government action, it piles up a lot of change in short order, and consumes much of the society's psychic energy. But sustained public action is emotionally exhausting and frequently produces less than is promised. Disillusion follows. The body politic needs time to digest the innovations that have been introduced. People seek a period of rest and recuperation, wanting to immerse themselves in the privacies of life. Class and interest politics subside. Materialism takes over, and cultural politics (ethnicity, religion, social status, morality) come to the fore. An era of individualism follows, but in such an era not everyone succeeds. Some segments of the population fall behind in the acquisitive race. Neglected problems become acute. The priority of wealth over commonwealth nourishes a propensity to corruption in government. Intellectuals are estranged. People are weary of materialism and begin to look for meaning in life beyond themselves. Each public/private cycle, Schlesinger believes, lasts a generation. "Each swing of the cycle produced Presidents responsive to the national mood, some against their own inclination," he wrote (ibid., p. 32). He said he could not find any relationship to the Kondratiev wave, but this is understandable because what is clear from his examples is that his "generations" are synchronized with Kuznets cycles: private interest has prevailed in each Kuznets growth upswing; public purpose has come to the fore after the upswing peaks, as growth rates descend to a trough. There thus must be two alternations of public purpose and private interest per Kondratiev wave.

What is involved here is *cyclical change in social values,* according to J. Zvi Namenwirth's "Wheels of Time and the Interdependence of Value Change in America" (1973). Namenwirth argues that the long-wave upswing moves through *progressive* and *cosmopolitan* stages (roughly approximating the acceleration and deceleration phases of an inflationary Kuznets growth cycle), and that the long-wave downswing moves through *conservative* and *parochial* stages (approximating the acceleration and deceleration phases of a deflationary Kuznets growth cycle). The progressive-cosmopolitan and conservative-parochial shifts, coinciding with turning-point crises at Kuznets-cycle peaks, are from periods of growth acceleration to periods of deceleration. As the first of these shifts occurs, the agenda switches from economic growth to the extrovert use of power in global politics. The second shift is from individual enterprise to more introvert and parochial concerns for security and belonging.

A picture emerges of political behavior phased in lockstep with the synchronized Kondratiev-Kuznets rhythms of growth and prices. Growth accelerations are dominated by private interest and are either progressive in inflationary epochs or conservative when the prevailing environment is deflationary. Growth decelerations, dominated by public purpose, are either cosmopolitan in an inflationary environment or parochial when conditions are deflationary. Such hypothesized phasing is surely worthy of more analysis, for *if the arguments are valid, a powerful theory of the cyclical dynamics of the political economy is likely to emerge.* I find the prospect both exciting and challenging, but worry whether there can ever be more than rhetorical "proof."

The Concept of Critical Elections

One element of such a theory that has been researched by a succession of American political scientists is the notion of critical elections.[1] The idea was initially advanced by V. O. Key in 1955 in his article "A Theory of Critical Elections." In it he defined *critical elections* as "a type of election in which there occurs a sharp and durable electoral realignment between parties" brought about by a cross-cutting cleavage of national importance and scope (p. 16). Subsequently, Angus M. Campbell (1966) developed a broader, fourfold classification of elections ("maintaining," "deviating," and "reinstating," as well as "realigning"); Walter J. Burnham (*Critical Elections and the Mainsprings of American Politics* [1970]) pointed to the relationship between critical elections and major shifts in the public-policy agenda; James L. Sundquist (*Dynamics of the Party System* [1973]) suggested that the precipitating cleavage is usually a new one on the political agenda; and Jerome L. Clubb, William H. Flanigan, and Nancy H. Zingdale (*Partisan Realignment: Voters, Parties, and Government in American History* [1980]) developed the idea that a necessary precondition for realignment is progressive "dealignment," in which the existing parties provide insufficiently differentiated signals to prospective voters.

The most recent development has been to link policy shifts to the institutions most directly related to policymaking, Congress and the Supreme Court. Schmidhauser, for example, in *Constitutional Law in American Politics* (1984), explores the consequences of turning-point shifts in political attitudes for the conflicts that arise between the president and Congress on the one hand, and between the president and the Supreme Court on the other (since the Court is not ordinarily affected immediately by a transition of power and carries appointees selected by advocates of one set of policies long into the tenure of executives and legislators who advocate alternatives).

As yet no one has explored the relationship between the timing of critical elections and the rhythms of the long wave, however. This is what I will attempt here. I begin by drawing together the ideas of Key (1955), Burnham (1970), and Campbell (1966). What these authors argue is that in specific periods, the American electoral pattern has been dominated by particular political regimes, coalitions that operate the federal government and maintain their dominant positions through the development of distinctive institutional arrangements and approaches to policy questions. (See also Stephen Skowronek's "Presidential

---

1. I am indebted to Edward J. Harpham, Greg Thielemann, and Royce Hanson for helping me with this formulation.

Leadership in Political Time" [1984] and "Notes on the Presidency in the Political Order" [1986]). During these periods of hegemony, *maintaining elections* (in which the presidential candidate of the majority party is elected and the pattern of party alignment and strength continues unchanged) are the most common. At times of crisis, *deviating elections* occur; in these, the minority party gains power, but basic party alignment remains unchanged. Once the crisis passes, the majority party resumes control in a *reinstating election*.

Eras between realignments are thus seen as having their own party systems. *Critical elections*, however, bring about realignments in which voting behavior, institutional roles, and policy outputs undergo substantial modifications. At this kind of juncture it is not a matter of choice of one party over another; a fundamental reorganization takes place. The elections most commonly cited are those of 1800, 1828, 1860, 1896, and 1932. Once a stable pattern of voting behavior and generalized leadership recruitment has been reestablished after the realignment, it continues with only short-term deviations until the next period of stress and abrupt transformation. Critical realignments are thus associated with:

• short-lived but intense disruptions of traditional patterns of voting behavior.

• unusually high intensity in the party-nominating and platform-writing process, when accepted rules of the game are flouted, contributing to a sharpening of ideological polarization and leading to unusually high voter participation.

• remarkably uniform periodicity: "*it is sufficient to assert that this periodicity has an objective existence, that it is one of the most striking historically conditioned facts associated with the evolution of American electoral politics, and that it is of very great analytical importance*" (Burnham, *Critical Elections*, p. 8).

Critical elections arise when "politics as usual" cannot cope adequately with major societal and economic crises. Involving constitutional readjustments in the broadest sense of the term, they are intimately associated with and followed by transformations in large clusters of policies which produce correspondingly profound alternations in the grand institutional structures of American government. What results is a broadly repetitive pattern of oscillation between the normal inertia of mass electoral politics and the ruptures of the normal which realignments bring about. "One is led to suspect that the truly 'normal' structure of American electoral politics at the mass base is precisely this dynamic, even dialectic polarization between long-term inertia and concentrated bursts of change" (ibid., p. 27).

According to David W. Brady (*Critical Elections and Congressional Policy Making* [1988]), all realignments appear to have shared several elements in common:

1. The parties take polarized positions on the cross-cutting issues.

2. The election results are national.

3. There is majority control of Congress for at least a decade.

4. There are high degrees of committee turnover.

5. There is party-structured voting in Congress.

In my view, James L. Sundquist offers the most carefully crafted summary of the realignment process that takes place during these concentrated bursts of change. In his 1973 book, *Dynamics of the Party System,* he agreed that American political parties have great stability, resilience, and adaptability, and that an upheaval in the party system comes only when events generated in the society are strong enough to shatter the party system's characteristic inertia. Thus, he argued (pp. 275ff.):

1. A realignment is precipitated by the rise of a new political issue (or cluster of related issues).

2. To bring about a realignment, the new issue must be one that cuts across the existing line of party cleavage, and must also be powerful enough to dominate political debate and polarize the community.

3. The issue must be one on which the major political groups take distinct and opposing policy positions that are easily dramatized and understood. And even then, whether a new issue becomes dominant depends not only on its intrinsic power but also on the extent to which the older issues underlying the party system have faded with the passage of time.

4. Usually, the new issue is likely to have a greater inherent appeal to the voters of one of the major parties and thus is potentially more disruptive for that party than for the other.

5. The normal response of both major parties at the outset is to straddle the new issue, but within each of the parties there are at each pole political groups more concerned with victory for their position than with their party's electoral success. The polar forces coalesce most rapidly if the party out of power has the greater predisposition to the new issue. If both major parties persist in their straddle or come under the control of the polar forces opposing change, supporters of the new issue form a third party.

6. The realignment process is precipitated when the moderate centrists lose control of one or both of the major parties (i.e., of party policy and nominations) to one or the other of the polar forces. If the forces supporting the new issue gain control of a major party, realignment will be averted if they also capture control of the other party. In any other circumstance, however, the crisis precipitates a realignment.

7. The form of realignment is determined by the degree of difficulty of the new forces in gaining control of a major party. If control is gained early, a third party does not emerge. If later, after a third party has been formed, realignment may occur through absorption of the new party by one of the old ones,

or replacement of one of the existing parties by the third party. At the extreme, both existing parties can be replaced.

8. The realignment reaches its climax in one or more critical elections that center on the realigning issue and resolve it, but the realigning process may extend over a considerable period before and after the critical election.

9. After the critical elections(s), polarization gives way to conciliation, the parties move from the poles to the center, the distance between them narrows, and the country returns to "politics as usual." If new issues arise that coincide with the existing line of party cleavage, they strengthen party cohesion and reinforce the existing alignment. Change comes with the next significant cleavage-crossing issue.

What differentiates critical realignments from normal party succession, Sundquist said, is that a broader social and economic transformation is occurring to which the system of parties and politics responds. On the one hand, American electoral life has involved a succession of hegemonistic epochs of politics-as-usual in which the opposition party may briefly come to power. On the other hand, at regular intervals, critical elections have occurred in which the party system has been realigned.

Is the *timing* of these critical elections related to the rhythms of the long wave? Figure 80 provides insights:

- Whereas Kondratiev-peak stagflation crises have been marked by cosmopolitan (liberal)-conservative transitions within the framework of existing party cleavages (Madison-Monroe, Lincoln-Grant, Wilson-Harding), *critical elections have occurred in association with every other long-wave turning-point crisis or depression: 1825 (1828), 1840s, 1857 (1860), 1873, 1890s (1896), 1907, 1929 (1932), 1954, 1972–(?).*

- The critical elections of 1828 and 1932, which brought about Jacksonian democracy and the New Deal, occurred amidst the turning-point crises at the peaking of deflationary growth accelerations and the plunge of prices into a primary vortex. The 1932 turning-point crisis was, of course, converted into the Great Depression by a variety of ill-advised interventions.

- The critical elections of 1800 and 1860, which addressed issues of federalism and the survival of the Union, occurred during the turning-point crises associated with the peaking of inflationary growth accelerations.

- Kondratiev-trough deflationary depressions have been accompanied by one critical election, that of 1896, in which the Republican party restructured itself.

The appearance of critical realignments in every other Kuznets-peak or Kondratiev-trough crisis results in a realignment roughly once every 40 years. What appears to be involved is a generation of consolidation of the new hegemony following the realignment, a challenge (perhaps realized briefly via a deviating election) in the succeeding long wave crisis, and a generation of dealignment and

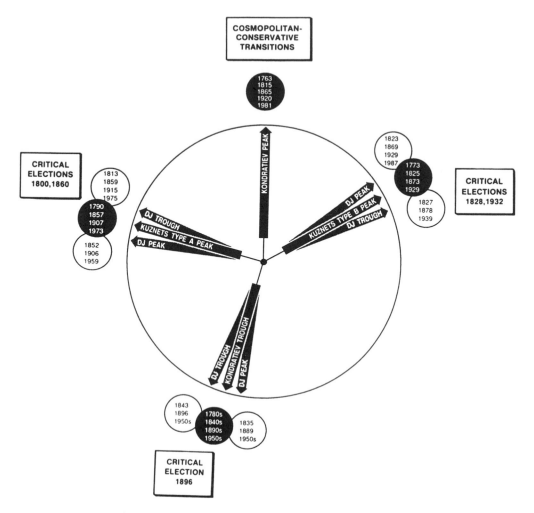

Figure 80. The Timing of Critical Elections

Critical elections involving a shift in hegemony have occurred toward the end of every other Kuznets turning-point crisis and deflationary depression. Each stagflation crisis has been accompanied by a cosmopolitan/conservative transition. Clear long-wave synchronicity is apparent.

sharpening party competition which is ended by the long-wave crisis that follows, when another cross-cutting issue provides the formula for restructuring the party system.

The critical election of 1896 came amidst a depression at the end of a long deflationary slowdown; a central issue in the political debate was gold. One might hypothesize that the coincidence of the democratizing critical elections of 1828 and 1932 in the turning-point crises of deflationary growth epochs arose from the growing *inequality and distress* that emerged during the preceding periods of deflationary growth acceleration. Similarly, it is possible to hypothesize that the coincidence of the critical elections of 1800 and 1860 in the turning-point crises of inflationary growth cycles involved questions of *power*—its distribution between federal and state governments, and between the executive and congressional branches. Deflationary growth cycles are driven by the supply side and favor entrepreneurs and innovators; when an economic crisis occurs amidst a disintegrating political hegemony, the reaction is to put into place institutions and programs that favor the underprivileged. Inflationary growth cycles are driven by demand and favor large-scale corporations and central government; when an economic crisis occurs amidst a disintegrating political hegemony, the reaction is to focus on government institutions, seeking to create structures capable of providing checks and balances to the excessive concentration of power that developed during the inflationary upwave. Andre Gunder Frank and Maria Fuentes agree with the first of these hypotheses, arguing that social movements espousing egalitarian ideals are stronger and more numerous in Kondratiev downwaves ("Social Movements in Recent World History" [1988]).

As noted earlier, inappropriate interventions quickly turned the 1929–1930 turning point into the deepest deflationary depression in U.S. history, and, indeed, the 1932 realignment and the policy response of the New Deal had characteristics in common with the realignments of 1896 and 1828. One side of the New Deal was concerned with economic inequality, just as the 1828 realignment had focused on political inequality. The other side involved issues of the collapse of prices and the need for reflation, just as a prime concern in 1896 had been gold. Major gold discoveries helped spark the post-1896 recovery; another source of "gold"—Keynesian deficit spending—took over after 1932.

The every-other-crisis timing suggests that another realignment should have occurred in the mid-1970s. There has been much disagreement as to whether a realignment began under Nixon. Dealignment of Roosevelt's coalition was already well under way. It had begun with the Dixiecrat rebellion in the Democratic Party and the ensuing alliance between the Republican Party and the Southern Democrats, reinforced by the Kennedy-Johnson era of civil rights. When reelected in 1972, Nixon was able to extend the electoral appeal of the Republican Party to white Southerners, to the growing numbers of upwardly mobile suburban voters, and, by appealing to patriotism and latent racism, to blue-collar workers. With his call for a New Federalism, the stage seemed set for another realignment; many Southern senators and congressmen were ready to switch parties when the Watergate affair occurred and Nixon was forced to resign.

In "Political Gridlock" (1988), Walter Dean Burnham concluded that "instead of a completed revolution, we got a bastard mix of old interest-group liberalism—with all the entitlements and transfer payments it has imbricated in the budget—and a really perverse kind of right-wing macro-Keynesianism that has lifted budget deficits to the stratosphere." I disagree with this interpretation. Although delayed until the "Reagan Revolution" brought it to full fruition, the realignment that began with the critical election of 1972, like the realignments of 1800 and 1860, centered on the role of government and the division of powers, although the recasting of the role of the parties took a new and unfamiliar form.

Some would argue that since the New Deal, politics has had less and less to do with economics and progressively more to do with social issues, and that "party" has become less salient as a determinant of voting behavior—that political parties have ceased to exist as viable elements of governance. Contrariwise, I believe that the realignment begun by Nixon, reinforced by the disastrous Carter interlude and completed by Reagan, resulted in a *national* (Republican) *presidential party* with hegemonistic control of the White House and the executive branch of government and a *local* (Democratic) *congressional party* which, via the power of special-interest-financed incumbency, maintains hegemonistic control of the legislative branch of government. The key issues involved in this realignment were those of power—the size of the federal government, and the centralization or decentralization of authority and responsibility. The resultant restructuring has brought new meaning to the system of checks and balances between the executive and legislative branches, typified no more vividly than in the contest over the proposal to appoint Robert Bork to the Supreme Court. It also has led to a shorter-term partisan cyclicality (Alberto Alesina and Howard Rosenthal, "Partisan Cycles in Congressional Elections and the Macroeconomy" [1989]). In presidential elections voters choose between two polarized candidates, but use midterm elections to counterbalance the president's policies by strengthening the opposition in Congress. (Somewhat tongue in cheek, Robert Erikson argues that it is now in the best interest of the Democrats for them to lose presidential elections, because this guarantees their control of Congress; see "Economic Conditions and the Presidential Vote" [1989]). Apparently in confirmation of a completed realignment, the Bush/Dukakis race of 1988 was, in Dukakis's words, "about competence, not ideology." In keeping with Sundquist's ninth stage, George Bush has pursued the politics of conciliation as opinions converge on such issues as pollution, drugs, and crime.

I see clear relationships of political cycles and realignments to the long-wave rhythms summarized in Chapters 5 and 6. As Calvin Jillson notes in his 1988 paper, "The Intellectual Context of Critical Realignment and Governmental Response," the American political system responds to the problems posed by economic and social development by instituting new systems of policy. Jillson sees the response occurring on several distinct but interrelated levels:

1. Broad adjustments at the constitutional level set the structure, tone, and character of American national politics. Periods of reform have been episodic since the Revolution, separating three distinct constitutional epochs: the first, that of the "Politics of Democratization"; the second, that of the "Politics of

Party Competition" extending from the 1840s to the 1890s; and the third, that of the "Politics of Interest-group Liberalism," which has been under severe pressure since the 1970s (Samuel Huntington, *American Politics* [1981]). The major reform episodes were those of 1776, 1828, and 1896.

2. Within these constitutional epochs, partisan struggle for control of political institutions has been subject to development and change, producing realignments in the relations of social forces and political institutions. The major mid-epoch realignments occurred in 1800, 1860, and 1932.

3. Halfway into each realignment period, a mid-sequence adjustment produces two distinct phases of roughly equal length, most clearly distinguished by the presence or absence of consistent control of national political institutions by the major party. Psychological, social, and economic tensions in the individual and in the patterns of association within which the individual is enmeshed lead to different types of "politically relevant change" in each of these phases. New generations, in particular, break partisan continuity between the past and the future and force changes in the policy agenda (Paul Beck, "A Socialization Theory of Political Realignment" [1974]). The process begins after a mid-sequence adjustment, as the dominant party loses its grip. A period of unstable, competitive, two-party politics begins as a rising generation emerges with alternative aspirations. The second phase comes after a realignment or a deviating election, when a political party that succeeds in capturing the rising generation's concerns comes to power and exacts its policy agenda (Daniel Elazar, "The Generational Rhythm of American Politics" [1976]).

What Jillson's phasing of political change lacks is the trigger of economic crisis. Periods of stable economic change are also phases in which American politics has a distinctive character. Phase-shifts in politics coincide with economic crises. Each crisis is marked by a deviating election. Every other crisis involves a realignment. Every other realignment separates constitutional epochs. In their turn, the political phase-shifts produce the distinctive institutional arrangements and approaches to policy questions that ratify and reinforce the new direction of economic change. The circle is complete.

CHAPTER 9

CYCLES OF WAR AND WORLD LEADERSHIP

KONDRATIEV WAVES AS WAR CYCLES

We are not finished with the world of political science. At least two groups of students of international relations believe that recurrent major wars are central to the long wave, although there is disagreement about cause and effect. The most comprehensive recent treatment of war cycles is that of Joshua Goldstein in *Long Cycles: Prosperity and War in the Modern Age* (1988). Confirming the 1941 investigations of econometrician Harold T. Davis, Goldstein concludes (after a great deal of statistical analysis) that an escalatory great-power war upswing recurs roughly every 50–55 years, coinciding with the Kondratiev upswing; that the upturn in price increases precedes major wars; and that there is a one-to-one correspondence between war peaks and long-wave price peaks. He says that great-power wars "apparently play a central role in the economic long wave, especially in connection with inflationary periods on long wave upswings" (p. 411).

Beckman agrees, saying in *The Downwave* (1983): "Each upwave produces two major wars, one at the beginning and one at the end. . . . The long-wave tendencies govern war-like attitudes" (pp. 29–32). Vincent Tarascio reaches similar conclusions in "Economic and War Cycles" (1989): "What emerges is a remarkable pattern of wars occurring at the beginning and later stage of the expansionary phase of the long wave. . . . we may tentatively agree with Kondratieff that wars are not the consequences of blind social and economic forces, but patterned according to long economic cycles" (p. 100). Trough wars help in the recovery from depression; peak wars add to the runaway inflation that terminates the upwave. All of the most pronounced instances of inflation have occurred during or shortly after great wars. Trough wars are short, decisive, and easily financed when commodity prices and interest rates have just bottomed out; peak wars last longer than predicted, have indecisive results, carry a high price tag in terms of lives and money, spur inflation via massive deficit spending, and engender countervailing attitudes in the postwar period. During major war periods, consumption rises and production falls, and demand moves out ahead of supply to push up prices. The inflationary jolt becomes globalized in prolonged wars involving the world's major powers. "War is a symptom of the social and economic pressures which build up in the system. . . . Wars at the end of the upwave are due in part to the same social tensions associated with hyperactivity during high inflation, generating exceptionally strong emotions. Wars at the early stage of the upwave are far less popular and are more or less accepted as a *fait accompli* by the electorate" (Beckman, p. 29). "In the years before the peak, tensions build with the excitement of prosperity. The great issues that develop are both national and international" (Nathan Mager, *The Kondratieff Wave,* pp. 50–51). Deep-seated passions and pent-up repressions gush out in an emotional peak, a national catharsis. People seem unable to cope with mounting complications of life as the long-wave peak approaches; they have no stamina for keeping up with the accelerated rate of change. Peak wars start with a crusader fervor. Trough wars, on the other hand, are taken in stride; depression forces people to be predominantly concerned with their own well-being (ibid.; see also David McClelland, *Power: The Inner Experience*).

GLOBAL WARS AND CYCLES OF WORLD LEADERSHIP

The idea of a cycle of major wars that is synchronous with the Kondratiev wave appeared most forcefully in the work of Quincy Wright, whose 1942 book, *A Study of War,* occupies a position in the war-cycle literature similar to that of Kondratiev's works with respect to long waves of prices. Wright dated major concentrations of international warfare at 1701–1714, 1756–1763, 1795–1815, 1853–1856 and 1914–1918. His idea of great-power war cycles has been taken one step further by two different groups of scholars, in both cases largely rhetorically. The question that is raised is whether the behavior of nation-states tends to recur in specific phases. One school of thought rests on George Modelski's theory of long cycles of world leadership,[1] the other on Immanuel Wallerstein's four-phased cycle of hegemony/rivalry in the world system.[2]

---

1. Typical of the world-leadership-school literature are George Modelski's "The Long Cycle of Global Politics and the Nation-State" (1978), "Long Cycles, Kondratieffs, and Alternating Innova-

The World-Leadership School

According to advocates of the world-leadership idea, every other 55-year concentration of war has been a much more severe period of global war. These periods alternate with less severe war concentrations, making an approximately 115-year cycle in all. According to historian Arnold J. Toynbee, this cycle of war, spanning two Kondratiev waves, has been repeated five times since 1494 (*The Study of History* [1954]).

Modelski associates the double-Kondratiev pattern with the rise and decline of "world leaders"—nations with predominantly *global-reach capabilities* (primarily naval power until the twentieth century) which maintain the international political and social order. It is this global reach, Modelski says, that displays periodicity: long waves emerged along with the modern world system around the year 1500. According to Modelski, the first phase, *global war,* occurs at intervals of roughly a century. Out of these devastating struggles between major contenders for global dominance, a single state emerges as the provider of security and the manager of internal economic relations. During the second, *world-power* phase, there is a tight relationship between the dominant power's economic capabilities and military power, and that power reaps the fruits of its ascendancy. As memories of war fade, contenders emerge, and *delegitimization* takes place. *Imperial overstretch* occurs as the dominant power discovers that its global commitments exceed the capability of its economic system to support them. The dominant state comes under attack; nationalistic reaction to great-power dominance emerges and "intermediate warfare" develops. In the next phase, that of *deconcentration,* the dominant power retrenches and the system

---

tions: Implications for U.S. Foreign Policy" (1981), "Long Cycles of World Leadership" (1983), and *Exploring Long Cycles* (1987). See also George A. Raymond and Charles W. Kegley, Jr., "Long Cycles and Internationalized Civil War" (1987). An associated idea is that of the "dominant economy," developed by François Perroux in "Outline of a Theory of the Dominant Economy" (1948). In "From Hegemony to Competition: Cycles at the Core?" (1980), Nicole Bosquet suggests that long cycles arise because innovations promote productive superiority in a core country—Dutch shipbuilding and sea transport, British textiles, mining, and mechanization, and U.S. management superiority in the mass production of automobiles, aircraft, electronics, and computers.

2. Works by Immanuel Wallerstein: *The Modern World-System: Capitalist Agriculture and the Origins of the European World-Economy in the Sixteenth Century* (1974), *The Modern World-System: Mercantilism and the Consolidation of the European World-Economy* (1980), and "The Three Instances of Hegemony in the History of the Capitalist World Economy" (1984). Wallerstein's formulation rests heavily upon Lenin's theory of imperialism: V. I. Lenin, *Imperialism: The Highest Stage of Capitalism.* See also R. Värynen, "Economic Cycles, Power Transitions, Political Management, and Wars between Major Powers" (1983); Terrence K. Hopkins, Immanuel Wallerstein, et al., "Cyclical Rhythms and Secular Trends in the Capitalist World-Economy" (1982); and Albert Bergeson and Ronald Schoenberg, "Long Waves of Colonial Expansion and Contraction, 1415–1969" (1980). The crucial relationship of economic to military power as it affects the rise and fall of empires is the subject of Paul Kennedy's recent treatise *The Rise and Fall of the Great Powers* (1987). William R. Thompson discusses the difference between Modelski's and Wallerstein's "world-system time" in "The World Economy, the Long Cycle, and the Questions of World-System Time" (1983).

Table 4. Modelski's Phases of "Global-Reach Capabilities"

Global War	World Power	Delegitimation	Deconcentration
Portuguese Cycle: 1491–1516 Italian and Indian Ocean Wars	1516–1539 Portugal	1540–1560	1560–1580 Spain, France, and England
Dutch Cycle: 1580–1609 Spanish-Dutch Wars	1609–1639 Netherlands	1640–1660	1660–1688 France, England
First British Cycle: 1688–1713 Wars of Louis XIV	1714–1739 Britain I	1740–1763	1764–1792 France, Spain, Netherlands, Russia
Second British Cycle: 1792–1815 Wars of French Revolution and Napoleon	1815–1849 Britain II	1850–1873	1874–1914 France, Russia, Germany, United States
American Cycle: 1914–1945 World Wars I & II	1945–1973 United States	1973–2000	2000–2030 Soviet Union, Japan

shifts to multipolarity; rivalries intensify among established and aspirant world powers and ultimately erupt into another *global war,* beginning another cycle. The whole sequence takes two Kondratiev waves.

Modelski suggests that different types of war are associated with the different phases of world leadership. When a world power is dominant, wars represent interventions to preserve its concept of global order; the role is that of the policeman. In a period of deconcentration, wars may be instigated by contending powers to enhance their world position. In Modelski's view, the modern world system has gone through five complete cycles since the Italian Wars of 1494–1516. The cyclical phases of global-reach capabilities that he asserts are presented in Table 4.

Figure 81 is a rendering of Modelski's long cycles of global power. In Figure 82 I have attempted a schematic synthesis, overlaying Modelski's five hypothesized cycles of world leadership since the late fifteenth century on pairs of Kondratiev price waves, and these on pairs of Kuznets growth cycles—rhythms within rhythms within rhythms—extending the Kondratiev-Kuznets synthesis presented in Chapter 5. Whether I believe the extension is correct is another matter. Goldstein does: "Superficially, the long wave is an economic phenomenon and the hegemony cycle is a political one. But in fact the long wave contains

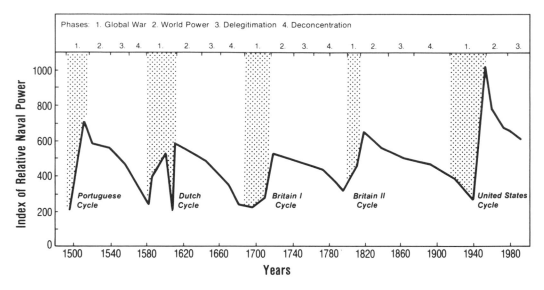

Figure 81. Modelski's Long Cycles of Global Power

key political elements (war plays a central role), and the hegemony cycle contains economic elements (economic hegemony and competition)" (*Long Cycles*, p. 7). "Growth creates the economic surplus required to sustain major wars among core powers. But these large-scale wars drain surplus and disrupt long-term economic growth" (ibid., pp. 15–16). Goldstein dates the ten Kondratiev waves he says have unfolded since the late fifteenth century as follows:

Trough	Peak	Trough	Trough	Peak	Trough
—		1509	1747	1762	1790
1509	1529	1539	1790	1814	1848
1539	1559	1575	1848	1872	1893
1575	1595	1621	1893	1917	1940
1621	1650	1689	1940	1968	—
1689	1720	1747			

This dating scheme is taken from Fernand Braudel and Frank C. Spooner, "Prices in Europe from 1450 to 1750" (1967); and Andre Gunder Frank, *World Accumulation, 1492–1789* (1978). Gaston Imbert identifies five earlier long waves (from 1268 to 1510) in *Des mouvements de longue durée Kondratieff* (1959), apparently giving lie to Modelski's idea that long waves did not appear until the emergence of the modern capitalist world system in the sixteenth century.

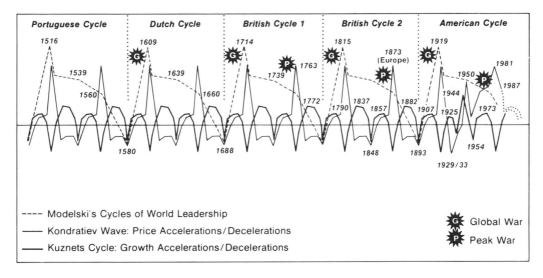

Figure 82. World-Leadership Cycles and the Kondratiev/Kuznets Rhythms

The World-Systems School

A central concept of Wallerstein's world-systems school is that each cycle of world power involves structural shifts in the nature of capitalism. Like Modelski, Wallerstein believes that the 115-year cycles of double Kondratievs are rooted in the rise and decline of hegemonic powers, but as befits his Marxian underpinnings, he believes that this pattern is rooted in the economic foundations of the expanding system of world capitalism. Wallerstein's view is that capitalist world-economies have emerged centered on core states that achieve productive, commercial, and financial superiority over their rivals and that exercise hegemonic control over weaker states in the periphery. But hegemony is difficult to maintain: innovations diffuse, competitors develop, and the costs of maintaining global order frequently rise more rapidly than the economic power of the state that must pay them. Wallerstein's phases (which will surely be familiar to those who have read Paul Kennedy's *Rise and Fall of the Great Powers* [1987]) are thus those of *ascending hegemony* as core states expand economically and compete to achieve dominance, *hegemonic victory* when a new hegemon eclipses the old, *hegemonic maturity* as the new hegemon establishes itself as the core of a new world order and exercises its productive, commercial, and financial superiority, and *declining hegemony* as conflict breaks out between the hegemon and its potential successors. In Wallerstein's view, three full cycles have unfolded since the United Provinces revolted against Philip II of Spain, and he offers the summary of paired Kondratievs and hegemony/rivalry shown in Table 5.

Table 5. Wallerstein's Cycles of Global Hegemony

Hegemonic power	I: Dorsal spine (Hapsburgs)	II: Netherlands (United Provinces)	III: Great Britain	IV: United States
A ascending hegemony	1450–	1575–1590	1798–1815	1897–1913/1920
B hegemonic victory		1590–1620	1815–1850	1913/1920–1945
A hegemonic maturity	–1559	1620–1650	1850–1873	1945–1967
B declining hegemony	1559–1575	1650–1672	1873–1897	1967–(?)

Source: Terence K. Hopkins, Immanuel Wallerstein, et al., "Cyclical Rhythms and Trends of the Capitalist World-Economy," in *World-System Analysis: Theory and Methodology*, ed. Hopkins, Wallerstein, et al. (Beverly Hills, Calif.: Sage Publications, 1982), p. 18.

BACK TO RHYTHMS WITHIN RHYTHMS: THE CYCLE OF WAR

I return now to the question of whether long waves are impelled by an internal dynamic or, as Marxists argue, have external causes. The literature abounds with rhetorical flourishes, and the arguments are at best cavalier. Is war a cause of the long wave, or is it internally generated as part of the long-wave dynamic? Kondratiev believed the latter. This viewpoint is also supported by Thompson and Zuk, who, in "War, Inflation, and the Kondratieff Long Wave" (1982), found that, at least for Britain and the United States, price upswings resulting from raw-materials shortages and resource contention preceded major wars, rather than the converse. Major wars come, they say, toward the end of the price upswing, contributing an abrupt and temporary impact that ends in the downswing, producing the extreme inflationary "spikes" that were so apparent in the earlier graphs. Alvin Hansen had stated this idea earlier, in *Economic Stabilization in an Unbalanced World* (1932): "Nations do not fight wars after prolonged periods of depression. . . . In periods of long-wave upswing war chests are accumulated, navies are built, and armies are equipped and trained. . . . it is the long-wave upswing that produces favorable conditions for the waging of wars" (pp. 96–97). In a similar vein, Rose argues that war is an innovative force that creates new potential for economic growth from the demands of warfare and reconstruction. Postwar demand dissipates, leading to a depression. With depression, conditions become ripe for a new cluster of innovations, which gives rise to new military programs, a new upswing, and more war ("Wars, Innovations, and Long Cycles: A Brief Comment" [1941]).

The countervailing view was that of Trotsky, who asserted that external conditions such as wars determine alternating periods in the development of capitalism (Värynen, "Economic Cycles, Power Transitions, Political Management, and Wars between Major Powers" [1983]). In Trotsky's view, world capitalism is separated historically and qualitatively into distinct stages by crises such as war, rather than being an internally regenerated sequence of cyclical upswings and downturns. Norman J. Silberling, in *The Dynamics of Business* (1943), and J. Akerman, in *Ekonomisk Teori* (1944), also have argued that wars introduce major inflationary shocks to the world economy, and that these shocks produce the long wave of prices. Their view was initially supported by Goldstein, who concluded quite boldly in *Long Cycles* (p. 252) that his analysis demonstrates significant causality from war to prices, but not vice versa, since 1790. But Goldstein then went on to develop a more elaborate long-wave theory, which begins with an idealized sequence of events in what he calls "cycle time" (Figure 83). From this, he adduces two-way causality between war and production: a sustained rise in production supports an upturn in great-power war, but increased

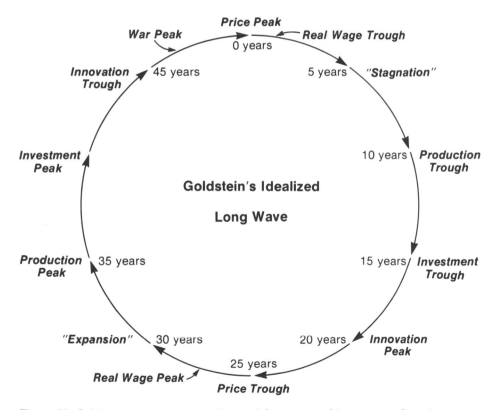

Figure 83. Goldstein's Idealized Long Wave of Sequences of Investment, Growth, Inflation, and Wars, in "Cycle Time"

war contributes to a downturn in production growth; economic stagnation curtails war severity, but low war severity contributes to the resumption of sustained economic growth. The sequence takes 50 years to complete. Prices are among the secondary variables that react to the relationship of growth and war, lagging behind production by 10–15 years and peaking most sharply in the severest war. So are innovation (which Goldstein says varies inversely with production), investment (which is disrupted by war), and real wages (which vary inversely with prices).

Much as I like some sections of Goldstein's work, I cannot accept this Kondratiev-phased war-production hypothesis. As I demonstrated earlier, production oscillates with Kuznets, not Kondratiev, periodicity, a rhythmicity that Goldstein did not explore. Erring on this, Goldstein's central two-way causality is wrong as hypothesized, because prices and production do not vary synchronously. His seemingly attractive theory thus fails, as Kuznets would have predicted.

Goldstein's model also lacks a central driving force. He appears to rely on Quincy Wright's view that psychological and economic factors embedded within an international system which continually tends toward war explain war cycles: "Fluctuations in the intensity of war . . . tend to assume a definite periodicity if the international system exerts a persistent pressure toward war and if the economic and technological period necessary to recover from a severe war and to prepare for another is identical with the psychological and political period necessary to efface the anti-war sentiment after such a war and to restore national morale" (*A Study of War*, p. 231).

I must admit to being deeply troubled by this notion of innate bellicosity as the central driving force in the international system. If it is true, the prognosis for long-run survival of our civilization is not good. Yet the idea remains central to the work of both the leadership-cycle and world-systems schools. The world-systems school, with its Marxist leanings, sees hegemony rooted in an economic system that requires external forces to reshape it as it lapses into periodic crises. In a more complex view, Modelski argues that economy and polity have autonomous rhythms. Kondratiev waves are embedded in a world-leadership cycle which brings global wars during every other Kondratiev upswing, synchronous with Arnold Toynbee's 115-year cycle of war. What Modelski believes is at work is the "counterplay of alternating innovations," the endogenous outcomes of a "deep structure":

1. There are alternating periods of resource abundance and resource scarcity, as evidenced by the long waves of prices.

2. Waves of political problems and political innovations coincide with problems of resource scarcity, bringing the reordering of political structures and the rise of new regimes, states, world powers, and international organizations. Wars—particularly global wars—are most frequently initiated by newly de-

veloping powers as they challenge the hegemon for supremacy. But this can come about only in the deconcentration phase of hegemonic power. During a deconcentration Kondratiev, the upswing phase of a Type A/Inflationary Kuznets cycle brings competition for markets, resources, and strategic territory, as well as the long-term prosperity that supports higher military expenditures and arms races. It is also in such phases that aggressive, expansionist psychological moods are at work.

3. Economic innovations tend to move toward fruition in periods of relative abundance when prices are on the downswing, finding embodiment in new leading sectors that drive economic growth.

4. The global polity and the world economy thus advance in counterposed rhythms, but political processes preponderate in each second phase of price upswing, leading to the establishment of a new world power.

5. Overall, political and economic processes appear to act as a synchronized but contrapuntal movement, evidence of one underlying deep structure.

KONDRATIEV WAVES AND WORLD POWER: THE "DEEPER STRUCTURE"

What are the facts? I have no evidence for cycles longer than the Kondratiev wave save the suggestions of Wright and Toynbee, Modelski and Wallerstein, and the empirical work of Goldstein, and much of their "proof" has been rhetorical. If the rhetoric is to be believed,

• Major periods of global warfare have broken out in the speculative growth phase of inflationary Kuznets cycles, when contention for control of scarce resources is at its maximum, when aggressive upwave attitudes turn expansionary, when concern for the national interest comes to the fore, and when funds are available to build up the armed forces. During such periods, there is frequently a turn toward charismatic political leadership. Adventures turn into crusades backed by moralistic fervor.

• Alternating periods of upwave warfare see the ascendancy of a leading economic power established in one Kondratiev wave, and the legitimacy of its hegemony challenged in the next. In the first wave, succession to leadership enables the hegemon to structure the world's economic and political order. In the second, that structure is fragmented by the growth of rivals; the world becomes polycentric and prone to global warfare.

• Each successive hegemon has been able to translate the power derived from technological advances in one Kondratiev wave into superior power derived from superior economic growth in the next. Both growth and power result from technological superiority: each successive hegemon has been the one with the highest rates of technical progress during the preceding hegemon's period of dominance. But power, once achieved, is the enemy of progress: maintenance of order encourages stasis, not change. It is those who are without power—who do not control existing resources and means of production—who must become innovative to succeed, inventing new ways of doing business that require new resources that are not under the hegemon's watchful eye.

- The controlling factors appear to be the speculatory epoch of resource contention in the Kondratiev upwave and the timing of the next rounds of growth that enable competitors to emerge. Thus, structured from the bottom up by Kondratiev-Kuznets relationships, the world-leadership cycle of *necessity* lasts for at least two Kondratiev waves. The British experience suggests that a hegemon that remains innovative should be able to maintain its world-leadership position for a longer span of time; the critical variable is the rate of technical progress and its translation into superior economic power.

That the "proof" of such a deeper structure is rhetorical, not evidentiary, needs to be re-emphasized. A majority of historians, I conjecture, would react to the above ideas on a scale somewhere between extreme unease and outright rejection, and would prefer that I place the discussion among the mirages and myths to which Chapter 10 will be devoted.

THE STARS OR THE GENES?
IMAGES OF PREDESTINATION

With so many groups asserting that so many phenomena display Kondratiev-wave rhythmicity, but lacking a theory to explain why, the mystics and the determinists have been in their element. Predestination is as big a business today as it has been in historic religions. When individuals sense that they are unable to control the forces that affect their lives, they seek solace in an opiate. If the previous chapters seemed to traverse shifting sands, this one drifts into hallucinogenic smoke. Bear with me: there are people out there who smoke the weed! We should learn to spot their hallucinations. I deal with what they have to say not because I believe it, but because the existence of such mirages must be acknowledged. The myths must be confronted and set aside if the long-wave idea is to achieve credibility.

A 52-year long wave would not have surprised the ancient Maya. They lived in a world defined by two cycles of time. One was the *tzolkin*, a sacred almanac of 260 days which used 20 day names, each prefixed with a number from 1 to 13. The other was a 365-day civil calendar composed of 18 months (20 days each) plus a final 5-day segment, the inevitably evil *nayeb*. When the two calendars were meshed, each day was specified in terms of its day name and number and its month name and position; a particular day so specified could repeat only once every 18,980 days—that is, every 52 years. The 52-year cycle was known as the *calendar round*. It served as the basis of a rigorous system of predestination: all events were believed to be linked to particular named time periods. Mayan astronomer-priests monitored the passage of time, predicted untoward futures, and recommended the appropriate rituals and sacrifices to propitiate the gods. Their world was cyclical, repetitive, and predestined; all shorter-term cycles were embedded within the calendar round.

The Maya were not alone. The life-rhythms of most early civilizations were guided by astronomer-priests, and 50-year cycles were common. The great astronomical clock at Stonehenge, for example, has an outer ring of 56 Aubrey holes. And even today there are those who are comforted by the certainty of predestination and who turn to cosmology to explain long cycles. The ideas of Hindu guru P. D. Sarkar, leader of the Ananda Marg cult, banned in India for its extremism, were the underpinning of best-selling economist Ravi Batra's prediction of another Great Depression in 1990! How many of you read your horoscope in the newspaper each day? I find it astounding that consultation of astrologers occurs today, even at "the highest levels of government," in societies that espouse big science. What price cognitive dissonance?

THE STARS: CLIMATIC CYCLES AS CAUSE

Among the determinists are those who seek external causes for long waves in natural phenomena, particularly in solar-system dynamics, extending the logic of biorhythms, day and night, monthly hormonal shifts, and seasonality to higher orders of fluctuation.

As early as 1927, Dewey and Dakin asserted (in *Cycles: The Science of Prediction*) that there was a relationship between the 11.14-year sunspot cycle and the 11-year Juglar business cycle (Figure 84). This thesis has been repeated by other climatic determinists—for example, by Michael Zahorchak in *Climate: The Key to Understanding Business Cycles . . . The Raymond H. Wheeler Papers* (1983). Most recently, in *Sun—Earth—Man* (1989) and other publications, Theodor Landscheidt has suggested a relationship between climatic variation and impulses in the torque of the sun's motion. (For a good review of sun-weather relationships see John R. Herman and Richard A. Goldberg, *Sun, Weather, and Climate* [1978]).

Grant Noble is typical of the stock market numerologists who have picked up on Zahorchak's idea, arguing that the sunspot cycle is the basis of cycles of the Fibonacci derivatives of 11.14: 22.28, 33.42, 55.7, 89.12, 144.82, 233.94, etc. (*The Ultimate Dow Top* [1988]), and that these are the apparent periodicities in Raymond Wheeler's famous "Drought Clock" (Figure 85). Parenthetically, the 11-22-33-55 Fibonacci series was also the basis of Ralph N. Elliott's asserted relationship between five 11-year Juglar cycles and a 55-year "supercycle" (discussed in Chapter 7; see Frost and Prechter, *The Elliott Wave Principle* [1985]).

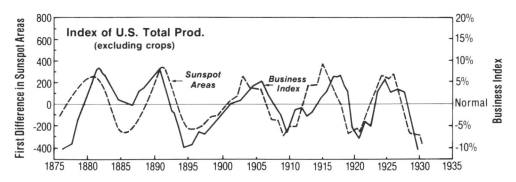

Figure 84. Dewey and Dakin's Correlation of the 11.14-year Sunspot Cycle and the 11-year Juglar Business Cycles, 1875–1930

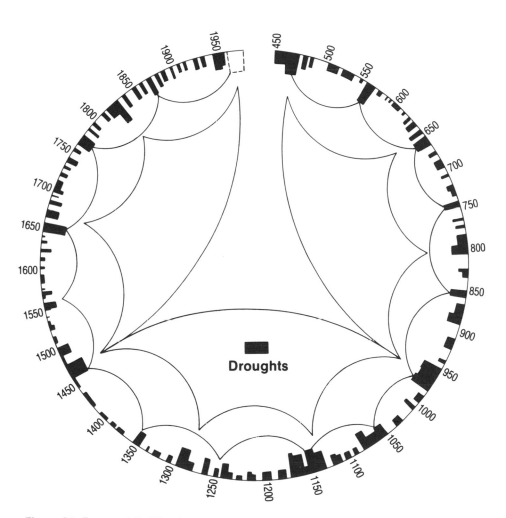

Figure 85. Raymond H. Wheeler's "Drought Clock"

Numerology soon degenerates into astrology and mysticism. A single quotation should suffice: "It appears that the origin of these rhythmic cycles and their phase reversals is of solar system origin and may be related to the rhythmic movements of the planets Uranus and Saturn relative to each other and to the Sun" (L. Peter Cogan, *The Rhythmic Cycles of Optimism and Pessimism* [1969], p. 43). Whoopee!

Other leaps from solar rhythms to human affairs are no less abrupt. Wheeler said, in a manner reminiscent of the advocates of the world-leadership cycle, that his 100-year climatic cycle should actually be viewed as pairs of Kondratiev waves composed of four quarter-century-long building blocks of climatic history: warm-wet, warm-dry, cold-wet, cold-dry. The first "K-wave," he said, has always been a warm-weather phenomenon, divided into a warm-wet upswing and a warm-dry downswing. The second K-wave occupies the cold half of the century, alternating between a cold-wet upswing and a cold-dry downswing. Reflecting broad climatic conditioning, the wet-weather upswings are times of prosperity, but the warm-wet upswing is longer, more vigorous, and more prosperous than the cold-wet upswing. Dry-weather downswings are times of depression, the warm-dry downswing being shorter and more intense than the cold-dry downswing. Of the two waves of prosperity, Wheeler asserted that the first has been associated with nation-building and imperialism, the second with the decline of great powers and the trend back toward pluralism. Of the two waves of depression, the first comes when "centralizing trends reach a climax economically and politically." The second is associated with economic collapse "during periods of inadequate government and trends toward anarchy and chaos" (Zahorchak, *Climate . . . The Raymond H. Wheeler Papers*, pp. 191, 237ff.). The world-leadership advocates call Wheeler's ideas "crackpot."

More recently, the sunspot-weather correlation has received firmer empirical support (Richard A. Kerr, "Sunspot-Weather Correlation Found" [1987], citing Karin Labitzke, "Sunspots, the QBO, and the Stratospheric Temperature in the North Polar Region" [1987]). Some scholars, however, argue that the drought cycle is 22 rather than 11 years—the solar magnetic cycle in which the sunspot number peaks twice but the magnetic polarity of the sunspots reverses once (Roger Lewin, "Relax, the Sun Is Brightening Again" [1988]).

Others see not simply the sun at work but also the moon. They argue that the 22-year solar cycle accounts for only 10 percent of the variance of the drought record, and that a bigger signal within an admittedly noisy record is accounted for by the moon's 18.6-year cycle of changing declination, during which its maximum height in the sky varies by twenty of its diameters, significantly affecting atmospheric tidal accelerations (Richard A. Kerr, "The Moon Influences Western U.S. Drought" [1984]). Dewey and Dakin (*Cycles*, pp. 115ff.) feature an 18-year rhythm associated with the rhythm of real estate activity. In *Building Cycles and the Theory of Investment* (1940) Clarence D. Long, Jr., says that "the cycles vary over time [and] in each locality there is great variability [but] long cycles do appear in all cities and the agreement in the turning points of these cycles is surprisingly high, especially with respect to the troughs" (pp. 145–149).

An 18.6-year cycle yields the Fibonacci derivatives 37.2, 55.8, 93.0, 148.8, etc. The maximum coincidence of the sunspot and the lunar derivatives occurs in a cycle of 55.7/55.8 years. The lunar and solar cycles were close to being superposed in 1934, amidst the severe and widespread drought of the 1930s. The previous superpositions were in 1878, 1822, and 1766. The most recent near-superposition occurred in 1989, amidst a drought of a severity not seen since the 1930s.

Each of the recent 55-year drought episodes has arrived during the downturn following a stagflation crisis (Figure 86), helping push the economy toward recession via the effects in agriculture, an especially vulnerable sector with multiple linkages to the rest of the economic system. ("Perhaps," John Kenneth Galbraith said of 1929, "trouble was transmitted to the economy as a whole from some weak sector like agriculture" [*The Great Crash, 1929*, p. 181]). The correlation between long-wave phasing and the drought cycle is far from perfect, however, and I am not persuaded by climatic determinism, even though climatic cycles may have been the cause of long waves of agricultural output and prices

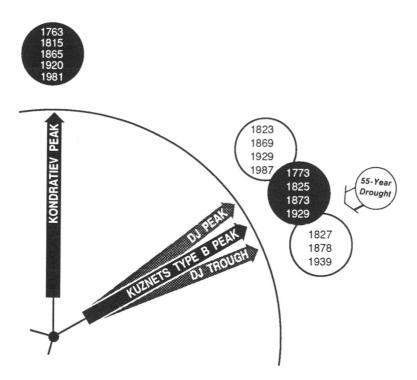

Figure 86. Recurrent Drought Episodes Repeat during the Same Phase on the Long-Wave Clock

in preindustrial societies. Recall that Lord Beveridge suggested that there had been 50-year long waves in English grain prices at least as far back as the fifteenth century. Joshua Goldstein says that a 50-year weather cycle in the preindustrial period could have affected harvests, hence economic surplus, and hence also the capacity to wage war.

Yet I must admit to some unease because there do appear to be drought-downwave correlations, and I even toyed with one proposition: that the intertwined economic and political processes that produce the long wave maintain their rhythmicity because during the synchronous descent of prices, growth, and stocks into depressions, the economic system is given a regular "nudge" by the 55-year cycle of droughts at a juncture that further depresses an already depressed agricultural economy. Such a nudge would not have to be large—just enough to establish direction. This would explain the continuity of long waves of prices throughout the past five centuries, despite the replacement of an agrarian by an urban-industrial society. It would also help explain why social and economic processes that have no inherent tendency toward 55-year oscillations are drawn back to fluctuations of that frequency after they have drifted away. The drought cycle could be the metronome. Far-wiser heads than mine ask whether a series as noisy as that of drought is capable of exciting such regular discipline, however. Absent a better sense of mechanism, the speculation must remain just that. After all, we're drifting in that hallucinogenic haze, and it may have made me see mirages too! Thank heavens, sometimes, for the naysayers' antidotes to speculation.

THE GENES: LONG WAVES AS MASS PSYCHOLOGICAL PHENOMENA

In *The Downwave* (1983) (and again in *Into the Upwave* [1988]) Robert Beckman advances a Shakespearean theory of long waves predicated not on external forces but on a deeper endogeneity. ("The fault, dear Brutus, is not in our stars but in ourselves.") "The causes," Beckman says, "lie deep within the psyche of our human race. We can look at inflation, wars, political trends, speculative manias, etc., but these are not causes. They are the effects of mass psychological phenomena involving long term swings of pessimism and optimism that occur in short term rhythmical patterns within a longer term rhythmical pattern and within a still longer term rhythmical pattern, like wheels and circles in a spiral" (*The Downwave*, pp. 46–47). His description of upwaves, manias, downwaves, and depressions is worth a brief review because, as in so many analogous formulations, there is enough that sounds familiar to give the whole idea seeming credibility, but Beckman, too, may have been hallucinating.

"Upwave" Characteristics

Upwaves, says Beckman, begin in depressions, when confidence is at its nadir. They are "up" waves because they are periods in which both prices and growth increase after their long slide into the depression. The initial impetus is often a "trough war," which starts the adrenaline flowing again. Expectations rise as the economy becomes more prosperous, and rise again with the transition to a peacetime economy. Attitudes shift from fear to optimism. People become willing to assume more risk, and as prosperity increases they become more outgoing and gregarious.

Mass psychology is at work: attitudes and behavior diffuse and intensify. Progressively, a consumer mentality comes to dominate. Fashion, music, literature, theater, and dance all fall under the influence of the upwave. There is greater hedonism and a quest for pleasure, leisure, and freedom of individual expression. As the upswing progresses further, liberty becomes self-indulgent license. Clothing becomes extreme, even bizarre. Sex life turns libertarian.

With continuing expansion, economy and society are primed for an inflationary orgy. A generation learns that wealth can be acquired by debt. A nouveau riche emerges, wealthy from speculative gains. Beckman argues that the upwave spans a period of psychological desolation to a period of excessive optimism, covering the full spectrum of people's greed and fear.

Manias: Speculative Bubbles That Burst

Excessive optimism turns to greed when speculative profits are to be made, fed by an expansion of bank credit that enlarges the money supply—easy money that encourages people to speculate beyond their means in an atmosphere of accelerating inflation. Credit produces demand for goods or financial assets that are in short supply; prices increase and produce new profit opportunities, drawing in new investors. Positive feedback drives an upward price spiral: investment increases incomes, higher incomes increase investment, further investment increases incomes. Feverish speculation ensues; there is a manic desire to "get rich quick," as Charles P. Kindleberger shows in *Manias, Panics, and Crashes* (1978). He says (p. 28) that manias and panics are associated with general irrationality and mob psychology—with hysteria, with bandwagon effects, as documented so graphically in Charles MacKay's *Memoirs of Extraordinary Delusions and the Madness of Crowds* (1932) (an account of the South Sea Bubble of 1720) and John Carswell's *The South Sea Bubble* (1960).

The impending bursting of the bubble is sensed by insiders who become queasy about get-rich-quick schemes and decide to take their profits and withdraw. As others follow, a rush for liquidity begins, and the prices of assets—goods, securities, land—drop. As the asset base falls, both individuals and firms are unable to cover their liabilities. Frequently, the crisis is signaled by the failure of an overextended bank or the revelation of a swindle. The bubble bursts, bank failures multiply, and a general panic ensues.

"Downwave" Behavior

As the bubble bursts, greed turns to fear, and the crowd seeks security. A downwave begins "following the interaction of several unsustainable phenomena: the effect of war, a surge in prices, a speculative bubble, over-expansion by industry, and profligate monetary policy," and the "world is turned upside down" (Beckman, *The Downwave,* p. 67). Optimism turns to pessimism, conservatism to parochialism. Security rather than risk becomes the order of the day. After the panics and banking failures, risk-taking subsides, investment slackens, and the economy slows down.

From Recession to Depression

Recession turns to depression when slowdown becomes a self-reinforcing downward spiral: lack of investment means cutbacks, unemployment, loss of income, falling demand, and reduction of investment opportunities (Theodore E. Burton, *Financial Crises and Periods of Industrial and Commercial Depression* [1910]). As the vortex pulls the economy downward, mass bankruptcies in industry occur, capital markets collapse, and land and property values steadily decline. Businessmen respond to the profit and price squeeze by cutting wages and attempting to reduce competition (Kindleberger, *Manias, Panics, and Crashes*).

Those who find it difficult to cope with circumstances that appear to be beyond their control look for someone to blame. These are years of "devil" theories: someone or something must be blamed. Some turn to religion for solace: an underlying American religiosity surfaced in the millenarian, anti-papist, and social reform movements of the 1840s, 1890s, and 1920s, as it has in the evangelical Christian upsurge of the 1970s, 1980s, and early 1990s. Michael Barkun reports that of 270 utopian communities founded in the United States between 1787 and 1919, one-third were started in two 7-year-long concentrations, 1842–1848 and 1894–1900, in conjunction with millenarian movements ("Communal Societies as Cyclical Phenomena" [1984]). Each of the movements jelled in a period of depression, but the resulting religious revivals contributed to the mood shift in the subsequent upswing (Walter Dean Burnham, "The 1980 Earthquake: Realignment, Reaction, or What?" [1981]). Both prices and growth bottom out in a depression, but the vortex spins too far, and a basis is laid for the next upsurge.

In Beckman's view, upwave liberalism and downwave conservatism are mass psychological phenomena arising from deeply lodged optimism-pessimism swings. To C. H. Powers ("Pareto's Theory of Society" [1981], cited by Robert Philip Weber, "Cyclical Theories of Crisis in the World-System" [1983]), the liberal-conservative cycle instead arises straightforwardly from a relationship between belief systems and productivity:

1. The greater the rate of increase in productivity, the more likely are increasing complexity of life and of experiences to bring traditional beliefs into conflict with actual experience, with the result that belief orientations become more innovative.

2. The more innovative the belief orientations, the more likely are investment and the consumption of available resources to increase and savings to decline,

reducing the potential for capital accumulation, with the result that productivity can be expected to decline.

3. The more pronounced the decline in productivity, the fewer are the opportunities for personal advancement and the more likely are innovative orientations to come into conflict with actual experience, with the result that beliefs become more traditional in orientation.

4. The more traditional the beliefs, the less likely the investment of available resources in productive activities and the greater the volume of savings, increasing the potential for capital accumulation, with the result that productivity can be expected to increase.

I could go on—there's much more out there in the haze—but I suspect that the marginal returns from further exploration turned negative some time ago. One thing is clear: there are lots of "long wavers" who believe that the rhythms have external causes and that we are therefore predestined to repeat history. I should not be numbered among those determinists. I believe that we first demonstrated our ability to modify these rhythms during the New Deal. I believe that we have an even greater opportunity to craft alternatives today. Therefore, in Chapters 11 and 12 I will turn from analysis and theory to an assessment of where we are now and where we might be heading—both if the doomsayers who see another Great Depression ahead are correct, and if we use the potentialities of the information age to craft alternative futures capable of carrying us into new rounds of growth and development that are free of the periodic crises of the past.

CHAPTER 11

WHAT TIME IS IT NOW?

On schedule in 1981, amidst a stagflation crisis, a conservative U.S. president replaced one who was more liberal. Signaling that transition, Ronald Reagan promised tax cuts, a reduction in the role of government, a return to the spirit of enterprise, and a reaffirmation of traditional American values. With the economy on its knees, drastic intervention by the Federal Reserve brought down inflation, turning upwave mania into downwave disinflation, and then, by reducing interest rates, enabled a new investment-and-profit cycle to take off, spurred by deficit-spending military Keynesianism. What followed was an epoch of disinflationary growth acceleration marked by a high rate of technical progress, the recovery of real profits, and an accompanying bull market (Figure 87). The Reagan Era seems destined to take its place among similar growth epochs in the nation's history.

The end of the epoch was signaled by the stock market crash of October 19, 1987. That crash came at a time when the 55-year drought was bearing down severely on the nation's grain-producing regions, presaging the slowdown of growth and pressures for a secondary price recovery which appeared in 1989. New venture-capital commitments peaked at $5 billion in 1987, but dropped to $2 billion in 1988. Amidst the incipient turning point phase, the election of 1988 reaffirmed the political realignment that had begun to take shape in

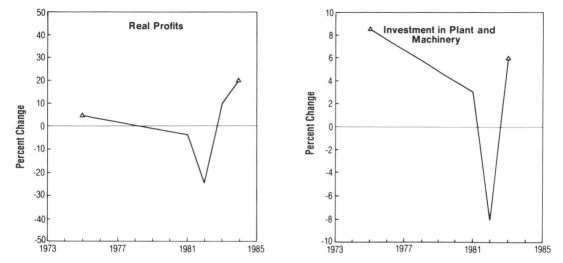

Figure 87. Real Profits and Investment in Plant and Machinery, 1974–1984

Adapted from *The Economist,* March 24, 1985, p. 24, this illustration reveals the economy's long slowdown from the turning-point crisis of 1973, its collapse during the stagflation crisis, and its subsequent recovery.

1972, conforming to the expectation that critical elections occur in every other growth-peak crisis or deflationary depression. A Republican president was safely returned to the White House, but Democrat majorities were returned to the House and Senate in elections in which more than 98 percent of the incumbents seeking to retain their seats were reelected, supported by abundant special-interest financing.

If we chart these events on the long-wave clock, as in Figure 88, we see that they have occurred in phase and on time, adding fuel to the doomsayers' assertions that a crisis cannot be far behind. Before accepting such a prognosis, however, it behooves us to delve more deeply into what actually unfolded in the 1980s, because the transition provides important insights into what has been programmed to emerge in the 1990s, and what degrees of freedom might be available to create alternative futures in the twenty-first century.

THE 1980s TRANSITION

During the 1980s, a technology transformation that was already unfolding in the U.S. economy was reinforced and brought to full realization, marking the end of the mass-production Kondratiev. This transformation changed the

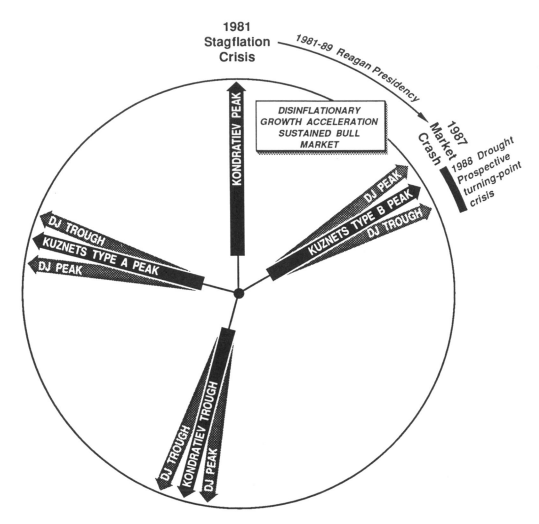

Figure 88. Political and Economic Events of the Last Decade Appear to Be "in Phase" on the Long-Wave Clock

economy from one in which employment growth is dominated by manufacturing to one in which the principal sources of new employment are in service production and the management of information. A diverse bundle of advanced service industries emerged as the economy's leading sectors, some devoted to intermediate rather than final outputs, many knowledge-based, and all divided between different private, public, and nonprofit settings:

Industrial Corporations, Publishing, and Transportation	*Specialized Technical and Business Service Firms*	*Public and Not-for-Profit Organizations*
Corporate headquarters	Law	Federal agencies
Research and development	Engineering	State agencies
Regional offices	Accounting	Universities
Computer centers	Finance	Musical arts
Training centers	Advertising	Hospitals and clinics
	Public relations	Cancer centers
	Insurance	Professional associations
	Seminars	Federal Reserve bank
	Communications	Museums
	Airlines	Consultants
	Consultants	
	Business information	

A similar transition in favor of knowledge-based high-technology manufacturing occurred, resulting in a new hierarchy of manufacturing enterprises:

High-technology: Production of goods that require much research and development or that employ many technically trained personnel (scientists and engineers).

Capital-intensive: Production of goods that require a high proportion of capital to labor.

Labor-intensive: Production of goods that require a high proportion of labor to capital.

Resource-intensive: Production of goods that require an intensive use of raw materials.

Foundations for the Transition

Between 1960 and 1980, employment in traditional services had already increased from 32.1 percent to 34.0 percent of the U.S. labor force, but in knowledge-based services the jump was from 23.8 percent to 33.0 percent. In the same two decades, the change in value added and employment by the four industry groups was:

Industry Group	Value Added (%)	Employment (%)
High-technology	+40.7	+22.2
Capital-intensive	−15.6	− 3.4
Labor-intensive	− 7.7	− 9.5
Resource-intensive	−17.9	−13.0

Accompanying these shifts were changes in the mix of occupations:

Occupation	Growth, 1960–1980 (%)
Professional and technical	+49.0
Managers	+39.0
Clerical	+31.4
Service	+19.4
Craft work	− 5.2
Sales	−10.1
Laborers	−11.4
Operatives	−24.8

As the occupational mix changed, so, between 1960 and 1975, did the distribution of earnings. Relative to the top and the bottom of the distribution, the middle class shrank:

Earnings Class (% of average earnings)	Distribution of Total U.S. Labor Force, 1960 and 1975 (%)		Increase in Jobs in Services, 1960–1975	
	1960	1975	No. of Jobs Added (in thousands)	%
120 and above	31.6	34.2	7,171	35.0
119 to 80	35.9	27.8	2,311	11.2
79 or below	32.5	38.0	10,034	53.8
Total	100.0	100.0	20,516	100.0

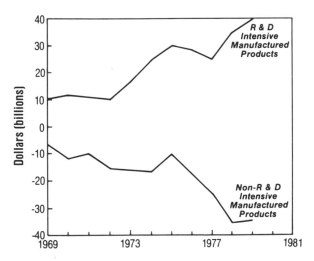

Figure 89. U.S. Trade Balance in R&D-intensive and Non-R&D-intensive Products, 1968–1980

The sources for this figure are *Science Indicators, 1980*; and Joan Spero, "Barriers to U.S. Services Trade," statement before the Subcommittee on International Finance and Monetary Policy of the Senate Committee on Banking, Housing, and Urban Affairs, November 1981.

Already, then, by the onset of the Reagan Era, the shift to a *knowledge-based information society* was well under way. The technology succession was from agriculture, mining, and mature manufacturing industries as principal sources of new employment to the knowledge-based economy of high-technology manufacturing, producer services, nonprofits, and the government at one extreme, and low-skill, minimum-wage employment at the other. It was from blue-collar and craft jobs to white-collar, professional, and technical occupations at the top and "fast food" service industries at the bottom, and it pushed the nation's income distribution toward the extremes, increasing inequality since there was relative shrinkage of the middle class. As the succession unfolded, the U.S. trade balance shifted, especially during the late 1970s, from non-R&D-intensive manufactured goods to those that are R&D-intensive (Figure 89). The foundations were laid for the new-growth epoch of the 1980s.

The 1981 stagflation crisis brought the economy to its knees, but then another investment-and-profit cycle began. As Lawrence R. Klein (1988) has shown, the expected upwave-downwave shifts in productivity and labor costs occurred:

Annual Percentage Changes in:	1973–1979	1978–1986	1985
Hourly compensation	9.5	6.4	5.3
Output per hour	1.4	3.5	5.1
Unit labor costs	8.0	2.8	0.2

The country was primed for another growth epoch embodying a high rate of technical progress.

Growth of the Venture-Capital Industry

Growth in this epoch was quarterbacked by an emergent venture-capital industry, itself a major organizational innovation that has revolutionized the process of technological change. Venture-backed firms are especially prominent in the fields of semiconductors, personal computers, CAD-CAM, software, and artificial intelligence. Of particular importance is "photonics"—the field concerned with the gathering, transmission, and processing of speech, data, pictures, and other information by means of light, and with the four key related areas of telecommunications: information processing, optical storage and display, and optical sensors. A second arena, but one that has been slower to emerge because of the longer lead times required for its development, is biotechnology—the science of manipulating the information contained in the genetic code to produce recombinant DNA.

Many of these growth directions reflect the priorities built into military research and development and procurement and the spinoffs from them (Figure 90). Just as World War II speeded the development of the transistor and the integrated circuit, which in the ensuing years gave the United States a massive lead in microelectronics-based industries, there is immense spillover potential in

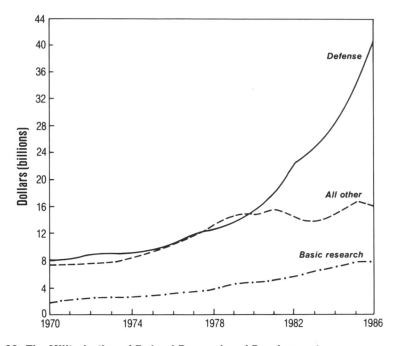

Figure 90. The Militarization of Federal Research and Development
Defense priorities played a major role in shaping the Reagan-era technology transition, as military research and development came to dominate basic research.

the telecommunications that enhance the power and instantaneous nature of global communications; in lasers; in software engineering, which is routinizing the programmers' art into system-production technology; in parallel supercomputing, which is permitting major advances to be made in such fields as artificial intelligence; and in the modeling and simulation of complex systems, a process that enriches the long-term view and provides enhanced hands-on experience in experimenting with social interventions. These military-funded advances are central to the design of the integrated network systems that are, in turn, the keys to the evolving development of information technology.

The growth of the venture-capital industry can be seen in the dramatic increase in capital committed annually by the industry's limited partnerships:

Year	Millions of Dollars
1978	216
1980	661
1984	3,185
1987	5,000

By 1988, approximately $20 billion was under commitment by the 61 most active venture-capital firms in an industry composed of 505 firms: 270 limited partnerships, 50 subsidiaries of financial institutions, 45 subsidiaries of industrial firms, and 140 small-business investment companies. The total industry commitment was $31 billion. However, as noted, new commitments peaked at $5 billion in 1987 and dropped to $2 billion in 1988 as returns dropped and an industry shakeout began.

Consistent with Joseph Schumpeter's theory, the venture-capital industry has financed a new burst of innovation, but has put into place a different context in which that innovation occurs. Gone is the old dichotomy between individual entrepreneurs who episodically launch new products, generating bandwagon effects in waves of innovation that create new industries, and the continuously managed research and development that takes place within large corporations. Today, the large corporations and universities establish the necessary scientific and technological context, functioning as incubators for technological change, but the small entrepreneurial companies exploit and commercialize the technological opportunities. The interplay is facilitated by transfers of personnel and exchanges of information, and by professional relations among manufacturers, suppliers, and vendors, with venture capitalists sitting at the center of the resulting innovation networks, actively fostering the interconnection. These venture capitalists serve as *technological gatekeepers*, setting the direction of technical change by their choices of what and what not to support, because *once a cluster of innovations is set in motion and a set of dominant designs is achieved, sociotechnical constraints are created that limit and guide further technological progress, squeezing out alternatives.*

Such a technological squeeze occurred in the 1980s as another of Schumpeter's clusters of innovations was put into place. The next growth surge will reflect the work of this cluster—the knowledge-based technologies—acting as gatekeeper and pushing the systems that are under active development toward market saturation. Whether better knowledge also means that the surge will be less prone to excessive overshoot remains to be seen. The possibility of a stabler growth path is there. It remains for the community of venture capitalists to curb their speculative appetites by building the likelihood of overshoot and the consequences of collapse into their screening process.

Three distinct types of venture-capital complexes have grown:

1. *Technology-oriented complexes,* which exist around concentrations of high-technology business, the outstanding case being San Francisco/Silicon Valley, with $5.3 billion of venture capital committed in 1985. Local venture capitalists invest locally and attract funds from elsewhere.

2. *Finance-oriented complexes*—for example, New York and Chicago, with $3.3 billion and $800 million committed, respectively, in 1985. These are organized around concentrations of financial institutions and tend to be capital exporters.

3. *Hybrid complexes,* which combine finance- and technology-oriented venturing. Major examples include Massachusetts and Connecticut, with $2.85 billion committed in 1985; Texas, with $775 million committed; and Minneapolis, with $380 million.

The kinds of funds that have become available have varied, with each kind having its accompanying funding specialists:

1. Early-Stage Financing
   a. Seed financing: a relatively small amount of capital provided to an investor or entrepreneur to prove a concept. It may involve product development, but rarely involves initial marketing. This kind of investment is sometimes referred to as "adventure financing."
   b. Start-up financing: used for product development and initial marketing. Firms may be in the process of organizing or have been in existence for only a short time (usually less than one year).
   c. First-stage financing: for companies that have expended their initial capital and require funds to initiate commercial production and sales.

2. Expansion Financing
   a. Second-stage financing: provides working capital for the initial expansion of a firm that is producing and shipping and has growing accounts receivable and inventories. The firm may not yet be showing a profit.
   b. Third-stage financing: allows for the major expansion of a growing firm that is breaking even or is profitable. These funds are utilized for plant expansion, marketing, working capital, or further product development.
   c. Fourth-stage (bridge) financing: for a company expecting to go public or to be bought out within six months to one year.

3. Acquisition/Management Buyout Financing
   a. Management-leveraged buyout: funds to permit operating management to acquire a firm or division for the purpose of entrepreneurial expansion.
   b. Acquisition.

Venture capitalists reduce investment uncertainty through careful screening of business proposals and by playing an active role in the management of portfolio companies. The use of equity investment instead of debt eliminates the problem of scheduled repayment. It allows young companies to reinvest their earnings and provides an asset base that can be used to attract outside capital and enhance a company's credibility with financial institutions. Equity financing enables venture capitalists to assume substantial risk over the longer term since one real success can offset a series of break-even investments or outright losses. Of the 526 investments made by the 10 largest venture-capital funds between 1972 and 1983, 56 successes generated half of the value held in portfolio, while 266 broke even or lost money (Florida and Kenney 1987a, 1987b, 1988). The problem is that this leads to the temptation to push new ideas to the limits of market saturation, producing periodic overload and industry shakeout, such as now appears to be the case. On the one hand, it might be argued that shakeouts increase efficiency. On the other hand, the result is the periodic economic crisis. If one of the benefits of the new information society is to cause venture capitalists to curb the worst of their speculative excesses, both they and society at large will benefit, for the consequence will be a stabler path of growth.

Unfortunately, as G. W. F. Hegel (1770–1831) said so cogently in the introduction to his *Philosophy of History,* "What experience and history teach is . . . that people and governments never have learned anything from history, or acted on principles deduced from it." Perhaps software engineering, artificial intelligence, telecommunications, and lasers will provide the information technologies that are needed to break the cycles of overshoot and collapse, and thereby ensure stabler growth in the years to come. But if they do, people and governments will have to learn from history and act on one principle that may be deduced from it: long-wave rhythms will continue as long as the cycle of speculative frenzy, overshoot, and collapse continues—that is, as long as individual greed produces the "boom and bustiness" that deflects the inherent tendency of the economic system to seek a stable path of long-term growth.

CHAPTER 12

WHAT LIES AHEAD?
IS THERE FREEDOM TO CHOOSE?

Do we really have this freedom to choose? We were once faced with a dialectic. At one extreme there was the doomsayers' notion of a completely determined periodic system in which we are predestined to live through the long wave time and again, phase by phase. At the other extreme there were the implications of the idea of a random walk: the belief that nothing is predictable, because a multiplicity of idiosyncratic forces is at work, and that individual choice is therefore irrelevant to social outcomes. Today, however, there is a third possibility, suggested by the idea of deterministic chaos—the theory that while underlying mechanisms do exist, rapid and unexpected state changes are possible, and thus, predictability and therefore choice exist only within bounds.

I reject the traditional bipolar extremes. Instead, Pollyanna-ish, I accept the notion that there are technological imperatives that carry with them both a modicum of predictability and unknown consequences that are akin to chaotic jumps. Because there is uncertainty, we both overshoot and undershoot in the search for stable growth. Within the bounds of the imperatives, we have been able to introduce policies that have modified the rhythms of overshoot and collapse. The New Deal safety net raised the floor of the price cycle. Institutions such as the Federal Reserve stabilized the path of growth. Yet we can do more. New technologies provide us with the potential to reduce uncertainty, and thereby help us to perfect markets by perfecting information about the future consequences of present and contemplated commitments.

If we realize this potential, the future is far from bleak. The cycle of overshoot and collapse will continue only if we fail to learn from history. We must begin to use the new information technologies to better inform our choices and thereby to modify investor behavior.

TECHNOLOGICAL IMPERATIVES

Actually, writes another Pollyanna, Peter Hall, in *The Carrier Wave: New Information Technology and the Geography of Information, 1846–2003* (1988), what is unfolding is a logical outgrowth of several "critical technological chains" that evolved in three successive Kondratiev waves. Those technological chains were:

1. Invention of the *telegraph* (1837–1839). Aided by innovation of the undersea cable, the telegraph created an important industry that made the railroads and steamships more efficient and effective.

2. Innovation of *electrical generating and transmission systems* (1870–1890). Diffusion entailing the development of local, regional, and national networks required the development and imposition of uniform technical standards. Invention of the *telephone* (1876), plus its associated switching systems and exchanges. Invention of *office machines* (typewriter, phonograph, duplicating machine, accounting machine) (1870–1890). Invention of the *radio* (1904–1906), although the organizational innovation of broadcasting did not come until the 1920s.

3. Key *electronics* innovations (sound films, television, FM radio, xerography, high-fidelity recording, radar, the computer) (1935–1948). After 1950, these innovations produced major consumer-goods industries and producer-goods industries for both commercial and military applications.

Each of these clusters of innovations occurred in a deflationary growth cycle such as has recently occurred. Each produced significant growth in the succeeding inflationary growth cycle of the type that is likely to occur early in the next century if events progress in phase according to the long-wave clock. The result in each case, Hall argues, was not a swarm of individual innovations, Schumpeter style, but chains of related inventions ('technology systems') that stemmed from one or two major technological breakthroughs. In this process, organizational and institutional innovations proved to be important. State action, involving major adaptations in the wider society, also played a crucial role—in the society's ability to generate the entrepreneurial figures, in the training and aptitude of its work force, in its capacity to develop patterns of consumption, and in the state's ability to provide the necessary infrastructural and regulatory framework.

What was important in the history of each of these technology systems, Hall and Preston noted, was that each depended for its exploitation on the creation of an infrastructural network (railways, telegraph and telephone, electricity grids, highways, airports and air-traffic control), which to be successful could be achieved only comprehensively and in a relatively short time. This required organization, massive capitalization, and technical standardization. It resulted in the creation of large-scale enterprises, often the largest of their day, and required state provision or major state concessions to ensure their success (the early railways, the electrical utilities, the telephone companies, the airlines). The key to maintaining leadership was the ability to develop strong, large-scale, corporately managed enterprises with integrated research-and-development and marketing functions, a capacity to develop and diffuse new technologies, and access to long-term risk capital.

This link between long-term risk capital and organizational structures has been a fundamental feature of technological developments in the last decade, and carries with it the likelihood that we will benefit from the fruits of changing technologies in a manner similar to that seen in previous waves. As noted in Chapter 11, the key organizational innovation has been that of the venture-capital industry itself. The emergence of this industry has been paralleled by a combination of *downsizing* of massive vertically integrated firms and their replacement by *network corporations* on the leading edge of development. At the core of such corporations are centers of creativity and entrepreneurial activity which are linked to diverse networks of independent manufacturers, subcomponent suppliers, distributors, and sales organizations. Local networks are linked to transnational networks: the developed world has become one in terms of technology. All developed countries are equally capable of doing everything, doing it equally well, and doing it equally fast. All can share instant information. All participate in global financial and stock markets. All major transnational corporations therefore seek what Kenichi Ohmae calls *triad power:* a significant presence in Asia, North America, and Europe. At the core are 505 major public corporations whose headquarters are distributed in nineteen urban regions that together constitute the single interlinked *polycenter of the global urban network:*

Region	Urban Complex	Number of Headquarters
North America	New York	90
	Chicago	28
	Los Angeles	22
	San Francisco	15
	Philadelphia-Wilmington	14
	Dallas–Fort Worth	14
	Houston	13
	St. Louis	10
	Detroit	9
	Pittsburgh	9
Asia	Tokyo	88
	Osaka-Kobe	37
	Seoul	9
Europe	London	63
	Paris	39
	Ruhrgebiet	21
	Frankfurt	13
	Randstadt	9
	Rome	4

It is from this polycenter that the networks of dispersed interdependent specialists are controlled and managed. For the participant corporations, global interest now transcends national interest, while global networks both tighten and make more immediate global interdependence. Note in Figure 91 how the emergent AT&T fiberoptic system links the U.S. polycenter to this world of instantaneous communication and data transmission.

The creative potential in this development is more than merely economic, and it is in this potential that the opportunity for crafting alternatives resides. Global organizations and institutions can transcend the political-power games of self-interested nation-states that have fought global wars in 55-year cycles in the past five centuries, producing successive hegemons and hegemonistic challenges and the final inflationary spikes of Kondratiev peaks.

In the absence of such emergence, Joshua Goldstein believes (*Long Cycles* [1988], p. 353) that the next phases of the long-wave clock will be:

1995–2020	Next upswing of production
2000/2005–2025/2030	Next upswing of war

The current hegemon, the United States, Goldstein says, is in decline: between 1950 and 1980 the U.S. share of the industrial world's GNP fell from 70 percent to 40 percent, as did its share of capital formation by the world's core countries. The permanent war economy since 1945 has created a particularly dangerous situation: every historical precedent in which there has been an arms race in which both sides have sought deterrence via a balance of terror has led in the long run to catastrophic war. But the current arms race embodies mutually assured destruction: MAD. The problem, Goldstein says, is that hegemonic war

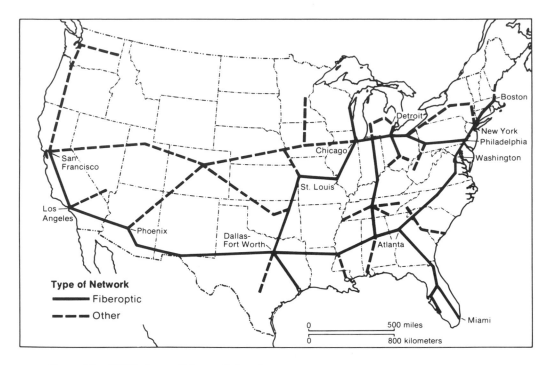

Figure 91. AT&T's Long-distance Network

This network, completed in 1990, combines fiberoptics and microwave, coaxial cable and radio lines, into a first-generation integrated-services digital system for voice and data transmission.

recurs because of the underlying practices of international politics at the core of the world system. Nation-states attempt to gain power, or to prevent others from gaining power, by military means. Power politics is the use of force, or the threat to use it, to maximize national self-interest. But any balance of power is short lived, for the source of power is economic growth, while the exercise of power suppresses the innovation that is the source of growth, and resulting changes in the locus of innovation change the locus of growth and therefore the balance of power. The decline of a hegemon inevitably degenerates into a war involving the great powers' pursuit of hegemonistic succession. "If a global alternative to hegemony is to emerge, new structures at the international and global levels will need to be created. The proliferation of international regimes— tacit or explicit agreements among countries (based on shared norms and rules) governing the operation of the international system—is a hopeful trend in this direction" (ibid., p. 375). "Only major changes in world politics can temper the dangers. . . . Evolving patterns of international relations are bringing a global-ization in which the only security is common security. The next world order will be built around this common security, not power politics, if the cycle of great power war is finally to be broken" (ibid., p. 17).

I choose to be optimistic. Perhaps the needed globalization will emerge from the potentials embedded within the new technologies. The venture-capital industry is betting on further developments in electronics—semiconductors and superconductors, telecommunications, personal computers, and artificial intelligence. The contemporary technology-system development that parallels previous experience is the creation of integrated network systems (fully integrated broadband digital networks based on high-capacity fiberoptic cable). Such systems, which are a natural extension of the continuing revolution in electronics, permit massive increases in instantaneous data traffic and equivalent reductions in paper transactions. The key innovations are in place. For deployment, very large large-scale organizations will be necessary to deploy the massive supportive infrastructure development that is required. Within AT&T's evolving Integrated Services Digital Network (ISDN), for example, each new switching center costs $3 million, putting the nationwide cost in the billions. Customers must install costly interfaces on their premises. Huge software-programming tasks remain. The Bell regional operating companies had a total of 200,000 lines capable of handling ISDN signals in place by 1989, and that number will exceed 2 million lines in 1992, according to current AT&T estimates.

Japan will have a first-generation integrated network system in place in the early 1990s, as will AT&T in the United States. Already, we have in place the Electronic Document Exchange that permits facsimile transmission (the current growth of fax machines parallels that of personal computers). What these developments suggest is that just as transport-building cycles were central to previous growth waves, we are primed for new rounds of transport-building and growth in the twenty-first century. And just as new transport and energy technologies transformed our way of life in the past, the new information technologies are capable of reshaping them, and possibly the long wave too, in the future.

To be sure, certain long-wave rhythms are already locked in. We know that the next upswing in entries to the labor market will occur in the first decade of the twenty-first century, after the decline in entries bottoms out in 1995. Refer to Figure 92, which reproduces key features of the lower panel of Figure 50 in Chapter 4. This demographic imperative probably dictates that the next (inflationary) growth cycle will take off in the first decade of the twenty-first century. Growth will center on the information technologies put into place in the 1980s. It is conceivable that these information technologies will be used to stabilize that growth and reduce the risk of overshoot—both economic and political.

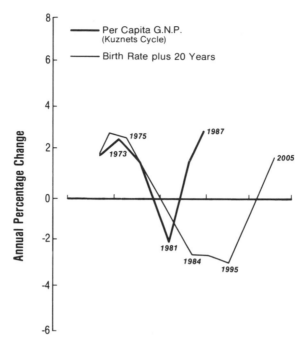

Figure 92. The Timing of the Next Inflationary Growth Cycle Is Suggested by the Correlation between Cycles of Labor-Market Entrants and Kuznets Cycles

This figure is adapted from the lower panel of Figure 50.

BUT ARE WE FREE TO CHOOSE?

The determinists among us deny that we have this freedom of choice, and those who link uncertainty to randomness say that choice is irrelevant to social outcomes; but the success of safety-net amelioration belies their images of Armageddon or the precedence of thermodynamics' second law.

The Doomsayers

Doomsayers such as Paul Erdman and Ravi Batra are the worst of the determinists. It is inevitable, they say, that history will repeat itself: the long wave embodies a future that is both cyclical and predestined.

In *What's Next? How to Prepare Yourself for the Crash of '89 and Profit in the 1990s* (1988), Erdman looked at the overleveraging of corporations and developing nations, advancing what he called a "convergence theory" pointing to a second Great Depression. Six events, he said, will converge, each reinforcing the one before to culminate in a financial crisis of unprecedented proportions:

1. The end of the Reagan recovery will signal that a recession is about to begin.

2. The inauguration of a new president (Erdman said probably a liberal Democrat) will bring to the White House a leader whose responses to the recession will be those of a left-of-center liberal, cutting military spending and raising taxes to support social programs and to balance the federal budget.

3. A resultant worsening of the economic outlook will trigger a cascade of bankruptcies accompanied by a rapid contraction of consumer spending as unemployment spreads from weak companies that are in trouble because of their overleveraged financial positions to much stronger companies and their suppliers.

4. The recession will spread rapidly from the United States to the other industrial nations of Europe and Asia. Information now flows instantaneously between markets, making movements more rapid and more extreme, and global markets mean global euphoria and global panics. The United States was the center of job creation globally in the 1980s, as well as the strategic link in the global system of economics and finance. An American recession will quickly become a global depression throughout the industrial world.

5. A global depression will precipitate the financial collapse of the Third World's major debtor nations—Brazil, Mexico, etc. As demand in the industrial world shrinks, so will the developing nations' markets. No longer will they be able to service their debt, despite extensive rescheduling. The spiral will produce widespread international default.

6. This process will be further impelled by reductions in the price of oil as the Iran-Iraq peace leads these nations to pump more oil to rebuild their war-shattered economies. Oil producers' earnings will shrink; if they are debtors like Mexico, so will their ability to repay.

As these events converged in 1989, Erdman believed the world would crash into a depression that was far wider and deeper than that of the 1930s. Just as the stock market crash of 1929 signaled the onset of the Great Depression, the market crash of 1987 signaled, in his mind, an approaching Armageddon. But 1989 is over as I write this sentence, and the forces of destruction have yet to gather at Megiddo. Erdman made the fatal mistake of all unsuccessful soothsayers: he predicted real events in the immediate future. Successful soothsaying demands the technique of a Nostradamus: predict events in the distant future using language that permits multiple interpretations.

Another soothsayer, his Hindu heritage making him comfortable with cyclicality and predestination, is Ravi Batra. Arguing by analogy in *The Great Depression of 1990* (1987), Batra listed what he believed was a significant consistency of trends in the periods 1920–1926 and 1980–1986:

1920	High inflation, interest rates, and unemployment.	1980	Same combination.
1921	Huge tax cut favoring the rich	1981	Major pro-business, pro-affluent tax cut.
1922	Sharp decline in inflation and interest rates; sharp rise in stock market averages.	1982	Same combination.
1923	Banks offer interest on checking accounts for first time in history. Employment declines sharply. Bull market continues.	1983	Checking accounts bear interest for first time since 1930s. Rapid drop in unemployment. Rising stock market averages.
1924	Low inflation and interest rates. Bull market.	1984	Same combination.
1925	Unemployment drops further. Stock market averages rise. Inflation unchanged. Number of bank failures increases sharply.	1985	Same combination.
1926	Stock market breaks records, unemployment drops sharply, tax reform reduces rates for poor and raises rates for corporations; bank failures increase, energy prices fall.	1986	Same combination.

He concluded that "the stock market will continue to rise, but its total percentage gain by the end of 1987 may not be as strong as its gain in 1986. The market fever will resume in 1988, with occasional retreats and pauses, lasting almost to the end of 1989. . . . if no remedial measures are taken, then 1989 will be like 1929. This means that at the end of 1989 or in the first half of 1990, the stock market will crash and will be followed by an abysmal decline in business activity and a sharply higher rate of unemployment. The low point of this great depression will come in 1994" (pp. 139–140).

Safety-net Amelioration

Batra's crystal ball appears to be cloudy. The market did crash on October 19, 1987, with a 508-point drop in the Dow Jones Industrials average, followed quickly by similar drops on most of the world's major stock exchanges. The reason a major financial crisis did not ensue was that *we learned from the Great Depression*. Batra's analogies are inappropriate because the institutional innovations of the New Deal and the advent of Keynesian macroeconomic management enabled us to intervene, thereby assuring a stabler path of growth and price supports that ameliorated the worst consequences of the crash. As Figure 93 reaffirms, while the essential rhythms of the long wave have not been changed, the oscillations of growth have been dampened and the level of inflation around which prices fluctuate has been raised so that the price phases move from infla-

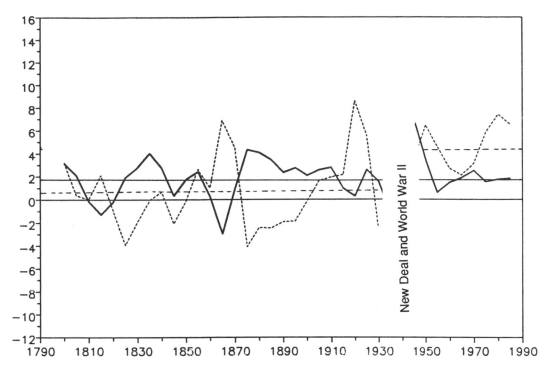

Figure 93. Transition of the Ten-Year Moving Averages of the Growth Rates of Prices (*dotted lines*) and Real Per Capita GNP (*solid lines*) after the New Deal and World War II

The long-term rate of economic growth has been 1.79 percent per annum throughout the two centuries graphed. Following the New Deal recovery, however, fluctuations around this average were dampened. In addition, the advent of Keynesian macroeconomics raised the long-term growth rate of prices from less than 1 percent to close to 5 percent per annum, with the result that fluctuations changed from an inflation-deflation range to a higher inflation-disinflation range.

tion-deflation to inflation-disinflation. A safety net has been put into place. Its efficacy was reaffirmed by the events of October 1989, when another dramatic fall in the stock market was immediately countered by the announcement that the Federal Reserve would ensure that adequate funds were available for banks and brokerage houses to meet their obligations in the event of a larger sell-off.

All of Schumpeter's, Galbraith's, and Kindleberger's supernormal sensitivities of 1929 were present in 1987: stock market excesses, banking-system weakness, a mortgage crisis, graft, dubious foreign balances, a reductionist Democratic Party platform, and pressures for protectionism, including new trade legislation. A major financial crisis did not occur after the crash of 1987 because both the government and business intervened vigorously. In 1987, the U.S. Federal Reserve drove down interest rates by pumping billions of dollars into the banking system. Major corporations announced share-repurchase programs that helped drive the market back up. The Japanese government urged its securities industry to support the Tokyo stock market. Federal deposit insurance companies ensured that bank failures did not bankrupt small savers. The banking system seemed safe because the government was both a guarantor of deposits and a lender of last resort.

Because huge amounts of liquidity were pumped into the system, strong economic growth continued. Consequently, the annihilation of consumer demand financed by unrealized capital gains was not as widespread as it had been in the 1930s. To be sure, high-priced housing and high-ticket consumer goods have been under severe pressure, and the number of personal bankruptcies has risen, but the impact has remained localized. Weaknesses in the U.S. banking system will continue to do harm, and the number of failures will mount as the reality of loans based on overvalued assets is realized, but Congress has passed the necessary legislation to underwrite the savings-and-loan bailout, and so there is every confidence that a banking crisis will continue to be avoided.

An agricultural-mortgage crisis also has arisen out of borrowing-and-lending practices that were based on unreasonable expectations regarding agricultural prices and land-value appreciation. This crisis has been compounded by the 55-year drought, especially in the nation's grain-producing regions, but again we have the institutional capacity to respond. Many price supports are still in place. Congress acted speedily to provide drought relief to the nation's productive farms, even if relief did not arrive quickly enough to prevent the demise of the weak. Institutional changes once again reduced the supernormal sensitivities that were present in 1929.

Globally, too, there has been institutional development. The world's industrial nations—the "Group of Seven"—have proved that they can act in concert to manage exchange and interest rates in order to maintain and redistribute growth. The idea of *shared leadership* may just be gaining strength. The question is whether the International Monetary Fund can negotiate additional rescheduling of the debt of many developing countries, particularly such major debtors as Brazil and Mexico, to avoid both an international banking crisis and political instability in those nations.

The fly in the ointment is domestic politics. Ultimately, what will prevent another Great Depression is our ability to prevent the disastrous deflation of the 1930s. Some, like Davis Weis in "Why Elliott, Kondratieff See Deflation Ahead" (1988), conclude that "the fear of inflation will be echoed all the way down" by a Federal Reserve that is so intent on solving yesterday's problems that it will continue to take anti-inflationary actions despite the longer-term pressures moving in the opposite direction. The countervailing force is that of Lord Keynes, who showed that growth produced by deficit spending guarantees that turndowns are accompanied by *disinflation* rather than *deflation*. Much of the net that holds up Keynesian macroeconomics is woven of military expenditures, however. A retreat from military Keynesianism through budget-balancing spending cuts without an effective transition to an innovative peacetime-growth economy could easily turn disinflation into deflation and a downturn into a vortex.

LONG-WAVE CLOCKS IN A DIGITAL AGE

The institutional innovations of the New Deal reduced some oscillations and raised the levels around which others unfold. Can the long-wave rhythms that remain be changed by further ameliorating the continuing cycle of overshoot and collapse, or are they so fundamental to the capitalist process that the only alternative is, as the Marxists say, an alternative socioeconomic system?

The potential for change lies, I believe, not in any disastrous Marxist alternative, but in the information age. Central to Kuznets cycles is the problem of mismatch between investors' expectations and the realities of investment opportunities, a mismatch that results in the repetition of overshoot and collapse. Better and more immediately available information about capital commitments and construction could be effective in dampening investors' overenthusiastic estimates of future market opportunities, easing the alternations of mass euphoria and despair, moving us from clockwork motions to the stabler rhythms of the digital age. Better and more widely available information might also help reduce the speculatory cycles in which demand is produced by easy credit, which is itself predicated on overenthusiastic estimates of potential speculatory gains and inflation-boosted asset values. Better and more closely monitored information could help reduce the abuses of insider trading schemes and corrupt kiting. A beginning has been made in attempts to monitor for, and to control, insider trading on the New York Stock Exchange, and to place limits on the daily swings produced by the program traders. A more aggressive role by a Federal Reserve that takes a longer-term view is needed. While we lack the tools to engineer complete stability, we do have within our grasp the information technology to make the economy a far smoother oscillator, one that is freer of episodic suffering and offers more opportunities for those on whom our future depends.

Central to the final inflationary spirals of Kondratiev waves is another factor—the use of the printing press to finance arms races and wars. Better information-gathering, information-disseminating, and communications technologies should help reduce misperceptions about intentions, and therefore the risk of global war. The direct Moscow-to-Washington communications link is just one step in that direction, as is the advent of space-based monitoring systems and on-sight inspection: *glasnost* is a positive sign.

Such information is useful only if there are organizations to use it, however. There is great hope that transnational enterprises whose interests transcend those of individual nation-states will become a driving force in promoting the concept of a more collective security. There is hope, too, that other international organizations will play a role in crafting an international order that formerly was the right of a militarily successful hegemon. A more active United Nations has helped bring an end to the Iraq-Iran war. The Association of South East Asian Nations (ASEAN) has made some progress in promoting progress toward a Kampuchean settlement in that troubled region. Latin leaders are taking the lead in negotiating peace in Central America. And finally the Great Powers are coming to realize not simply the costs of arms races and the opportunities for domestic and international development that are thereby foregone, but also the senselessness of the oblivion to which all of us will be consigned if nuclear arsenals are ever unleashed. How much better a world would it be if the arms race could be converted into a disarmament race, and if alternative uses could be found for the $1 trillion spent annually by the military-industrial complex? Would we then be faced with an international debt crisis? Would we then be unable to provide a minimum level of decency and a broad-based floor of opportunity for all? Might the resources then be available to seriously address the problems of world hunger and global inequality? Might we then be able to address global warming and the other equally profound threats to our survival that are our doing and that are likely to afflict us by default?

The problem, as always, is the ignorance of consequences which clouds choices in a world where individuals and nations pursue wealth and power. The dilemma is that the drive to maximize individual advantage under conditions of uncertainty converts races to frenzies that end in overshoot and collapse, whether the race be that of the entrepreneur or that of the militarist. Yet a knowledge-based society could be aware of the collective consequences of individual actions and should be able to curb those that are undesirable, placing the net of collective security over the arena of individual choice.

A knowledge-based society is ultimately only as good as the quality of its minds. These minds must have access to sound information. They must get it in a timely fashion. They must know how to use it when they have it. And they must be infected with the magic of creativity which enables them to imagine—and create—the new knowledge upon which our future will be based. We have the resources to ensure that the ultimate resource, our minds, is not wasted, but we misallocate them. Any effort to increase collective survivability will not only increase the likelihood of more stable future growth; it will also create the opportunity to achieve the real potential of a knowledge-based society, the fullest development of its minds. This is the promise of the digital age: that the alternating swings of prosperity and despair can be dampened; that growth can be stabilized; that we can be more knowing about ourselves and produce a future that is free of the collective consequences of individual excess.

PRICE DYNAMICS: THE GROWTH RATES OF PRICES SMOOTHED BY SUCCESSIVELY LONGER MOVING AVERAGES

In the succession of diagrams that follow, the graphs are arranged in pairs, two to a page. The upper graph always shows the relationship computed and plotted annually. The lower graph shows the relationship computed and plotted at five-year intervals. Thus, the first pair shows the annual growth rates of prices in the upper panel and the annual rates plotted for every fifth year in the lower level. The second pair shows two-year moving averages of the annual growth rates of prices computed and plotted annually and every fifth year. The process is repeated for four-, six-, eight-, ten-, twelve-, fourteen-, sixteen-, eighteen-, and twenty-year moving averages to enable the reader to compare the consequences of different smoothing intervals for the resulting patterns.

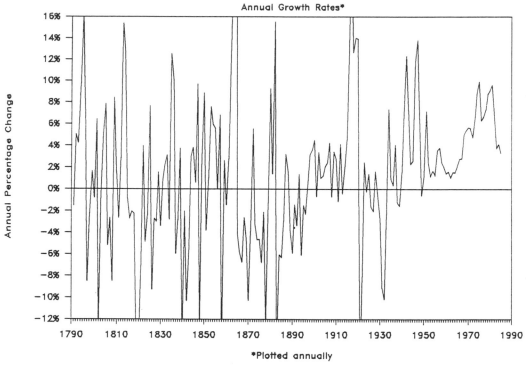

*Plotted annually

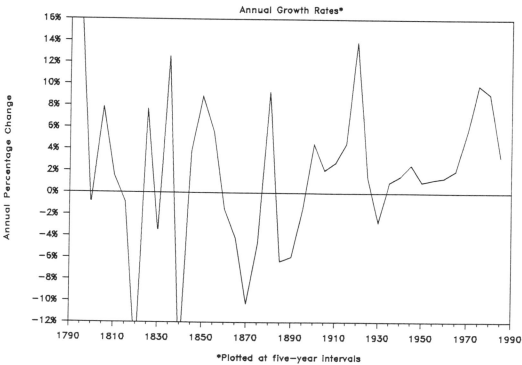

*Plotted at five-year intervals

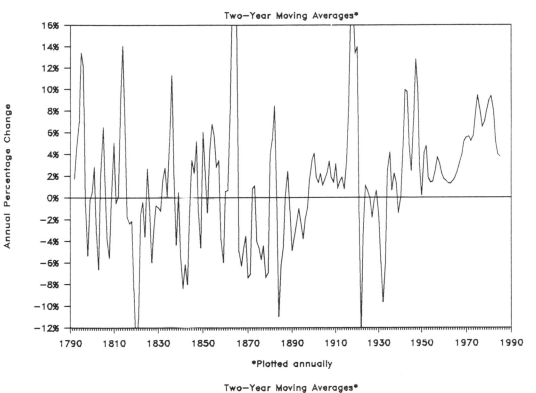

*Plotted annually

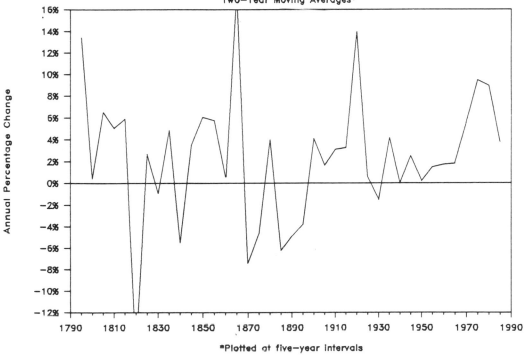

*Plotted at five-year intervals

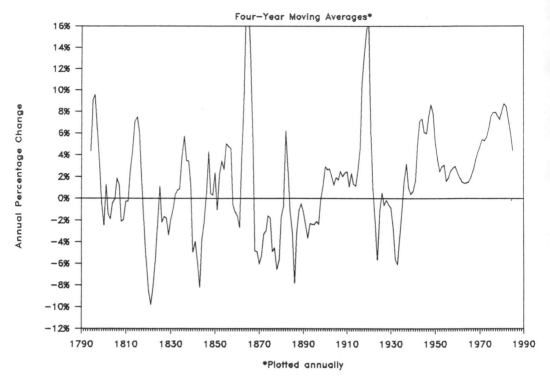

*Plotted annually

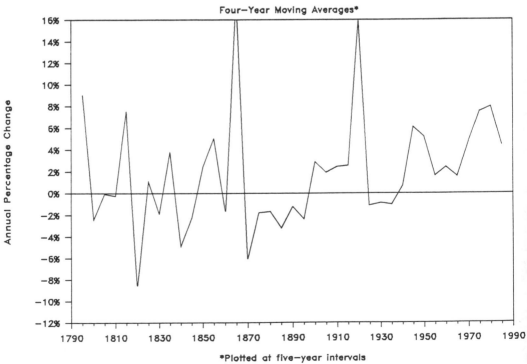

*Plotted at five-year intervals

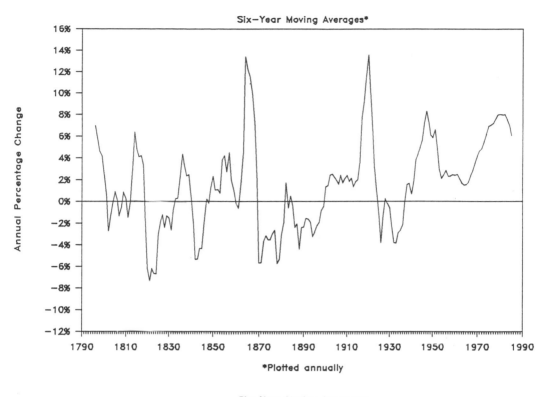

Six-Year Moving Averages*

*Plotted annually

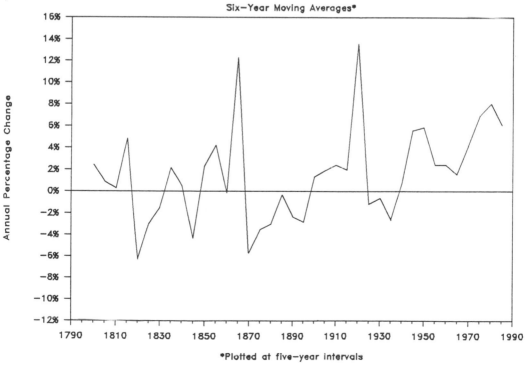

Six-Year Moving Averages*

*Plotted at five-year intervals

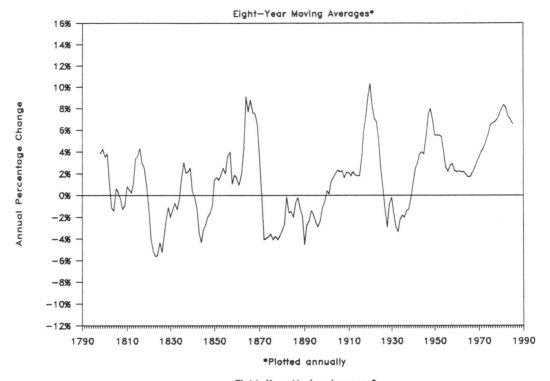

*Plotted annually

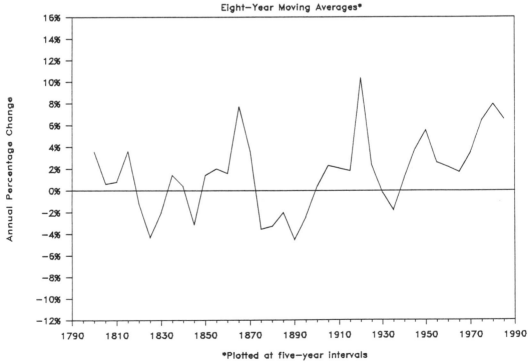

*Plotted at five-year intervals

Ten-Year Moving Averages*

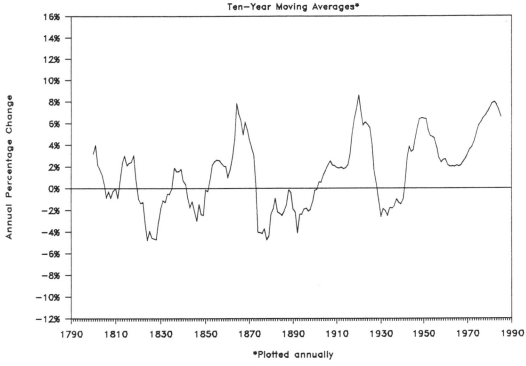

*Plotted annually

Ten-Year Moving Averages*

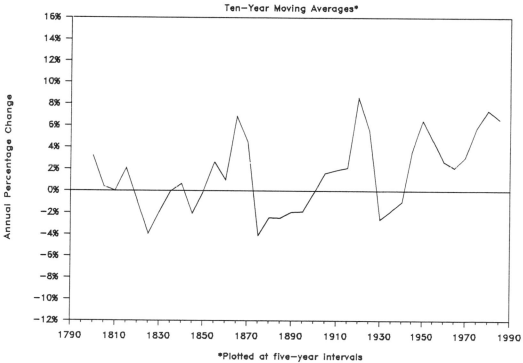

*Plotted at five-year intervals

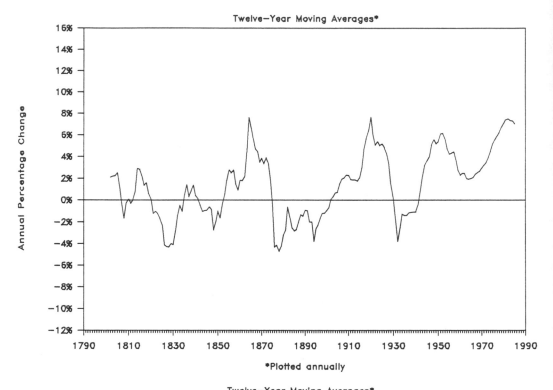

Twelve–Year Moving Averages*

*Plotted annually

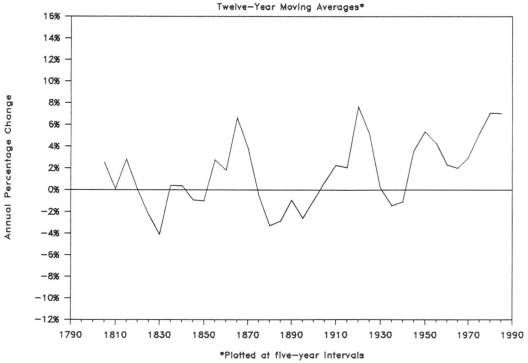

Twelve–Year Moving Averages*

*Plotted at five–year intervals

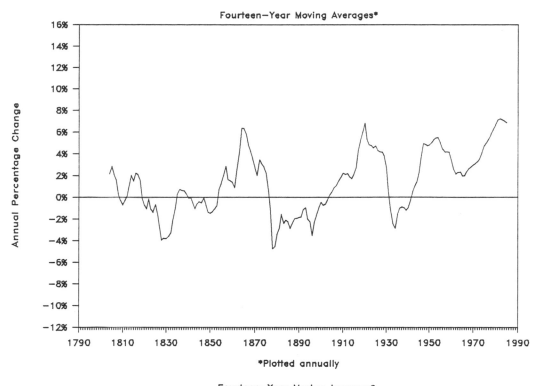

Fourteen—Year Moving Averages*

*Plotted annually

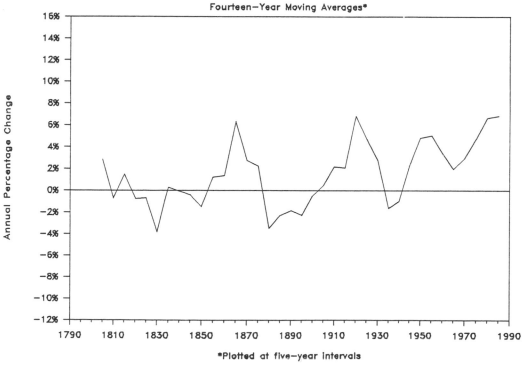

Fourteen—Year Moving Averages*

*Plotted at five—year intervals

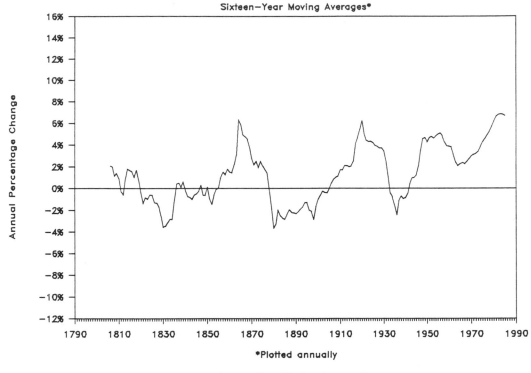

Sixteen—Year Moving Averages*

*Plotted annually

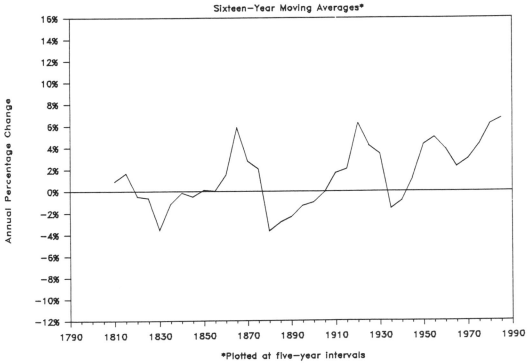

Sixteen—Year Moving Averages*

*Plotted at five—year intervals

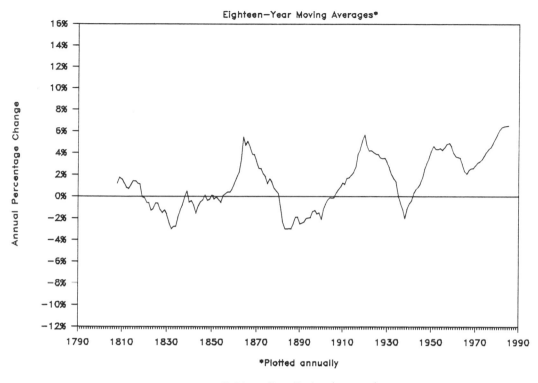

Eighteen—Year Moving Averages*

*Plotted annually

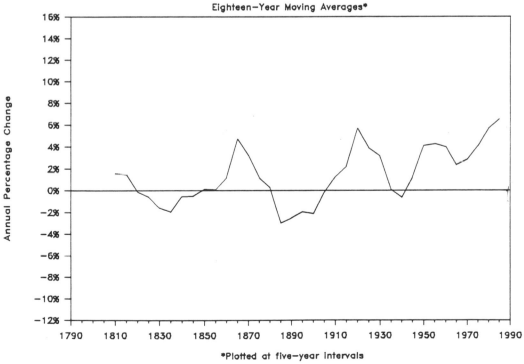

Eighteen—Year Moving Averages*

*Plotted at five—year intervals

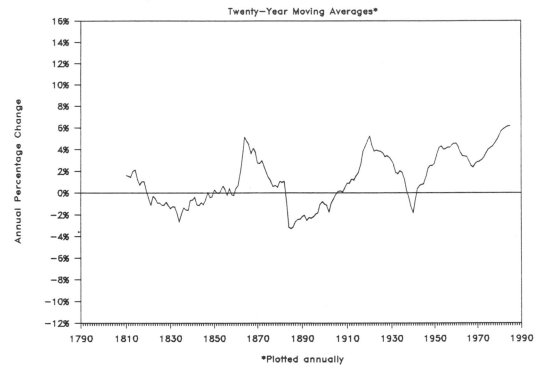

Twenty—Year Moving Averages*

*Plotted annually

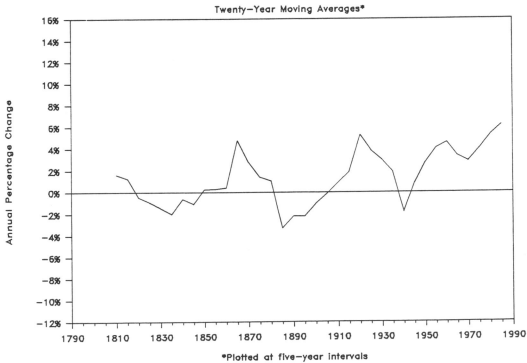

Twenty—Year Moving Averages*

*Plotted at five—year intervals

GROWTH DYNAMICS: THE GROWTH RATES OF REAL PER CAPITA GNP SMOOTHED BY SUCCESSIVELY LONGER MOVING AVERAGES

The graphs in this appendix mirror those in Appendix A, except that the data processed are the growth rates of real per capita GNP.

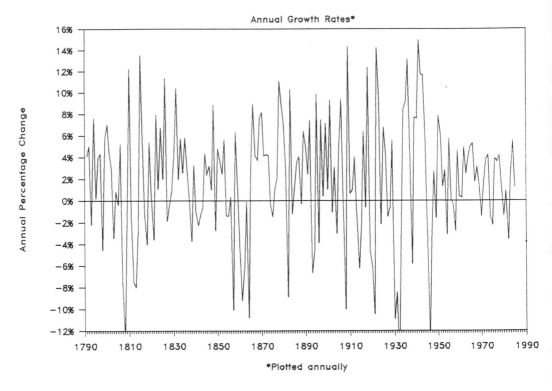

Annual Growth Rates*

*Plotted annually

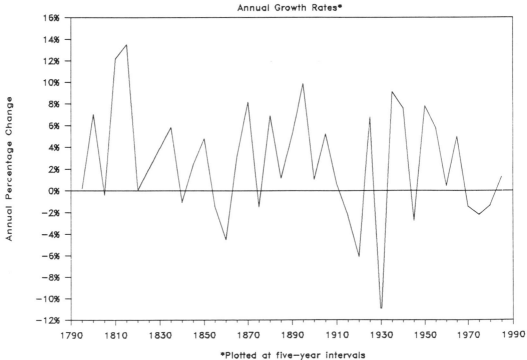

Annual Growth Rates*

*Plotted at five-year intervals

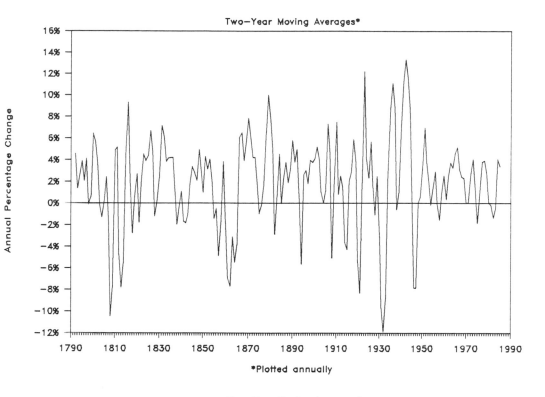

Two-Year Moving Averages*

*Plotted annually

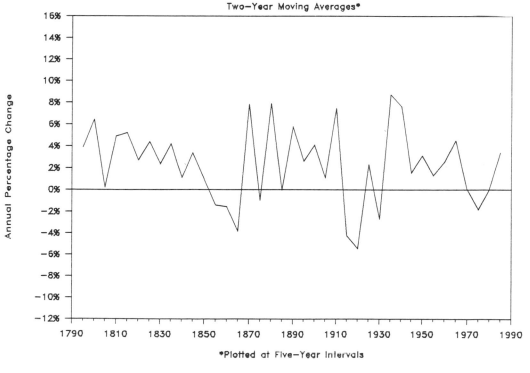

Two-Year Moving Averages*

*Plotted at Five-Year Intervals

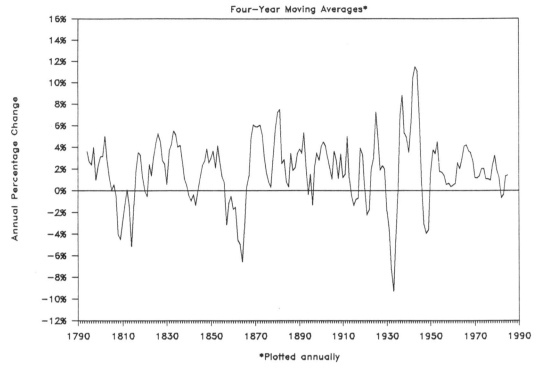

*Plotted annually

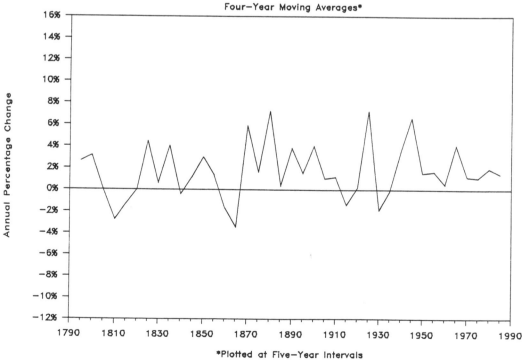

*Plotted at Five-Year Intervals

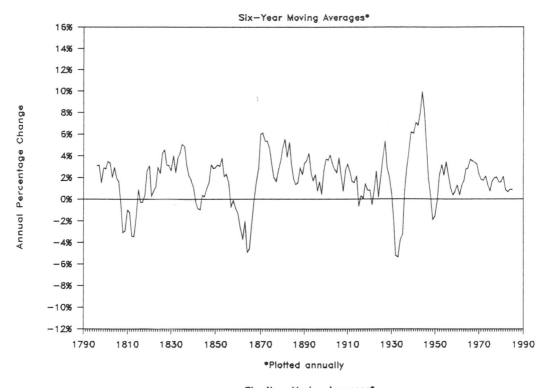

Six-Year Moving Averages*

*Plotted annually

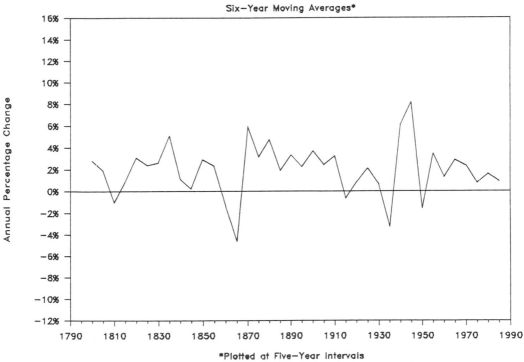

Six-Year Moving Averages*

*Plotted at Five-Year Intervals

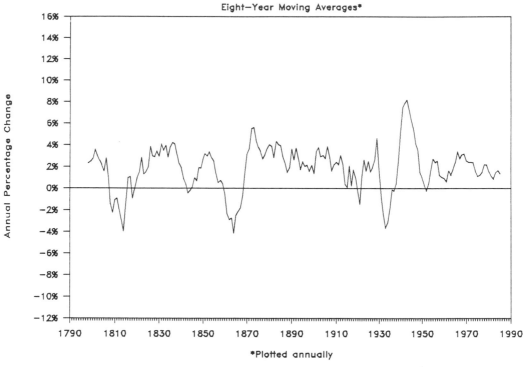

Eight—Year Moving Averages*

*Plotted annually

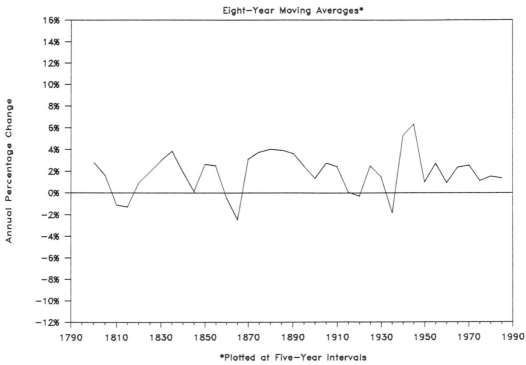

Eight—Year Moving Averages*

*Plotted at Five—Year Intervals

Ten-Year Moving Averages*

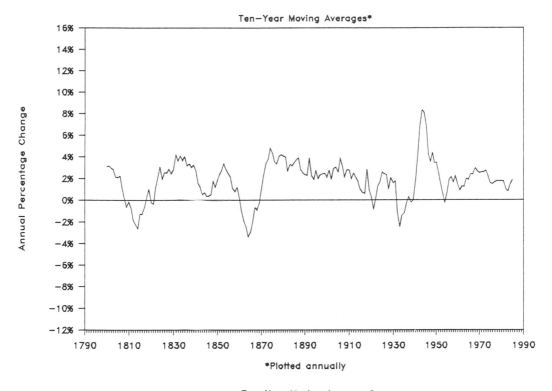

*Plotted annually

Ten-Year Moving Averages*

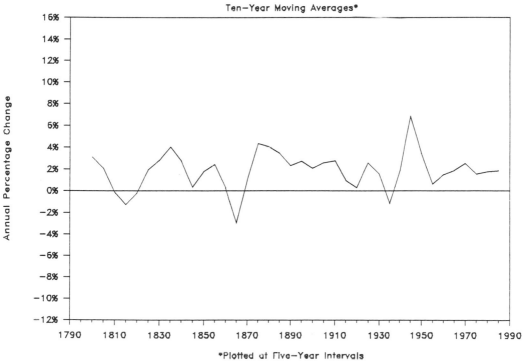

*Plotted at Five-Year Intervals

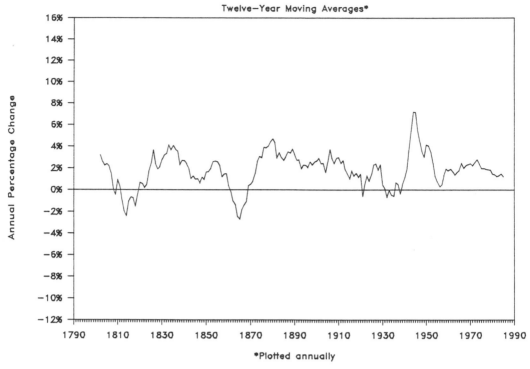

*Plotted annually

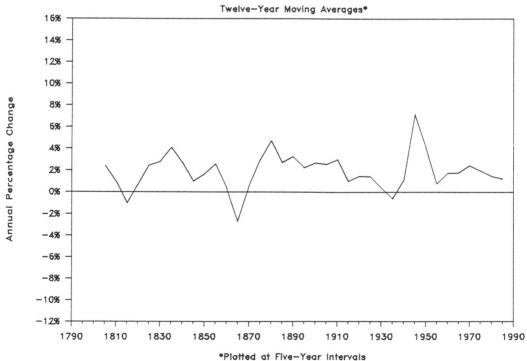

*Plotted at Five-Year Intervals

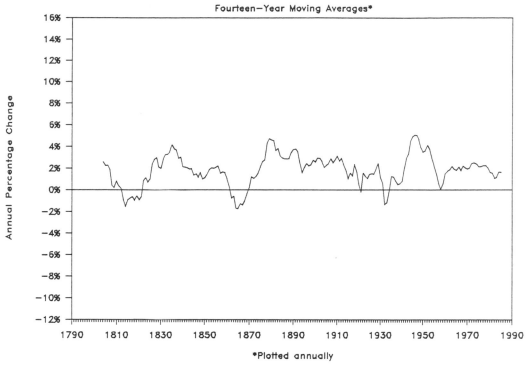

Fourteen—Year Moving Averages*

*Plotted annually

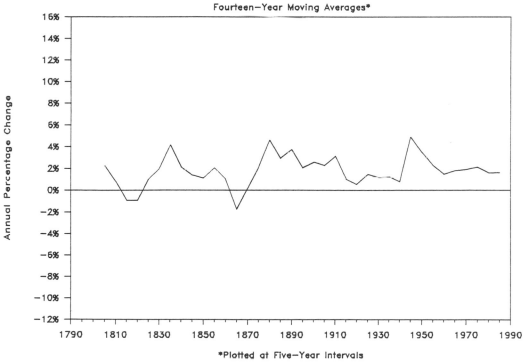

Fourteen—Year Moving Averages*

*Plotted at Five—Year Intervals

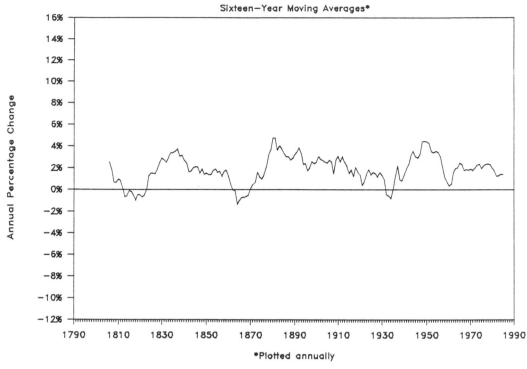

*Plotted annually

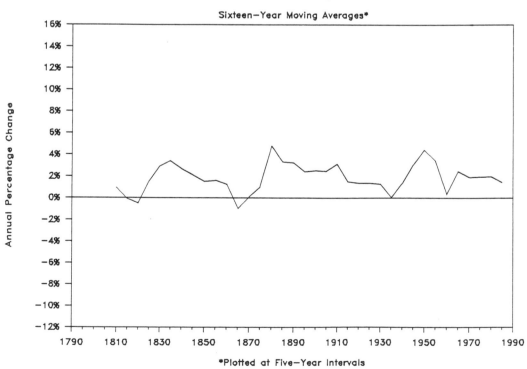

*Plotted at Five-Year Intervals

Eighteen–Year Moving Averages*

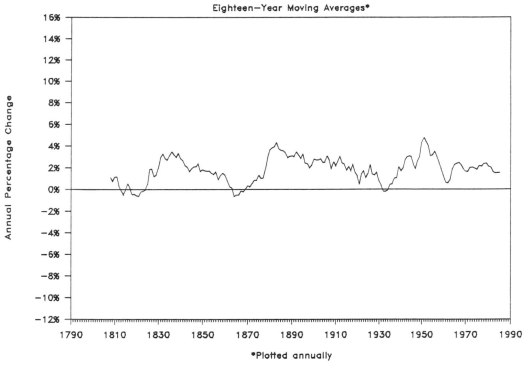

*Plotted annually

Eighteen–Year Moving Averages*

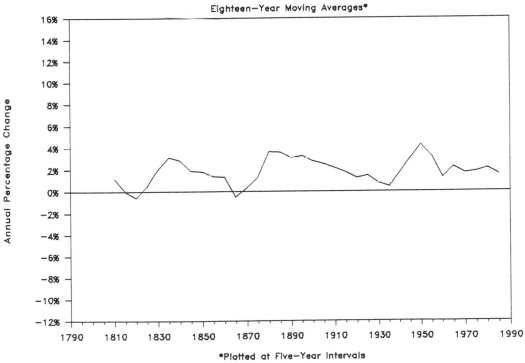

*Plotted at Five–Year Intervals

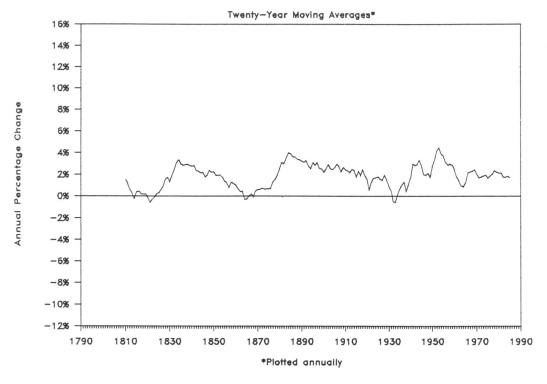

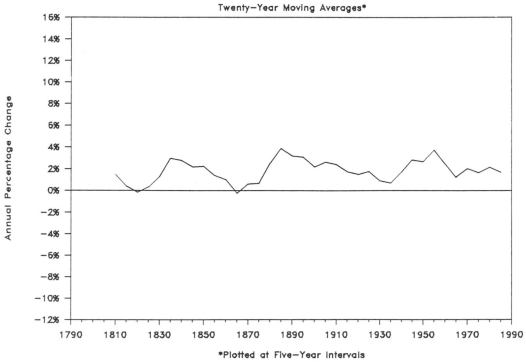

BIBLIOGRAPHY

Abramovitz, Moses. 1961. "The Nature and Significance of Kuznets Cycles." *Economic Development and Cultural Change* 9:225–268.

———. 1968. "The Passing of the Kuznets Cycle." *Economica* 34:349-367.

Adams, Robert McCormick. 1988. "Contexts of Technological Advance." Darryl Forde Lecture, University of London.

Aftalion, Albert. 1913. *Les Crises périodiques de surproduction.* 2 vols. Paris: Rivière.

Allan, Pierre. 1987. "Social Time." In *Interaction and Communication in Global Politics,* edited by C. Cioffi-Revilla, R. L. Merritt, and D. A. Zinnes, pp. 95–113. Beverly Hills, Calif.: Sage Publications.

Akerman, J. 1944. *Ekonomisk Teori.* Lund, Sweden: Gleerup.

Alesina, Alberto, and Howard Rosenthal. 1989. "Partisan Cycles in Congressional Elections and the Macroeconomy." *American Political Science Review* 83:373–398.

Amos, Orley M., Jr. 1989. "A Reevaluation of Long Cycle Theories: Development as the Satisfaction of Hierarchial Needs." *Social Science Quarterly* 70:341–355.

Arthur, W. Brian. 1988. "Self-reinforcing Methods in Economics." In *The Economy as an Evolving Complex System,* edited by P. W. Anderson and K. J. Arrow. New York: Addison-Wesley.

Awan, Akhtar A. 1985. "Marshallian and Schumpeterian Theories of Economic Evolution: Gradualism versus Punctualism." *Atlantic Economic Journal* 14:37–49.

Barber, James David. 1977. *The Presidential Character: Predicting Performance in the White House.* Englewood Cliffs, N.J.: Prentice-Hall.

Barkun, Michael. 1984. "Communal Societies as Cyclical Phenomena." *Communal Societies* 4:35–48.

Barnett, W., and P. Chen. 1986. "The Aggregate-Theoretic Monetary Aggregates Are Chaotic and Have Strange Attractors." In *Dynamic Econometric Modelling,* edited by W. Barnett, E. Berndt, and H. White. Cambridge: Cambridge University Press.

Barnett, W., John Gewecke, and Karl Shell. 1989. *Economic Complexity: Chaos, Sunspots, Bubbles, and Nonlinearity.* Cambridge: Cambridge University Press.

Batra, Ravi. 1987. *The Great Depression of 1990: Why It's Got to Happen. How to Protect Yourself.* New York: Simon & Schuster.

Baumol, William J., and Jess Benhabib. 1989. "Chaos: Significance, Mechanism, and Economic Applications." *Journal of Economic Perspectives* 3:77–105.

Beck, Paul. 1974. "A Socialization Theory of Political Realignment." In *The Politics of Future Citizens,* edited by Richard Niemi, pp. 199–219. San Francisco: Jossey-Bass.

Becker, Gary S. 1988. "Family Economics and Macro Behavior." *American Economic Review* 78:1–13.

Beckman, Robert. 1983. *The Downwave.* Portsmouth, England: Milestone Publications.

———. 1988. *Into the Upwave.* Portsmouth, England: Milestone Publications.

Bentson, George. 1980. *Conglomerate Mergers.* Washington, D.C.: American Enterprise Institute.

Bergeson, Albert, and Ronald Schoenberg. 1980. "Long Waves of Colonial Expansion and Contraction, 1415–1969." In *Studies of the Modern World-System,* edited by Albert Bergeson, pp. 231–277. New York: Academic Press.

Bernstein, E. M. 1940. "War and the Pattern of Business Cycles." *American Economic Review* 30:524–535.

Berry, Brian J. L. 1988. "Migration Reversals in Perspective: The Long-Wave Evidence." *International Regional Science Review* 11:245–251.

Berry, Brian J. L., Susan Walsh Sanderson, Susan Elster, Maryann Feldman, Holly Johnston, and Aydan Kutay. 1985. "Growth and Adjustment in an Economy Undergoing Structural Transformation." Prizewinning paper in 1985 General Motors Business Understanding Program, School of Urban and Public Affairs, Carnegie-Mellon University, Pittsburgh, Pa., April.

Bird, Roger C., Meghnad J. Desai, Jared J. Enzler, and Paul J. Taubman. 1985. "Kuznets Cycles in Growth Rates: The Meaning." *International Economic Review* 6:229–239.

Bloomfield, Arthur I. 1968. *Patterns of Fluctuation in International Investment before 1914.* Princeton Studies in International Finance, no. 21. Princeton: Princeton University Press.

Borchert, John R. 1961. "American Metropolitan Evolution." *Geographical Review* 57:301–332.

Bosquet, Nicole. 1980. "From Hegemony to Competition: Cycles at the Core?" In *Processes of the World-System,* edited by T. K. Hopkins and I. Wallerstein, pp. 4–-83. Beverly Hills, Calif.: Sage Publications.

Brady, David W. 1988. *Critical Elections and Congressional Policy Making.* Stanford: Stanford University Press.

Braudel, Fernand, and Frank C. Spooner. 1967. "Prices in Europe from 1450 to 1750." *Cambridge Economic History of Europe* 4:374–486.

Brock, W. A. 1988. "Hicksian Nonlinearity." Department of Economics, University of Wisconsin. Photocopy.

Brock, W. A., and G. Chamberlain. 1984. "Spectral Analysis Cannot Tell A Macro-Econometrician Whether His Time Series Came from a Stochastic Economy or a Deterministic Economy." Social Systems Research Institute, University of Wisconsin. Photocopy.

Brock, W. A., W. D. Dechert, and J. A. Scheinkman. 1987. "A Test for Independence Based on the Correlation Dimension." Working Paper 8702, Department of Economics, University of Wisconsin.

Brock, W. A., and A. G. Malliaris. 1988. *Differential Equations, Stability, and Chaos in Dynamic Economics.* New York: North-Holland Publishing Co.

Brock, W. A., and C. L. Sayers. 1987. "Is the Business Cycle Characterized by Deterministic Chaos?" Working Paper 87–15, Department of Economics, University of North Carolina, December.

Brozen, Yale. 1982. *Mergers in Perspective.* Washington, D.C.: American Enterprise Institute.

Burnham, Walter Dean. 1970. *Critical Elections and the Mainsprings of American Politics.* New York: W. W. Norton.

———. 1981. "The 1980 Earthquake: Realignment, Reaction, or What?" In *The Hidden Election: Politics and Economics in the 1980 Presidential Campaign,* edited by Thomas Ferguson and Joel Rogers, pp. 132–140. New York: Random House.

———. 1982. *The Current Crisis in American Politics.* Oxford: Oxford University Press.

———. 1988. "Political Gridlock." *New Perspectives Quarterly,* Spring, pp. 16–23.

Burns, Arthur F. 1934. *Production Trends in the United States since 1870*. New York: National Bureau of Economic and Social Research.

———. 1935. "Long Cycles in Residential Construction." In *Economic Essays in Honor of Wesley Clair Mitchell*. New York: National Bureau of Economic Research.

———. 1968. "Business Cycles." In *International Encyclopedia of the Social Sciences*, edited by David L. Sills, vol. 2, p. 227. New York: Macmillan and the Free Press.

Burns, Arthur F., and Wesley C. Mitchell. 1946. *Measuring Business Cycles*. New York: National Bureau of Economic Research.

Burton, Theodore E. 1910. *Financial Crises and Periods of Industrial and Commercial Depression*. New York: D. Appleton.

Butz, William P., and Michael P. Ward. 1979. "The Emergence of Countercyclical U.S. Fertility." *American Economic Review* 69:318–328.

Cairncross, A. K. 1953. *Home and Foreign Investment, 1870–1913: Studies in Capital Accumulation*. Cambridge: Cambridge University Press.

Campbell, Angus. 1966. "A Classification of Presidential Elections." In *Elections and the Political Order*, edited by Angus Campbell, Philip Converse, Warren E. Miller, and Donald E. Stokes, pp. 63–77. New York: John Wiley & Sons.

Carswell, John. 1960. *The South Sea Bubble*. London: Cresset Press.

Cassel, G. 1932. *Theoretische Sozialökonomie*. 5th ed. Jena: A. Deichertsche Verlagsbuchhandlung.

Cato, Ralph D. 1986. "I. Kondratieff the Man: The Marxist/Long-Wave Clash." *Futures. The Magazine of Commodities* 15 (March): 67–72.

———. 1986. "II. What Kondratieff's 1925 Paper Really Said about Waves." *Futures. The Magazine of Commodities* 15 (April): 76–80.

———. 1986. "III. How Today's Gurus See the K-Wave Theory." *Futures. The Magazine of Commodities* 15 (May): 76–80.

———. 1986. "IV. Why "the Killer Wave" May Not be Imminent." *Futures. The Magazine of Commodities* 15 (June): 62–66.

Chambers, William Nisbet, and Walter Dean Burnham, eds. 1967. *The American Party System: Stages of Political Development*. New York: Oxford University Press.

Clark, John, Christopher Freeman, and Luc Soete. 1981. "Long Waves, Inventions, and Innovations." *Futures* 13:308–322.

Clubb, Jerome W., William H. Flanigan, and Nancy H. Zingdale. 1980. *Partisan Realignment: Voters, Parties, and Government in American History*. Beverly Hills, Calif.: Sage Publications.

Cogan, L. Peter. 1969. *The Rhythmic Cycles of Optimism and Pessimism*. New York: William-Frederick Press.

Cooney, E. W. 1960. "Long Waves in Building in the British Economy of the Nineteenth Century." *Economic History Review* 13:257–269.

Dale, Charles. 1984. "A Search for Business Cycles with Spectral Analysis." *Proceedings of the Business and Economic Statistics Section, American Statistical Association*, pp. 267–272.

———. 1989. "Searching for Chaos in Economic Systems: The Worldwide Race to Be First." Paper presented at the Sixth General Assembly of the World Future Society, Washington, D.C., July 16–20.

Davis, Harold T. 1941. "The Fifty Year War Cycle." In *The Analysis of Economic Time Series*. San Antonio, Tex.: Privately printed.

Davis, Richard G. 1968. "The Role of Money Supply in Business Cycles." *Monthly Review* (Federal Reserve Bank of New York), April, pp. 63–73.

Day, Richard H. 1982. "Irregular Growth Cycles." *American Economic Review* 72: 406–414.

Day, Richard H., and Jean-Luc Walter. 1989. "Economic Growth in the Very Long Run: On the Multiple-Phase Interaction of Population, Technology, and Social Infrastructure." In *Economic Complexity,* edited by W. Barnett et al., pp. 253–289. Cambridge: Cambridge University Press.

Dewey, Edward R., and Edwin F. Dakin. 1927. *Cycles: The Science of Prediction.* New York: Henry Holt & Co.

De Wolff, Samuel. 1920. "Het economisch getif." In *Der Lebendige Marxismus,* edited by Otto Jensen. Festgavezum, 70 Geburstag von Karl Kautsky. Jena: Thuringer Verlagsanstalt.

———. 1924. "Prosperitats und depressionsperioden." In *Der Lebendige Marxismus,* edited by Otto Jensen. Festgavezum, 70 Geburstag von Karl Kautsky. Jena: Thuringer Verlagsanstalt.

Dominguez, Kathryn M., Ray C. Fair, and Matthew D. Shapiro. 1988. "Forecasting the Depression: Harvard versus Yale." *American Economic Review* 78:595–612.

Dupriez, L. H. 1935. Einwirkungen der langen Wellen auf die Entwicklung der Wirtschaft Seit 1800." *Weltwirtschaftliches Archiv* 37:1–12.

Easterlin, Richard A. 1968. *Population, Labor Force, and Long Swings in Economic Growth.* New York: National Bureau of Economic Research.

———. 1987. *Birth and Fortune: The Impact of Numbers on Personal Welfare.* 2d ed. Chicago: University of Chicago Press.

Ehrensaft, Philip. 1980. "Long Waves in the Transformation of North American Agriculture: A First Statement." *Cornell Journal of Social Relations* 15:65–83.

Ekelund, Robert B., Jr., and Mark Thornton. 1986. "Schumpeterian Analysis, Supply-Side Economics, and Macroeconomic Policy in the 1920s." *Review of Social Economy* 44:221–237.

Elazar, Daniel. 1976. "The Generational Rhythm of American Politics." Temple University Center for the Study of Federalism, Working Paper 13.

Elliott, Dave. 1986. "Technology and the Future: A New Look at Kondratieff Cycles." *Journal of Interdisciplinary Economics* 1:189–204.

England, P., and G. Farkas. 1986. *Households, Employment, and Gender.* New York: Aldine.

Erdman, Paul. 1988. *What's Next? How to Prepare Yourself for the Crash of '89 and Profit in the 1990s.* New York: Doubleday.

Erikson, Robert S. 1989. "Economic Conditions and the Presidential Vote." *American Political Science Review* 83:567–573.

Ewijk, C. Van. 1982. "A Spectral Analysis of the Kondratieff Cycle." *Kyklos* 35:468–499.

Fisher, Irving. 1923. "The Business Cycle Largely a 'Dance of the Dollar.'" *Journal of the American Statistical Association* 18:1024–1028.

Fisher, Kenneth L. *The Wall Street Waltz.* Chicago: Contemporary Books.

Florida, Richard L., and Martin Kenney. 1987a. "Venture Capital and High Technology Entrepreneurship." Working Paper, School of Urban and Public Affairs, Carnegie-Mellon University, October.

———. 1987b. "Venture Capital Financed Innovation and Technological Change in the U.S." Working Paper, School of Urban and Public Affairs, Carnegie-Mellon University, October.

———. 1988. "Venture Capital, High Technology, and Regional Development." *Regional Studies* 22:33–48.

Foley, Duncan K. 1989. "Endogenous Financial-Production Cycles in a Macroeconomic Model." In *Economic Complexity,* edited by W. Barnett et al., pp. 89–99. Cambridge: Cambridge University Press.

Forrester, Jay W. 1976. "Business Structure, Economic Cycles, and National Policy." *Futures* 8:195–214.

———. 1977. "Growth Cycles." *De Economist* 125:525–543.

———. 1979. "Innovation and the Economic Long Wave," *Management Review* 16:24.

Frank, Andre Gunder. 1978. *World Accumulation, 1492–1789*. New York: Monthly Review Press.

Frank, Andre Gunder, and Maria Fuentes. 1988. "Social Movements in Recent World History." Paper presented to Second International Karl Polanyi Conference, Montreal, November 10–13.

Freeman, Alan. 1989. "'29, '87, and the Rise and Fall of U.S. Hegemony." Paper presented at an international colloquium, "The Long Waves of the Economic Conjuncture," Vrije Universiteit Brussel, Brussels, January 12–14.

Freeman, Christopher. 1982. *The Economics of Industrial Innovation*. Cambridge, Mass.: MIT Press.

———. 1986. *Design, Innovation, and Long Cycles in Economic Development*. New York: St. Martin's Press.

———. 1989. "The Third Kondratieff Wave: Age of Steel, Electrification, and Imperialism." Paper presented at an international colloquium, "The Long Waves of the Economic Conjuncture," Vrije Universiteit Brussel, Brussels, January 12–14.

———, ed. 1984. *Long Waves in the World Economy*. London: Frances Pinter.

Freeman, Christopher, J. Clark, and L. Soete. 1982. *Unemployment and Technical Innovation*. London: Frances Pinter.

Friedman, Milton, and Anna J. Schwartz. 1963. "Money and Business Cycles." *Review of Economics and Statistics* 45 (Feb. suppl.): 32–78.

———. 1983. *A Monetary History of the United States*. Princeton: Princeton University Press.

Frost, Alfred J., and Robert R. Prechter, Jr. 1985. *The Elliott Wave Principle*. Gainesville, Ga.: New Classics Library.

Fry, Maxwell J. 1988. *Money, Interest, and Banking in Economic Development*. Baltimore: Johns Hopkins University Press.

Galbraith, John Kenneth. 1954. *The Great Crash, 1929*. Cambridge, Mass.: Riverside Press.

Garvy, George. 1943. "Kondratieff's Theory of Long Cycles." *Review of Economic Statistics* 25:203–220.

Gattei, Giorgio. 1989. "Every Twenty-five Years? Strike Waves and Long Economic Cycles." Paper presented at an international colloquium, "The Long Waves of the Economic Conjuncture," Vrije Universiteit Brussel, Brussels, January 12–14.

Gayer, A. D., W. W. Rostow, and A. J. Schwartz. 1953. *The Growth and Function of the British Economy, 1790–1850*. 2 vols. New York: Barnes & Noble.

Gerster, Hans J. 1989. "Econometric Tests on Long Waves in Price and Volume Series from Sixteen Countries." Paper presented at an international colloquium, "The Long Waves of the Economic Conjuncture," Vrije Universiteit Brussel, Brussels, January 12–14.

Glass, Leon, and Michael C. Mackey. 1988. *From Clocks to Chaos*. Princeton: Princeton University Press.

Gleick, James. 1987. *Chaos: Making a New Science*. London: Penguin Books.

Glisman, Hans H. 1987. "From Gold Field Discoveries to Institutional Sclerosis: Theories and Observations on Long Waves of Economics." *European Journal of Political Research* 15:223–240.

Glyn, A., and R. Sutcliffe. 1980. *The British Disaster*. London: Pluto Press.

Goldstein, Joshua S. 1985. "Kondratieff Cycles as War Cycles." *International Studies Quarterly* 29:411–444.

———. 1988. *Long Cycles: Prosperity and War in the Modern Age.* New Haven: Yale University Press.

———. 1989. "A War-Economy Theory of the Long Wave." Paper presented at an international colloquium, "The Long Waves of the Economic Conjuncture," Vrije Universiteit Brussel, Brussels, January 12–14.

Goodwin, Richard M. 1986. "The Economy as an Evolutionary Pulsator." *Journal of Economic Behavior and Organization* 7:341–349.

Gordon, David M. 1978. "Up and Down the Long Roller Coaster." In *U.S. Capitalism in Crisis,* compiled by the Union for Radical Political Economics, pp. 22–35. New York: URPE.

Gordon, David M., Thomas E. Weisskopf, and Samuel Bowles. 1983. "Long Swings and the Nonreproductive Cycle." *AEA Papers and Proceedings* 73:152–157.

———. 1989. "Inside and Outside the Long Swing: The Endogeneity/Exogeneity Debate." Paper presented at an international colloquium, "The Long Waves of the Economic Conjuncture," Vrije Universiteit Brussel, Brussels, January 12–14.

Gottlieb, Manuel. 1976. *Long Swings in Urban Development.* New York: National Bureau of Economic Research.

Graham, A. K., and P. M. Senge. 1980. "A Long-Wave Hypothesis on Innovation." *Technological Forecasting and Social Change* 17:283–311.

Grassberger, Peter, and Itamar Procaccia. 1983. "Characterization of Strange Attractors." *Physical Review Letters* 50:346–349.

———. 1983. "Estimation of the Kolmogorov Entropy from a Chaotic Signal." *Journal of Statistical Physics* 28:2591–2594.

Griliches, Z., and L. Hurwicz, eds. 1972. *Patents, Invention, and Economic Change.* Cambridge, Mass.: Harvard University Press.

Gurley, John G., and Edward S. Shaw. 1957. "The Growth of Debt and Money in the United States, 1800–1950: A Suggested Interpretation." *Review of Economics and Statistics* 39:250–262.

Hall, Peter, and Paschal Preston. 1988. *The Carrier Wave: New Information Technology and the Geography of Information, 1866–2003.* London: Unwin Hyman.

Hansen, Alvin H. 1932. *Economic Stabilization in an Unbalanced World.* New York: Harcourt Brace.

———. 1941. *Fiscal Policy and Business Cycles.* New York: W. W. Norton & Co.

Hartman, Raymond S., and David R. Wheeler. 1979. "Schumpeterian Waves of Innovation and Infrastructure Development in Great Britain and the United States: The Kondratieff Cycle Revisited." *Research in Economic History* 4:37–85.

Haubrich, Joseph, and Andrew Lo. 1989. *The Sources and Nature of Long-Term Memory in the Business Cycle.* National Bureau of Economic Research, Working Paper 2951. Cambridge, Mass.: NBER.

Haustein, Heinz-Dieter, and Erich Neuwirth. 1982. "Long Waves in World Industrial Production, Energy Consumption, Innovations, Inventions, and Patents and Their Identification by Spectral Analysis." *Technological Forecasting and Social Change* 22:53–89.

Heertje, A. 1977. *Economics and Technical Change.* London: Weidenfeld & Nicolson.

Henderson, H. 1985. "Post-Economic Policies for Post-Industrial Societies." In *The Global Economy: Today, Tomorrow, and the Transition,* edited by H. F. Didsbury, Jr. Bethesda, Md.: World Future Society.

Herman, John R., and Richard A. Goldberg. 1978. *Sun, Weather, and Climate.* Washington, D.C.: National Aeronautics and Space Administration.

Hoffman, Charles. 1970. *The Depression of the Nineties*. Westport, Conn.: Greenwood Press.

Holmes, Jack E. 1985. *The Mood/Interest Theory of American Foreign Policy*. Lexington: University Press of Kentucky.

Hopkins, Terrence K., Immanuel Wallerstein, et al. 1982. "Cyclical Rhythms and Secular Trends in the Capitalist World-Economy." In *World-System Analysis: Theory and Methodology*, edited by Hopkins, Wallerstein, et al. Beverly Hills, Calif.: Sage Publications.

Howard, Jeanne. 1989. "Long Wave Cycles and Cities in a Global Society." In *Cities in a Global Society*, edited by Richard V. Knight and Gary Gappert, pp. 169–180. Newbury Park, Calif.: Sage Publications.

Humphreys, D. 1982. "A Mineral Commodity Life Cycle?" *Resources Policy* 8:215–229.

Huntington, Samuel. 1981. *American Politics: The Promise of Disharmony*. Cambridge, Mass.: Harvard University Press.

Imbert, Gaston. 1959. *Des mouvements de longue durée Kondratieff*. Aix-en-Provence: La Pensée Universitaire.

Isard, Walter. 1942. "A Neglected Cycle: The Transport-building Cycle." *Review of Economic Statistics* 24:149–158.

Jantsch, Eric. 1967. *Technological Forecasting in Perspective*. Paris: Organization for Economic Cooperation and Development.

Jerome, H. 1926. *Migration and Business Cycles*. New York: National Bureau of Economic Research.

Jillson, Calvin. 1988. "The Intellectual Context of Critical Realignment and Governmental Response." Paper presented at the annual meeting of the Southwestern Political Science Association, Houston, Tex., March 23–26.

Johnson, Paul M., and William R. Thompson. 1985. *Rhythms in Politics and Economics*. New York: Praeger.

Juglar, Clement. 1862. *Des crises commerciales en leur retour périodique en France, en Angelterre et aux États-Unis*. Paris: Libraire Gillaumin et Cie.

Kalecki, Michal. 1939. *Essays in the Theory of Economic Fluctuations*. New York: Russell & Russell.

———. 1943. "Political Aspects of Full Employment." *Political Quarterly* 14:322–341.

Kelley, Allen C. 1969. "Demographic Cycles and Economic Growth: The Long Swing Reconsidered." *Journal of Economic History* 29:633–656.

Kennedy, Paul. 1987. *The Rise and Fall of the Great Powers*. New York: Random House.

Kerr, Richard A. 1984. "The Moon Influences Western U.S. Drought." *Science* 224:587.

———. 1987. "Sunspot-Weather Correlation Found." *Science* 238:479–480.

———. 1988. "Sunspot-Weather Link Holding Up." *Science* 242:1124–1151.

Key, V. O., Jr. 1955. "A Theory of Critical Elections." *Journal of Politics* 17:3–18.

Keynes, John Maynard. 1930. *Treatise on Money*. London: Macmillan.

Kindleberger, Charles P. 1973. *The World in Depression, 1929–1931*. Berkeley: University of California Press.

———. 1978. *Manias, Panics, and Crashes*. New York: Basic Books.

Kitchin, Joseph. 1923. "Cycles and Trends in Economic Factors." *Review of Economic Statistics* 5:10–16.

———. 1930. "Production et consommation de l'or dans le passé et dans l'avenir." *Rapport provisoire de la délégation de l'or du comité financier*, appendix 12, pp. 57–64.

Kitwood, Tom. 1986. "Long Waves in Economic Life: An Image without a Method." *Journal of Interdisciplinary Economics* 1:107–125.

Klein, Lawrence R. 1988. "Components of Competitiveness." *Science* 241:308–313.

Kleinknecht, Alfred. 1987. *Innovation Patterns in Crisis and Prosperity: Schumpeter's Long Cycle Reconsidered.* New York: St. Martin's Press.

Klingberg, Frank L. 1952. "The Historical Alternation of Moods in American Foreign Policy." *World Politics* 4:239–273.

———. 1983. *Cyclical Trends in American Foreign Policy Moods: The Unfolding of America's World Role.* Lanham, Md.: University Press of America.

Klotz, B. P., and L. Neal. 1973. "Spectral and Cross-Spectral Analysis of the Long-Swing Hypothesis." *Review of Economics and Statistics* 55:291–298.

Kondratiev, Nikolai D. 1922. *The World Economy and Its Condition during and after the War.* Moscow: Volgada.

———. 1923. "Some Controversial Questions Concerning the World Economy and the Crisis." *Economic Bulletin of the Conjuncture Institute.*

———. 1924. "On the Notion of Economic Statics, Dynamics, and Fluctuations." *Economic Bulletin of the Conjuncture Institute.*

———. 1925. "Long Business Cycles." *Problems of Economic Fluctuations* 1:28–79.

———. 1926a. "Die langen Wellen der Konjunktur." *Archiv für Sozialwissenschaft und Sozialpolitik* 56:573–609.

———. 1926b. "Major Economic Cycles." *Economic Bulletin of the Conjuncture Institute.*

———. 1928a. "Dynamics of Industrial and Agricultural Prices." *Economic Bulletin of the Conjuncture Institute.*

———. 1928b. "Die Preisdynamik der industriellen und landwirtschaftlichen Waren." *Archiv für Sozialwissenschaft und Sozialpolitik* 60:1–85.

———. 1935. "The Long Waves in Economic Life" (originally published in German, 1926). Translated by W. F. Stolper. *Review of Economic Statistics* 17:105–115.

———. 1984. *Nikolai Kondratieff's "The Long Wave Cycle"* (originally published in German, 1928). Translated by Guy Daniels, with an introduction by Julian M. Snyder. New York: Richardson & Snyder.

Kuczynski, Thomas. 1980. "Have There Been Differences between the Growth Rates in Different Periods of the Development of the Capitalist World Economy since 1850?" In *Historical Social Research*, edited by J. M. Clubb and E. K. Schench. Stuttgart: Klett-Cotta.

———. 1985. *Marx and Engels on Long Waves.* Berlin: Institute of Economic History.

———. 1989. "Great Depressions as Transitional Phases within the Capitalist Mode of Production: The Interaction of Socio-economic and Techno-economic Factors." Paper presented at an international colloquium, "The Long Waves of the Economic Conjuncture," Vrije Universiteit Brussel, Brussels, January 12–14.

Kuznets, Simon. 1930. *Secular Movements in Production and Prices: Their Nature and Their Bearing upon Cyclical Fluctuations.* Boston: Houghton Mifflin.

———. 1940. "Schumpeter's Business Cycles." *American Economic Review* 30:267.

———. 1953. *Economic Change.* New York: W. W. Norton.

———. 1958. "Long Swings in the Growth of Population and in Related Economic Variables." *Proceedings of the American Philosophical Society* 102:25–52.

Kuznets, Simon, and S. Rosen. 1954. *Immigration and the Foreign Born.* New York: National Bureau of Economic Research.

Labitzke, Karin. 1987. "Sunspots, the QBO, and the Stratospheric Temperature in the North Polar Region." *Geophysical Research Letters* 14:535.

Landscheidt, Theodor. 1988. "Solar Radiation Impulses of the Torque in the Sun's Motion, and Climatic Variation." *Climatic Change* 12:265–295.

———. 1989. *Sun—Earth—Man: A Mesh of Cosmic Oscillations.* London: Urania Trust.

Lasswell, H. 1935. *World Politics and Personal Insecurity*. Glencoe, Ill.: Free Press.

Lenin, V. I. 1973. *Imperialism: The Highest Stage of Capitalism*. Peking: Foreign Language Press.

Lewin, Roger. 1988. "Relax, the Sun Is Brightening Again." *Science* 240:1733–1734.

Lewis, J. Perry. 1965. *Building Cycles and Britain's Growth*. London: Macmillan.

Lewis, W. Arthur. 1978. *Growth and Fluctuations, 1870–1913*. London: George Allen & Unwin.

Lewis, W. Arthur, and P. J. O'Leary. 1955. "Secular Swings in Production and Trade." *Manchester School of Economics and Social Studies* 23:113–152.

Lloyd-Jones, Roger. 1987. "Innovation, Industrial Structure, and the Long Wave: The British Economy, c. 1873–1914." *Journal of European Economic History* 16: 315–333.

Long, Clarence D. 1940. *Building Cycles and the Theory of Investment*. Princeton: Princeton University Press.

Lorenz, H. W. 1987. "Strange Attractors in a Multisector Business Cycle Model." *Journal of Economic Behavior and Organization* 8:397–411.

McClelland, David C. 1975. *Power: The Inner Experience*. New York: Irvington Press.

McGrane, Reginald G. 1965. *The Panic of 1837*. New York: Russell & Russell.

Mackay, Charles. 1932. *Memoirs of Extraordinary Delusions and the Madness of Crowds*. Boston: L. C. Page.

Maddison, A. 1982. *Phases of Capitalist Development*. Oxford: Oxford University Press.

Mager, Nathan H. 1987. *The Kondratieff Wave*. New York: Praeger.

Malabre, Alfred L., Jr. 1987. *Beyond Our Means: How Reckless Borrowing Now Threatens to Overwhelm Us*. New York: Random House.

Malkiel, Burton G. 1989. "Is the Stock Market Efficient?" *Science* 243:1313–1318.

Mandel, Ernst. 1968. *Marxist Economy Theory*. London: Merlin.

———. 1975. *Late Capitalism*. London: New Left Books.

———. 1980. *Long Waves of Capitalist Development: The Marxist Interpretation*. London: Cambridge University Press.

———. 1983. "Explaining Long Waves of Capitalist Development." In *Long Waves in the World Economy*, edited by C. Freeman, pp. 195–201. London: Frances Pinter.

Mansfield, Edwin. 1987. "Long Waves and Technological Innovation." *AEA Papers and Proceedings* 73:141–145.

Marchetti, Cesare. 1980. "Society as a Learning System: Discovery, Invention, and Innovation Cycles Revisited." *Technological Forecasting and Social Change* 18:267–282.

———. 1983. *On a Fifty Year Pulsation in Human Affairs: Analysis of Some Physical Indicators*. Laxenburg, Austria: International Institute for Applied Systems Analysis.

———. 1988. "Infrastructures for Movement: Past and Future." In *Cities and Their Vital Systems: Infrastructure Past, Present, and Future*, edited by Jesse H. Ausubel and Robert Herman, pp. 146–174. Washington, D.C.: National Academy Press.

Markusen, Ann Roell. 1985. *Profit Cycles, Oligopoly, and Regional Development*. Cambridge, Mass.: MIT Press.

Marshall, Michael. 1987. *Long Waves of Regional Development*. New York: St. Martin's Press.

Mattick, Paul. 1981. *Economic Crisis and Crisis Theory*. London: Merlin.

Mensch, Gerhard. 1979. *Stalemate in Technology*. Cambridge, Mass.: Ballinger.

Menshikov, Stanislaw. 1989. "The Long Wave as an Endogenous Mechanism." Paper presented at an international colloquium, "The Long Waves of the Economic Conjuncture," Vrije Universiteit Brussel, Brussels, January 12–14.

Mills, Leonard. 1988. "Can Stock Prices Reliably Predict Recessions?" *Business Review of the Federal Reserve Bank of Philadelphia*, September/October, pp. 3–14.

Mitchell, B. R. 1983. *International Historical Statistics: The Americas and Australasia.* Detroit: Gale Research Co.

Modelski, George. 1978. "The Long Cycle of Global Politics and the Nation-State." *Comparative Studies in Society and History* 20:214–235.

———. 1981. "Long Cycles, Kondratieffs, and Alternating Innovations: Implications for U.S. Foreign Policy." In *The Political Economy of Foreign Policy Behavior,* edited by Charles W. Kegley, Jr., and Patrick MaGowan. Beverly Hills, Calif.: Sage Publications.

———. 1983. "Long Cycles of World Leadership." In *Contending Approaches to World System Analysis,* edited by William R. Thompson. Beverly Hills, Calif.: Sage Publications.

———. 1987. *Exploring Long Cycles.* London: Frances Pinter.

Nakicenovic, Nebojsa. 1988. "Dynamics and Replacement of U.S. Transport Infrastructures." In *Cities and Their Vital Systems: Infrastructure Past, Present, and Future,* edited by Jesse H. Ausubel and Robert Herman, pp. 175–221. Washington, D.C.: National Academy Press.

Namenwirth, J. Zvi. 1973. "Wheels of Time and the Interdependence of Value Change in America." *Journal of Interdisciplinary History* 3:649–683.

Nelson, Ralph L. 1959. *Merger Movements in American Industry, 1895–1956.* Princeton: Princeton University Press.

Noble, Grant D. 1988. *The Ultimate Dow Top.* Lake Forest, Ill.: By the author.

North, R. C., and R. Lagerstrom. 1971. *War and Domination.* New York: General Learning Press.

Noyelle, Thierry J. 1984. "The Service Era: Forming Public Policy on People and Places." *Economic Development Commentary* 8, no. 2.

Olsen, Mancur. 1982. *The Rise and Decline of Nations: Economic Growth, Stagflation, and Social Rigidities.* New Haven: Yale University Press.

Perez, Carlota. 1981. "Structural Change and the Assimilation of New Technologies in the Economic and Social Systems." *Futures* 13:357–375.

Perroux, François. 1976. "Outline of a Theory of the Dominant Economy" (originally published in French, 1948). English translation in *Transnational Corporations and the World Order,* edited by G. Modelski. San Francisco, Calif.: W. H. Freeman.

Pigou, A. C. 1927. *Industrial Fluctuations.* London: Macmillan.

Poletayev, Andrej V. 1989. "Long Waves in Profit Rates in Four Countries." Paper presented at an international colloquium, "The Long Waves of the Economic Conjuncture," Vrije Universiteit Brussel, Brussels, January 12–14.

Pool, Robert. 1989a. "Is It Chaos, or Is It Just Noise?" *Science* 243:25–28.

———. 1989b. "A Simple Model of Chaos." *Science* 243:311.

———. 1989c. "Where Strange Attractors Lurk." *Science* 243:1292.

Pope, David. 1984. "Rostow's Kondratieff Cycle in Australia." *Journal of Economic History* 44:729–754.

Powers, C. H. 1981. "Pareto's Theory of Society." *Revue Europeene des Sciences Sociales* 19:99–119.

Prechter, Robert R., Jr. 1986. *The Major Works of R. N. Elliott.* Gainesville, Ga.: New Classics Library.

Ramsey, J. B., C. L. Sayers, and P. Rothman. 1988. "The Statistical Properties of Dimension Calculations Using Small Data Sets: Some Economic Applications." Research Report 88–10, C. V. Starr Center for Applied Economics, New York University.

Ray, George F. 1980. "Innovation in the Long Cycle." *Lloyd's Bank Review* 135:14–28.

———. 1983. "Energy and the Long Cycles." *Energy Economics* 5:3–8.

Raymond, George A., and Charles W. Kegley, Jr. 1987. "Long Cycles and Internationalized Civil War." *Journal of Politics* 49:481–499.

Reijnders, Jan. 1988. "The Enigma of Long Waves." Ph.D. thesis, University of Groningen.

———. 1989. "Kondratieff in a Different Perspective." Paper presented at an international colloquium, "The Long Waves of the Economic Conjuncture," Vrije Universiteit Brussel, Brussels, January 12–14.

Resnick, David, and Norman C. Thomas. 1988. "Cycling through American Politics." Paper presented at the annual meeting of the Southwestern Political Science Association, Houston, Tex., March 23–26.

Richardson, L. F. 1960. *A Study of Deadly Quarrels*. Pittsburgh: Boxwood Press.

Rose, A. 1941. "Wars, Innovations, and Long Cycles: A Brief Comment." *American Economic Review* 30:195–197.

Rosenberg, Nathan, and Claudio R. Frischtak. 1983. "Long Waves and Economic Growth: A Critical Appraisal." *American Economic Review* 73:146–151.

Rostow, Walt Whitman. 1975. "Kondratieff, Schumpeter, and Kuznets: Trend Periods Revisited." *Journal of Economic History* 35:719–753.

———. 1978. *The World Economy*. Austin: University of Texas Press.

———. 1979. *Getting from Here to There: A Policy for the Post-Keynesian Age*. London: Macmillan.

———. 1980. *Why the Poor Get Richer and the Rich Slow Down*. Austin: University of Texas Press.

Sahlman, W. A., and H. A. Stevenson. 1985. "Capital Market Myopia." *Journal of Business Venturing* 1:7–30.

Saul, S. B. 1969. *The Myth of the Great Depression, 1873–1896*. London: Humanities Press.

Sayers, C. 1988. "Work Stoppages: Exploring the Nonlinear Dynamics." Working Paper, Department of Economics, University of Houston.

Scheinkman, J. A., and B. Le Baron. 1987. "Nonlinear Dynamics and Stock Returns." Working Paper, Department of Economics, University of Chicago.

———. 1989. "Nonlinear Dynamics and GNP Data." In *Economic Complexity*, edited by W. Barnett et al., pp. 213–227. Cambridge: Cambridge University Press.

Schlesinger, Arthur M., Jr. 1986. *The Cycles of American History*. Boston: Houghton Mifflin.

Schmidhauser, John R. 1984. *Constitutional Law in American Politics*. Monterey, Calif.: Brooks/Cole Publishing Co.

Schmookler, J. A. 1966. *Invention and Economic Growth*. Cambridge, Mass.: Harvard University Press.

Schnitzer, Martin. 1987. *Contemporary Government and Business Relations*. New York: Houghton Mifflin.

Schuman, James B., and David Rosenau. 1972. *The Kondratieff Wave*. New York: World Publishing.

Schumpeter, Elizabeth B. 1938. "English Prices and Public Finance, 1660–1882." *Review of Economics and Statistics* 20:21–37.

Schumpeter, Joseph A. 1934a. "Depressions—Can We Learn from Past Experiences?" *Economics of the Recovery Program*. New York: McGraw-Hill.

———. 1934b. *The Theory of Economic Development* (originally published in German, 1912). London: Cambridge University Press.

———. 1939. *Business Cycles: A Theoretical, Historical, and Statistical Analysis of the Capitalist Process*. 2 vols. London: McGraw-Hill.

———. [1942] 1976. *Capitalism, Socialism, and Democracy*. Reprint. London: George Allen & Unwin.

————. 1946. "The American Economy in the Interwar Period: The Decade of the Twenties." *American Economic Review* 36:1–10.

Shaikh, Anwar M. 1989. "The Long Term Profit Rate in U.S. Manufacturing, 1909–1985." Paper presented at an international colloquium, "The Long Waves of the Economic Conjuncture," Vrije Universiteit Brussel, Brussels, January 12–14.

Silberling, Norman J. 1943. *The Dynamics of Business.* New York: McGraw-Hill.

Simiand, F. 1932. *Les Fluctuations économiques a longue periode et la crise mondiale.* Paris: Alcan.

Simmie, James. 1986. "Kondratiev Waves and the Future of British Cities." *Futures* 18:787–794.

Skowronek, Stephen. 1984. "Presidential Leadership in Political Time." In *The Presidency and the Political System,* edited by Michael Nelson, pp. 8–-132. Washington, D.C.: Congressional Quarterly Press.

————. 1986. "Notes on the Presidency in the Political Order." *Studies in American Political Development* 1:286–302.

Slutsky, E. 1937. "The Summation of Random Causes as the Source of Cyclic Processes." *Econometrica* 5:107–146.

Solomou, Solomos. 1986a. "Innovation Clusters and Kondratieff Long Waves in Economic Growth." *Cambridge Journal of Economics* 10:101–112.

————. 1986b. "Non-balanced Growth and Kondratieff Waves in the World Economy, 1850–1913." *Journal of Economic History* 46:165–170.

————. 1987. *Phases of Economic Growth, 1850–1973.* Cambridge: Cambridge University Press.

————. 1989. "Long Waves in National and World Economic Growth, 1850–1973." Paper presented at an international colloquium, "The Long Waves of the Economic Conjuncture," Vrije Universiteit Brussel, Brussels, January 12–14.

Spiethoff, Arthur. 1938. *Die Wirtschaftlichen Wechesellogen, der stand und die nachte sukunff der Konjunktur forschung.* Munich: Dunckner & Humblot.

Sterman, John D. 1985. "A Behavioral Model of the Economic Long Wave." *Journal of Economic Behavior and Organization* 6:17–53.

Stevenson, Michael I. 1985. *Joseph Alois Schumpeter: A Bibliography, 1905–1984.* Westport, Conn.: Greenwood Press.

Sundquist, James L. 1973. *Dynamics of the Party System: Alignment and Realignment of the Political Parties of the United States.* Washington, D.C.: Brookings Institution.

Tarascio, Vincent J. 1988. "Kondratieff's Theory of Long Cycles." *Atlantic Economic Journal* 16:1–10.

————. 1989. "Economic and War Cycles." *History of Political Economy* 21:91–101.

Thomas, Brinley. 1954. *Migration and Economic Growth.* Rev. ed. Cambridge: Cambridge University Press.

————. 1973. *Migration and Urban Development.* London: Methuen.

Thomas, Dorothy S. 1956–1957. "Some Aspects of the Study of Population Redistribution in the United States, 1870–1950." *Proceedings of the World Population Conference, 1954,* vol. 2, pp. 667–713. New York: United Nations.

Thomas, Dorothy S., and K. C. Zachariah. 1963. "Some Temporal Variations in Internal Migration and Economic Activity, United States, 1880–1950." *International Population Conference, 1961,* vol. 1, pp. 525–532. London: International Council for the Scientific Study of Population.

Thompson, William R. 1983. "The World Economy, the Long Cycle, and the Question of World-System Time." In *Foreign Policy and the Modern World System,* edited by P. McGowan and Charles W. Kegley, Jr., pp. 35–62. Beverly Hills, Calif.: Sage Publications.

Thompson, William R., and L. G. Zuk. 1982. "War, Inflation, and the Kondratieff Long Wave." *Journal of Conflict Resolution* 26:621–644.

Toynbee, Arnold J. 1954. *A Study of History*, vol. 9, pp. 255, 322–326. London: Oxford University Press.

Trotsky, Leon D. [1923] 1979. "Report on the World Crisis and the New Task of the Communist International." Reprinted in *The First Five Years of the Communist International*, vol. 1, pp. 226–278. London: New Park.

Tufte, Edward R. 1978. *Political Control of the Economy*. Princeton: Princeton University Press.

Tugan-Baranovskij, Mikhail I. 1913. *Les Crises industrielles en Angleterre* (originally published in Russian, 1894). 2d ed. Paris: Giard & Breière.

Van Der Zwan, A. 1980. "On the Assessment of the Kondratieff Cycle and Related Issues." In *Prospects of Economic Growth*, edited by S. K. Kuipers and G. J. Lanjouw, pp. 183–222. Oxford: North-Holland Publishing Co.

Van Duijn, J. J. 1983. *The Long Wave in Economic Life*. London: George Allen & Unwin.

Van Gelderen, J. [J. Fedder, pseud.]. 1913. "Springvloed beschouwingen over industrielle ontwikeling en prijsbeweging." *De Nievwe Tijd* 18:253–257, 445–464.

Van Vlcck, George W. 1957. *The Panic of 1857*. New York: AMS Press.

Värynen, R. 1983. "Economic Cycles, Power Transitions, Political Management, and Wars between Major Powers." *International Studies Quarterly* 27:389–418.

Vasko, Tibor. 1985. *The Long Wave Debate*. Berlin: Springer Verlag.

Volland, Craig S. 1987. "A Comprehensive Theory of Long Wave Cycles." *Technological Forecasting and Social Change* 32:120–145.

Von Ciriacy-Wantrup, S. 1936. *Agrarkrisen und Stockungsspannen sur Frage der lange Welle in der Wirtschaftlichen Entwicklung*. Berlin: Paul Parey.

Waddell, Lorna M., and Walter C. Labys. 1987. *Transmaterialization: Technology and Materials Demand Cycles*. Morgantown: West Virginia University.

Wagemann, E. 1931. *Struktur und Rhythmus der Weltwirtschaft*. Berlin: R. Hobbing.

Wallerstein, Immanuel. 1974. *The Modern World-System: Capitalist Agriculture and the Origins of the European World-Economy in the Sixteenth Century*. New York: Academic Press.

———. 1980. *The Modern World-System: Mercantilism and the Consolidation of the European World-Economy*. New York: Academic Press.

———. 1984. "The Three Instances of Hegemony in the History of the Capitalist World Economy." *International Journal of Comparative Sociology* 24:100–108.

Wardwell, C. A. R. 1927. "An Investigation of Economic Data for Major Cycles." Ph.D. dissertation, University of Pennsylvania.

Warren, George F., and Frank A. Pearson. 1931. *Wholesale Prices in the United States for One Hundred Thirty-five Years, 1797 to 1932*. Cornell University Agricultural Experiment Station, Memoir 142, pt. 1. Ithaca, N.Y.: Cornell University, November.

———. 1935. *Gold and Prices*. New York: John Wiley & Sons.

Webcr, Robert Philip. 1983. "Cyclical Theories of Crisis in the World-System." In *Crises in the World-System*, edited by Albert Bergeson, pp. 37–56. Beverly Hills, Calif.: Sage Publications.

Weis, David. 1988. "Why Elliott, Kondratieff See Deflation Ahead." *Futures* 20:70–71.

Wiksell, Knut. 1936. *Interest and Prices: A Study of Causes Regulating the Price of Money* (originally published in German, 1896). London: Macmillan. *Geldzins und Guterpreise*.

Wilkinson, Maurice. 1967. "Evidences of Long Swings in the Growth of Swedish Population and Related Economic Variables, 1860–1965." *Journal of Economic History* 27:17–38.

———. 1970. "European Migration to the United States: An Econometric Analysis of Aggregate Labor Supply and Demand." *Review of Economics and Statistics* 52 272–279.

———. 1973. "An Econometric Analysis of Fertility in Sweden, 1870–1965." *Econometrica* 41:633–642.

Willett, Thomas D., ed. 1988. *Political Business Cycles*. Durham, N.C.: Duke University Press.

Williamson, J. G. 1974. *Late Nineteenth Century American Development: A General Equilibrium History*. New York: Cambridge University Press.

Woytinski-Lorenz, W. 1931. "Das Ratsel der langen Wellen." *Schmoller's Jahrbuch* 55:1–42.

Wright, Quincy. 1942. *A Study of War*. Chicago: University of Chicago Press.

Zahorchak, Michael, ed. 1983. *Climate: The Key to Understanding Business Cycles. With a Forecast of Trends into the Twenty-first Century. The Raymond H. Wheeler Papers*. Linden, N.J.: Tide Press.

Zarnowitz, V. 1989. *Facts and Factors in the Recent Evolution of Business Cycles in the U.S.* National Bureau of Economic Research, Working Paper 2865. Chicago: NBER.

INDEX

Abramowitz, Moses, on Kuznets cycles, 90–91

American growth cycles. *See* U.S. growth cycles

American economic history: phases of development in, 121–124; typology of crises in, 122

American politics: critical elections in, 148–155; cycles of public purpose vs private interest in, 146–147; liberal-conservative transitions during stagflation crises in, 145, 151; mood cycles in, 144–145; realignment process in, 150–151; types of elections in, 148

Batra, Ravi: and Ananda Marg cult, 168; data used, 6; inspired by guru P. D. Sarkar, 168; predicts Great Depression in 1990, 193–194

Baumol, William J., explanation of chaos theory offered by, 14–15, 22

BDS tests for chaos, 14–15, 73–74

Becker, Gary S., on data needed to validate long waves, 8

Beckman, Robert, on upwave and downwave behavior as mass psychological phenomena, 172–174

Birth and fortune, as related by Easterlin, 95–96

"Boom and bustiness" in chaotic systems, 22–24

Borchert, John R., on technology transitions and epochs of American development, 43–46

Brady, David W., on shared features of critical elections, 149–150

British growth cycles, compared to U.S., 78, 91–94; alleged inversion of, 91–92

Building cycles, 82–83, 86

Burnham, Walter J.: and concept of critical elections, 148; and idea of political gridlock, 153

Burns, Arthur F.: on measuring business cycles, 8; on oscillation of production trends in 25-year waveband, 79

Campbell, Angus, typology of elections, 148

Capital-lifespan theories, 51–53

Capital-market myopia, 85–86

Capitalist crises, in Marxist long-wave theory, 59–64

Chaos phase diagrams: of Kondratiev waves, 22–29; of Kuznets cycles, 73–74, 104, 106; of stock market fluctuations, 136–138

Chaos theory (*also* deterministic chaos): concept of, 10; discovery of, by Richard H. Day, 14; economic applications of, 14–15; uses of, in prediction, 186

City-building booms, 86

Clark, Dr. Hyde, 54-year long wave identified by, 3

Climatic cycles, 168–172

Cobweb diagrams of growth and price movements: 1800–1857, 107–108; 1857–1907, 109; 1907–1964, 110; 1964–1987, 111; schematic summary of, 112

Commodity-price fluctuations, Rostow's theory of, 41–42

Creative destruction: as phase in long-wave rhythms, 132; Schumpeter's concept of, 56

Crises in American economic history, typology of, 122

Critical elections: concept of, 148–151; related to long-wave rhythms, 151–155

"Curve of Capitalist Development," Trotsky's concept of, 59–60

Cycles. *See* Building cycles; Climatic cycles; Elliott; Fertility; Foreign investment cycles; Gross National Product; Hegemony; Immigration; Juglar investment cycles; Kitchin; Kondratiev waves; Kuznets cycles; Life cycles; Long-wave rhythms; Marxist long-wave theory; Mayan calendar round; Mood cycles; Political business cycles; Stock prices; Sunspot cycles; Toynbee; Transport-building cycles; Type A/Inflationary Growth Cycles;

Brian J. L. Berry is Founders Professor,
professor of political economy, and
director of the Bruton Center for Development Studies
at the University of Texas at Dallas.
He is a member of the National Academy of Sciences
and a fellow of the British Academy.